HOW TO FIND
YOUR IDEAL
COUNTRY HOME

HOW TO FIND YOUR IDEAL COUNTRY HOME

Ruralize Your Dreams

Gene GeRue

Heartwood Publications
Zanoni, Missouri

Copyright 1994
by Gene GeRue

All rights reserved

Heartwood Publications, HC 78, Box 1105, Zanoni, Missouri 65784
West coast address:
5808 #14, S. Pacific Coast Hwy., Redondo Beach, California 90277

This publication is designed to provide accurate and authoritative information in regard to the subject matter covered. It is sold with the understanding that neither the author nor the publisher is engaged in rendering legal, accounting, or other professional service. If legal advice or other expert assistance is required, the service of a competent professional person should be sought.
From a Declaration of Principles jointly adapted by a Committee of the American Bar Association and a Committee of Publishers and Associations.

ISBN 0-9641478-0-7

Library of Congress Catalog Card Number 94-76822

Printed on recycled paper

Printed by Malloy Lithographing, Ann Arbor, Michigan, USA

To Christina
a city girl
a country wife
who could write a book
on how to be
the ideal wife—anywhere

Contents

Part I — First things

Part II — Criteria and considerations

Part III — Finding your ideal country home

Reference illustrations

United States maps
(48 contiguous states)

State maps

(showing low-density population areas,
average state population density, the state flower and state tree,
the percentage of wooded land, and the state capital.)

Drawings

Forms

Reference illustrations were drawn by the author from sources noted. Woodcuts, daguerrotypes, pen-and-ink and crosshatch drawings, old plates, and old photographs derive primarily from public-domain graphics books published by Dover Publications, 31 East 2nd Street, Mineola, NY 11501.

Preface

Seeing in silence;
never the same twice,
but when you get it right,

you pass it on.

GARY SNYDER
WHAT HAVE I LEARNED

I grew up in rural Wisconsin. In 1963 I bought my first home, in Concord, California—a two-bedroom bungalow on a large lot for $11,200, payments $72 per month. I still remember feeling the natural high. I walked around my domain touching the trees and admiring how well the grass grew. My next-door neighbor appeared in his front yard. "Good morning, neighbor," I beamed. No answer. Thinking that he had not heard me, I raised my beam an octave and several decibels and repeated. He turned, looked at me—and turned his back. I was dumbfounded.

In the two decades following that bittersweet Saturday morning, I found that city living is "some different" from country life. In 25 years of northern California city living I went to college, raised a family and a business, bought several homes—and I never, ever, felt *at home*.

As a teen-aged Wisconsin farm boy, inspired by Louis Bromfield's *Malabar Farm*, I developed a naive dream of one day owning 1,000 acres and having my friends all live nearby, each of us contributing an essential skill. With great romantic idealism, that dream stayed with me.

In 1975 I took a TV course entitled: *Ready or Not*, designed to help individuals prepare for retirement. The final assignment was a written retirement plan, including an answer to the big question: where to live?

My method was first to compile criteria of my ideal home place. Using the criteria list at the local library, I narrowed my choices to seven states. After more research I chose one area, what I now know to be a bioregion, 2,000 miles away. I made contact with a large number of real estate agents and asked them to send me information on any listings they had that fit my criteria. In 1976 I took a two-week vacation/exploration trip to look at properties in my chosen area, a band approximately 60 miles wide and over 100 miles long.

The third day of looking revealed a property in a small valley with a year-round stream bubbling along 200 feet in front of a humble old farmhouse. It looked wonderful, but I still had over a week of appointments with agents who had properties for me to examine. A week and a half later I looked at the valley place a second time. Back in California, I wrote and mailed an offer. It was accepted.

For tax reasons, the sellers deferred the closing until 1977. On January third, I owned my permanent home, my ideal country place. In 1983 I moved to that place in southern Missouri, many hundreds of miles south of my growing-up place. I immediately felt at home.

I believe that part of my purpose in life is to help others get what they want by sharing what I have learned. This book is one attempt to serve that purpose. Here I have endeavored to bring together the cumulative knowledge of these various subjects that I have gained from personal experience and from reading the writings of others. The torrent of fresh information in the form of new books and periodicals has made this a challenging but enriching experience. I have subjected myself to the countryman's pain of city life by living and writing near the great libraries of the cities of Los Angeles County. Emerging computer and modem technology and electronic databases will hopefully make this a last.

Most of what I feel sure about has been learned by making many mistakes and experiencing some successes. Much of the information in this book comes from my experience as a real estate broker and teacher, from the successful personal quest for my ideal country place, and from living in the country for 26 of my years. Much also comes from knowing and talking to countless others who have moved from city to country.

I am indebted to my former real estate clients and students, who collectively helped me learn much of what I know about real estate; and to the friends, neighbors, and authors who have enhanced my knowledge and joy of life in the country. I acknowledge the valuable help and gratefully thank the many librarians who assisted me.

I am indebted to the readers-in-my-mind who will become the readers-in-reality. You have provided the motivation and the energy to make this book a tool which can help you live a simpler but higher-quality life by finding your own ideal country home.

Special acknowledgments

Sandra Bellinger

In addition to her editing skill, Sandra and her husband, Ron, are accomplished homesteaders who have successfully made the city-to-country transition. I am grateful for corrections, suggestions, constructive criticism, notification of latent pomposity, and for getting the editing accomplished quickly during new garden and broccoli harvest time. Thank you, Sandra.

Paurvi Trivedi

For proofreading, right-on design suggestions, production and marketing advice and assistance, and generous interest. And for doing all this in "spare time" during the distraction of arranging for her impending marriage. Thank you, Paurvi.

Craig J. Crawford

For being the on-call geographer and computer consultant, for essential help with the maps, for useful suggestions, and for sustained enthusiasm and encouragement. Thank you, Craig.

Christina GeRue

For unwavering support and encouragement. Thank you, sweetheart.

Alfred GeRue and Arlene GeRue

For gifts far too numerous to list and for passing down traditional values, my love and gratitude. Thanks Mom; thanks Dad.

Peter McWilliams

Peter provided inspiration and encouragement with *DO IT!: Let's Get Off Our Buts* before we ever knew him except through his books. He added knowledge and courage with *Self-Publishing, Self-Taught*. He helped us keep our focus with *You Can't Afford The Luxury of a Negative Thought*. He looked at the first design and made sensitive and sound suggestions for improvement. For all that and for sharing his wisdom, for computer hardware and software assistance, and for the use of his personal library, I am profoundly grateful. Thank you, Peter.

Notes on using this book

This is not a book for posterity—it is a tool to be used now. I strongly urge you to read with pen in hand. Circle or underline points you wish to be able to easily return to. Write key words and make notes in the margins. If you have borrowed this book or you simply cannot bring yourself to marking in it, use a pad of paper both as a bookmark and for notes. Perhaps like you, I used to keep book pages unmarked, unfolded, *unused*. It's a symptom of the same dis-ease that keeps us from removing mattress labels.

Throughout this book "you" should be understood to include you, your spouse/significant other/partner/companion/friend, and children or others you consider your family. Maximum involvement of all members of a family will generally result in the most agreeable choices. Parents know of the exceptions.

The gender-neutral challenge can often be handled by using "we," "our," "they," and other substitutes. Occasionally these do not work well. I respect women and men equally. I've done the best I can. If my use of "he" or "she" offends someone, I am truly sorry.

Before beginning reading, make a list of everything you want your ideal home place to have. This will get your brain operating in the right realm. Try to be open-minded. There will not be a test but there will be challenges.

From the feeling that there must be many like me,
who wanted a vantage point from which
they could survey the whole battlefield
before deciding where they would
stand the best chance of survival,
I came to believe that there must be
many veterans who would see what
an outsider has to make of them.
That is an author's job: to weigh the options,
clarify the objectives, balance the physical facts
against the convention and tradition.
Above all it is to identify the principles:
to reach the nub of the matter.
It is not easy to remain an outsider
from such an enthralling subject for long.

HUGH JOHNSON
THE PRINCIPLES OF GARDENING

*My point of view is, of course, that of the countryman,
and no doubt it has the countryman's bias.*

LIBERTY HYDE BAILEY
THE OUTLOOK TO NATURE

Introduction

*One of the most noted but unforeseen demographic trends
in the United States during the 1970s was the revival of population growth
in the rural and small town parts of the country. . . . There was both survey and
anecdotal evidence indicating that noneconomic quality-of-life reasons were
important for many thousands of people who decided either to remain in or
move to rural and small town areas. Even though the average family income in
nonmetropolitan areas has been about 20 percent less than that in metropolitan
areas, there was strong sentiment for the "simpler" life, expressed either in terms
of negative perceptions of life in the large cities and their suburbs or in terms of
positive conceptions of the merits of living in smaller communities.*

FUGUITT, BROWN, AND BEALE
RURAL AND SMALL TOWN AMERICA

The exodus of Americans to the countryside that began in the 1960s and 1970s continues unabated. Those disconnecting from urban and suburban life appear to be part of a large, quiet revolution, a backlash against social, economic, and environmental conditions resulting from materialistic values. The beatniks, the hippies, the soppies (semi-old professional persons—yuppies used to think we were all wet but now they're following our lead), and now the yuppies have found money success an empty house. The return to lower payments and higher values has become the province of the educated, the aware, the sensitive, the demanding—many of whom are turning to rural life as both a reaction against inhuman and environmentally destructive conditions and an attraction toward a lifestyle where nature and people are more important than big houses, Beemers, and the other trappings of financial affluence. As a nation we're starting to *get it*.

As suggested over 20 years ago by Alvin Toffler in *Future Shock,* we are imagining the future so we may shape our present. What we are now imagining is family and community meltdown—clearly evidenced by increasing crime and attendant widespread paranoia. More cops and more prisons are prescribed ("three strikes and you're out") because the honest diagnosis is overwhelming and painful—real solutions that treat the cause must confront unpleasant facts about ourselves and our living conditions.

We are also imagining environmental loss. Mounting evidence clearly shows that we are destroying our earth, our air, and our water—facts so alarming that environmentalism has become an international unifying force, a common goal, a cause that may yet save our species.

We are finding traditional values more sound than modern materialism. We are rejecting the madness that modern urban life has become and the worse hell it seems headed for. Toffler wrote: "We have set the stage for a completely new society and we are now racing toward it. . . . can we adapt to its imperatives?" Toffler's future new society has become the present and, for most Americans, the evolved answer to his question is: We don't want to.

American commerce and culture are rapidly decentralizing. People and businesses are leaving cities and their suburbs with insane high prices, filth, crime, and congestion and spreading out to small towns and rural areas with clean air, low prices, and lasting values. New concepts are imprinted on our consciousness: cities are sick—country is healthy—wilderness is safer than cities.

Commercial enterprises are leading *and* following the migration. Land is cheaper in rural areas. Lower wages are acceptable to workers with lower family overhead. And—no surprise: company executives and their families want to live away from the cities, too.

It is not just that cities have become unlivable, although many have. Cities have become unnecessary. Technology, the end of the industrial age and the beginning of the information age, plus widespread roads, electricity, telephones, and computers have made cities awkward, vestigial remnants of a society that is free for the first time in human history to live anywhere—but be instantly connectable to nearly any part of the world.

The new, very real American migration

The rural and small-town boom is not just the stuff of writers' imaginations, although it is one of the great stories of the waning years of this millennium. In the late 1960s, USDA senior demographer Calvin L. Beale first noticed that more people were leaving some metropolitan areas than moving there. His fellow demographers were skeptical. Not until the 1980 census was the national trend measured, confirmed, and finally accepted as fact. That census showed huge losses in city populations. For the first time since 1820, small town and rural area population was growing ahead of cities. In the 1970s, small towns and rural areas grew 15.5 percent faster than urban areas.

The 1990 census seemed to show that the flow from city to country had reversed. If so, the condition was short-lived. Kenneth M. Johnson and Calvin L. Beale presented a paper to the Southern Demographic Association in New Orleans, Louisiana, October 22, 1993 entitled *Nonmetropolitan Demographic Trends Since 1990.* They reported:

> In a reversal of the trend of the 1980s, population growth was widespread in nonmetropolitan areas of the United States during the early 1990s. More than 67 percent of the 2288 counties classified as nonmetropolitan in 1992 gained population between 1990 and 1991, compared to only 46 percent in the 1980s. In all, 500 more nonmetropolitan counties gained population than in the 1980s.

In *Megatrends 2000,* John Naisbitt and Patricia Aburdene spot the trends and predict the future.

> In the United States, for the first time in 200 years, more people are moving to rural areas than urban—many more. In the Northeast, West, Great Plains, and Southwest, everywhere, people are moving from cities and suburbs to rural areas. They are abandoning cities for quality-of-life reasons: low crime rates, comparatively low housing costs, recreational opportunities, and, perhaps most of all, a return to community values.

Naisbitt and Aburdene moved to Telluride, population 1,200, in southwest Colorado.

> Although we are six hours from Denver, with our computers, telephones, fax machine, and Federal Express we are as in touch with the rest of the world as if we were in downtown London or Tokyo.

During the 1980s as in the 1970s the population of most of the major central cities continued to fall, reported professor Jon C. Teaford, in *Cities of the Heartland.* According to Jack Lessinger, professor emeritus at the University of Washington, between one-third and one-half of the American and Canadian middle class will live outside metropolitan and suburban areas by 2010.

The historical westward movement has also reversed. Per *Newsweek* (7-19-93) United Van Lines and U-Haul figures show more native-born Americans leaving California than entering. For the first time in decades, California's adult population is growing only because of legal and illegal immigration from other countries, primarily Mexico and the Far East.

What is this thing called country?

My Webster's Ninth New Collegiate Dictionary defines *country* as "rural as distinguished from urban areas." Under *urban* we find "of, relating to, characteristic of, or constituting a city." *City* gives us "an inhabited place of greater size, population, or importance than a town or village." *Town* we find is "usually larger than a village but smaller than a city." We'll get to it any moment now, right? Aha! *Village* is "a settlement usually larger than a hamlet and smaller than a town." Onward; I feel we are closing in on the elusive thing. Here we are: a *hamlet* is "a small village." Gee, thanks a lot, Noah.

Sometimes the politics of place create unique definitions. Cities in Wyoming are communities with a population of at least 4,000. Those with between 150 and 3,999 are classified as towns.

One definition of country, or rural, is: sparsely populated and not directly influenced by a city. But even "sparsely" elicits diverse reactions. Each of us has a personal vision of country, and like "good" paintings, we know it when we see it. And that's what really counts.

Rural areas shrinking as metro areas adopt them

The dictionary is not the only reason for misunderstanding country. Towns and small cities have lobbied for the metropolitan designation to impress commercial interests and to tap federal programs. The federal designation "metropolitan area" now means a densely populated area that contains at least 50,000 people. These areas include much land that is rural or semirural, not urban. In fact, by census bureau manipulations that boggle the brain, *"39 percent of the rural population is metropolitan."* [My emphasis] (Fuguitt, Brown, and Beale, *Rural and Small Town America, 1989*) As an example, the St. Louis metropolitan area now includes ten counties, some of which exhibit bona-fide wilderness.

Metropolitan areas currently have such ballooned boundaries that they encompass approximately one-fifth of the total American land area. These artificial designations are one reason 1990 census figures are unreliable concerning the reported stall-out of city-to-country migration during the 1980s. Apparently, many people moved from city or suburb to true country, yet were included in the metropolitan count.

A model state?

North Carolina is often held forth as the shape of the future. The tenth most populous state, North Carolina has six million people but no large cities—at 350,000, Charlotte is the largest, with no other city over 200,000. With an extensive paved road system, a state university spread over sixteen campuses, and textile mills, furniture factories, and other manufacturing facilities scattered throughout the countryside, North Carolina is the result of purposeful planning and shaping by a succession of visionary leaders. As a result, the majority of the state is country in character.

And in definitional conclusion . . .

In this book, *country* means low-population-density areas lacking in the atmosphere, attitudes, and culture of a city. A home in the country may therefore be an old farmhouse on a large acreage, with the nearest neighbor miles away, or it may be a house on a lot in a town/village/hamlet, far enough from the nearest city that city atmosphere, attitudes, culture, and problems are not in evidence. In this book country does not include suburbs, edge cities, and master-planned communities. It is beyond what *The Last Landscape* author William H. Whyte referred to as the *greed line,* where the value of land has been reduced to its ability to create profit. By definition that leaves out agribusiness land, which you will learn to avoid.

The state maps in appendix B are shaded to show low-density areas, usually 50 persons per square mile but occasionally as low as ten. At 50 per square mile, that gives each person 12.8 acres. Take out space for roads and public places and we still have about 12.5, or 25 acres of elbow room for a couple, 50 acres for a family of four.

Motivations

The quest for quality of life, peace of mind, and living in harmony with one another is now combined with a growing understanding of our interconnectedness through nature. Awareness of the environmental crisis and the part each of us contributes to that problem is compelling us to reexamine our values, to seek to become part of the solution.

Sick cities: dirty air, undependable water, crime, schools and other social systems that just aren't working, high prices, and overcrowding. These are the apparent reasons why so many people are moving back to the country. I think the reasons are deeper, hidden within, sublimated for decades. I believe that our quest to understand our world and our condition is more difficult the more removed we are from nature. I believe we instinctively know that truth and beauty are most likely to be found in a natural environment.

I have lived in cities and I have lived in country. Cities offer greater economic opportunity, greater cultural offerings, and a greater number of services. Country living is cleaner, quieter, healthier, more crime-free, more stress-free, more independent, closer to nature, and, I believe, more conducive to personal growth.

Solid value systems derive from living close to nature. It is not by chance that the majority of our most successful leaders have come from low-population areas. Upon retirement from public service, they have often returned to rural living.

Those who study such things labor over the question: Are Americans repelled by the cities or drawn to the country? I think both are true. Where have we gone on vacations? Where have we dreamed of retiring to? Now that the providers of employment have figured out what we want, we don't have to wait for vacation or retirement time to be where we most desire. Now we can realize/ruralize our dreams.

Home computers and fax machines enable thousands to work at home, whether that home is on a mountaintop or deep in the woods. The completed national highway system and economical cars allow many more to move quickly from a country cottage to meaningful employment within a 30-minute drive. Living in the country is not only desirable, it is now economically realistic.

Are your motivations pragmatic or romantic? Mine were both. I'm a pragmatic romantic, very serious about romance. Living in the country provides more freedom to express myself and allows me to be in communion with nature, which I find essential for my well-being. City life seems abnormal, a denial of the natural factors of geography. My parents always gardened and the three places we lived while I was growing up were each progressively larger in acreage. Although I am on the west coast as I write this, my permanent home place is 130 acres of real country in the Midwest.

Many would find my place too remote. As one city visitor who slept there reacted, "It's awfully quiet at night." Too bad he wasn't there on one of the nights when the coyotes held a family reunion. The yipping, yapping, squealing (you haven't lived till you've heard grown coyotes squealing), yowling, and howling competes with the very highest attainment of punk rockers. But he wasn't and it was normal—very quiet. Not everyone likes that degree of quiet. To me, the city is outrageously noisy, with an ever-present background din. (The coyote parties only happen two or three times a year.) And more. As I write this in southern California, a man with a chain saw is pruning dead branches from the top of a palm tree two neighbors away. Actually, that sound makes me homesick. At my place I regularly use a chain saw to make firewood. But when my neighbors hear my saw, it is a muffled distant sound, as theirs is to me when they cut wood.

How much sound do you like? How close do you need to be to a supermarket, hardware store, or sports arena? As we explore these questions, you may find that what would please you most will be a place on a large lot at the edge of a small town. Or you may find that you want to be in a remote place, where supermarkets are nonexistent, where the nearest fast-food palace is a two-hour drive.

This book was produced for a wide range of people. It will be useful to retirees who have attained that secure status of knowing that a monthly check will follow them wherever they live and who have decided that they will plant their mailbox in front of a country home; to parents who want their children to understand that potatoes and carrots come from the ground, and eggs come from chickens—not from the supermarket back room; and for people of all ages who are disenchanted with city life and seek simpler, closer-to-nature lives in communities where natural human values are held in greater esteem than economic achievements.

Moving to the country may not create instant joy. After all, when we move, we take ourselves with us. Country living can be wonderful and it can be awful. Many people make life-altering moves based on decisions from emotional passion without due regard for commonsense considerations and practical knowledge. Such moves are seldom satisfactory. This book will assist you in making a sound, lasting decision. Your joy of country living will be ever so much greater for having made the effort to acquire the knowledge and do the planning.

The *premise* behind this book can be listed in four lines:
- If you clearly identify how and where you most want to live, and
- If you accordingly locate a property using *those criteria*, and
- If you acquire and live on that property, then
- Your life will be greatly enriched.

The place where one lives is a key factor contributing to overall happiness. Most people sense this. Surveys by the Gallup organization on national trends show an increasing preference for country living. A 1985 Gallup poll disclosed that "almost half of American adults would move to towns with fewer than 10,000 inhabitants or to rural areas." 1990 results showed an even stronger desire for rural life: 34 percent wanted a home in a small town; 24 percent picked a suburb; 22 percent desired a farm; and only 19 percent preferred a city.

Other studies have confirmed that, if they could, a majority of city dwellers would move to the country. What holds them back? Jobs, friends, family, and fear. Fear often comes from lack of knowledge.

As Pogo said, we are "confronted with insurmountable opportunities." And, as Robert Frost said, "You come, too."

. . . a child learns much,
and most of all that warmth
and love of Nature, which is perhaps
the greatest of all resources, not only because its
variety and beauty are inexhaustible but because slowly it creates
a sense of balance and of values, of philosophy and even of wise resignation
to man's own significance which bring the great rewards of wisdom
and understanding and tolerance. It is not by senseless accident
that the vast majority of the great men and women
of the nation and those who have built it
have come from farms or hamlets.

LOUIS BROMFIELD
OUT OF THE EARTH

On an occasion of this kind it becomes more than a moral duty
to speak one's mind; it becomes a pleasure.

<small>OSCAR WILDE</small>

Part I
First things

JOHN HENRY HILL
Meadow Lark's Nest, 1876. Etching.

Birth Place of.
Benjamin West.

1
The importance of place

*Perhaps the most psychologically significant
kind of movement that an individual can make
is geographical relocation of his home.*

ALVIN TOFFLER
FUTURE SHOCK

y concept of the ideal life is living in my ideal place, being
with whom I most wish to be, doing those things about which
I am most passionate, and having control over my basic needs
and my daily activities. A large order but possible—with
planning and focus, probable. And the first, vital requirement
is the right place.

The importance of place is overlooked, underestimated, and insuffi-
ciently acted upon. Most of us wait for an external push before opening
our minds to changing our home place. The most common happenings
are a job transfer or retirement but, increasingly, a major economic shock or
even criminal acts perpetrated against our property or loved ones.

*Try to live . . . deep in nature. Be native as trees to the wood,
as grass to the floor of the valley. Only then can the democratic spirit of man,
individual, rise out of the confusion of communal life in the city
to a creative civilization of the ground.*

FRANK LLOYD WRIGHT

*This return to nature is by no means a cure-all for the ills of civilization,
but it is one of the means of restoring the proper
balance and proportion in our lives.*

LIBERTY HYDE BAILEY
THE OUTLOOK TO NATURE

The value of natural surroundings is under-appreciated. The father of U.S. landscape design, Frederick Law Olmstead, who designed or co-designed numerous major parks, emphasized the importance of natural environments. From New York's Central Park to San Francisco's Golden Gate Park, millions of park visitors are proof not only of his skills but his wisdom.

There is a movie, *Enchanted April*, wherein four *disenchanted* English ladies pool their resources to rent for one month a villa in Italy. The unhappiness of all four is replaced by new and renewed love inspired by the beauty of the place—the trees, shrubs, flowers, and the views. The theme is timeless and persevering: whatever our psychological state, we are improved by the influence of a natural environment.

*Self-fulfillment comes more easily at the foot of a blue-gray mountain
and a few strides from a creek.*

JACK LESSINGER
REGIONS OF OPPORTUNITY

The importance of the place where we choose to live is beyond the kisses or kicks that climate delivers; it is more than the landform that shapes us; it is greater than the soil that feeds us and the water that washes us and replenishes our vital fluids; it is more than the natural and human community. It is all of these and it is more. Our place grounds us, steadies our posture to the world. It nurtures body and spirit. It gives us the strength to be what we would be.

*Our relationship with the places we know is a close bond, intricate in nature,
and not abstract, not remote at all . . . The danger . . . is that whenever
we make changes in our surroundings, we can all too easily shortchange
ourselves . . . The way to avoid the danger is to start doing three things at once:
Make sure that when we change a place, the change agreed upon nurtures
our growth as capable and responsible people, while also protecting
the natural environment, and developing jobs and homes enough for all.*

TONY HISS
THE EXPERIENCE OF PLACE

Opening one's mind, considering that any place is available to us, introspecting, developing criteria, conducting research, doing a lot of looking, and then purposefully moving to one's ideal place can be one of the most creative and rewarding experiences of a lifetime.

Beyond psychological nurture, a good natural environment raises intelligence. Really. Researchers at the University of California at Berkeley verified that rat brains grow larger when the animals are placed in an enriched environment. The brains of rats raised in a semi-natural outdoor environment grow larger still. So our quest is for a place where rat brains grow like crazy. Press on.

The place where a person lives
dramatically affects his happiness and success in life.
Living in a place which is not right for you
can be incredibly handicapping.
THOMAS F. BOWMAN, GEORGE A. GIULIANI, M. RONALD MINGE
FINDING YOUR BEST PLACE TO LIVE IN AMERICA

A girl and her ideal country home

2
The ideal country home

. . . a little nest that nestles where the roses bloom . . .
GEORGE WHITING AND WALTER DONALDSON
MY BLUE HEAVEN

In the beginning—dreams

Utopia is said to be impossible. That is likely a blessing—it would be terribly boring after the first day or three. For each of us though, there is a place that embodies the most of our wants and needs and the fewest of dislikes. With focus and persistence we each can find the place that is most ideal for us.

In our own mind, we can create any world we want. Reality begins with a dream. Daydream or nightdream, but dream. Those who dream and then focus on their dreams often attain them. Emerson said: "The ancestor of every action is a thought." Thoreau expounded: "If one advances confidently in the direction of his dreams, and endeavors to live the life which he has imagined, he will meet with a success unexpected in common hours."

One's imagined ideal place is often a blend of dreams and chance: lingering memories of childhood camps, vacations, books or movies, college or job experiences. I recently recalled that I made an emotional connection with place in January of 1970. My grandmother had died, and my brother and I were driving our "won't fly" parents and sister nonstop from California to Wisconsin for the funeral.

As we sped through the Missouri Ozarks I found myself increasingly captured by the scenery. And then I spotted a cabin on a hill, visible through the leafless trees, gray smoke twisting upward from a stone chimney. In only a few seconds an indelible connection was made. Seven years later, after considering the entire U.S. and carefully researching many states, never consciously remembering that cabin in the trees, I bought my ideal country place—smack dab in the middle of the Ozarks.

'Mid pleasures and palaces though we may roam,
Be it ever so humble, there's no place like home.

JOHN HOWARD PAYNE

Country home typically defines a house, a somewhat controlled area around the house, and a larger, more natural, maybe wild area expanding beyond—whether majestic mountains, undulating sands, shimmering waves of grasses, or the quiet, cool green of forest. It is more; it is the synergistic sum of house, garden, and landscape plus the magical, mystical aura common to a natural place. The whole can only be improved by working with instead of against nature.

The ideal country home place provides necessities: healthful air and water, climate wherein we thrive, and those utilities and services necessary to our chosen lifestyle. It provides space and conditions for our buildings and our activities, including food production and recreation. Located amidst natural beauty, the ideal home place provides mental and psychological well-being and it stimulates and nurtures our spiritual explorations. The ideal home inspires us to become more than we are. It elicits light, truth, and joy.

Location is paramount. The reason for the cliché: "The three most important elements of value are location, location, and location," is that almost anything about a place can be changed *except* its location. Terrain can be graded, trees and shrubs cut down or planted, and a house can be built, rebuilt, altered, razed, or moved. Only location and the attendant climate are unchangeable.

The ideal country home is located in an area that is economically stable. The income base is broad, with no dependence on a single industry. In many ideal rural counties, the three strongest sources of income are transfer payments (such as retirement checks), agriculture, and tourism.

Stability derives not only from economics but from community. The ideal home is located within a fair and nurturing community.

It is a deeply personal decision whether the ideal country home is in a tiny hamlet, a small town, near a town, or out in the boondocks. We will explore each of those options.

The ideal home site faces in a southerly direction, for maximum solar exposure. Whether it is in a valley or on a ridgetop will partly depend on whether you wish to look up or down at soaring birds—the kind of view you prefer. Other site considerations are detailed in chapter 10—*Land characteristics*.

Without leaving the contiguous 48 states you can find virtually any type of house, climate, topography, and demographics you prefer. An A-frame in the mountains; a cottage at the beach; a cabin in the woods, an adobe casa in the desert. Two hours from the nearest neighbor or tucked against a small town. On a thousand acres, a hundred acres, ten acres, an acre, or a large lot. Ski country, fishing country, farming country. But country.

Stability insurance—lots of land

On this I am firm: obtain as much land as you can afford to purchase and pay taxes on. *Nothing* will so guarantee your peace and privacy more than ownership of a substantial buffer around your home. Extra land provides the kind of privacy that makes window coverings redundant and the volume of Luciano Pavarotti or Willie Nelson while gardening strictly a matter of personal choice. To act as a steward for land in its natural state is also an honorable thing to do for our planet-home.

The Country Squire

If buying a large acreage seems beyond your means, you can look for a place that has characteristics highly undesirable to developers: remoteness, bad roads, rough terrain, steep access, and parcels too small to develop. Such land will usually be especially low-priced.

Like-minded persons can combine their dollars to buy a large acreage, deed housesites to each owner, and hold the rest of the land as common area, to be enjoyed by all and to be a buffer against intrusive development. If five buyers purchase an old 200-acre farm, and each uses five acres for house, outbuildings, and garden, that leaves 175 acres to ensure peace, quiet, and firewood forever. We have friends who did this. At first they had trouble getting bank financing for home construction because of legal questions regarding foreclosure and resale in case of default. They hired a lawyer who drafted an ownership agreement acceptable to the banks. They each now enjoy the use of a large, beautiful acreage that none of them could have purchased alone.

Now that is my viewpoint. There is another: buy only as much land as you need and wish to care for. This view comes from city people who treat country land like city land, busting their butts to prune forests and manicure pastures. Forget it. Manicure to your heart's content around the house, mow pastures a few times a year to thicken the grass and prevent erosion, and cut firewood judiciously, taking dead, dying, and crooked trees. Let the rest of your land be natural. If the natural landscape offends you, you probably would be unhappy living in real country.

There is in fact a great need for land to be protected from further human meddling. Forests, wetlands, grasslands, meadows, glades, and fens left in their natural states maintain biodiversity, protect watersheds, consume carbon dioxide, and preserve this bountiful and beautiful world for the future. That such land can also provide a buffer for serene living is a bonus.

In the next section we will explore the various factors that will help you identify *your* ideal country home place. As you choose your criteria, stretch your horizons. While considering climate, for instance, keep an open mind about areas extending beyond the edge of your first choice.

Now, look at the list you made when you finished *Notes on using this book*. You did make a list, didn't you? Does it include your fondest dreams, no matter how unrealistic they may seem? Write them down. And make any other additions you have thought of.

The happiness of the domestic fireside
is the first boon of heaven . . .
THOMAS JEFFERSON

Birthplace of Gilbert Stuart, North Kingstown, Rhode Island, c. 1886

3
Buy your land
as soon as you can

Buy land. They ain't makin' any more of the stuff.
WILL ROGERS

The population of our country is increasing. The domestic birth rate decline is more than offset by increased longevity and by immigration and immigrant birth rates. Since the 1960s, first hippies, then back-to-the-landers have moved from city to country. Now yuppies, soppies, and movie stars are doing it. Demographers tell us that the city-to-country migration is growing stronger.

I am not a star follower but I have noticed that celebrities often create trends. Notable among noticeables, Robert Redford, Ted Turner and Jane Fonda, Harrison Ford, Dennis Weaver, and, yes, Oprah, have all bought large acreages. Famous purchasers draw attention; their activities create followers; this drives prices up.

Baby boomers, the first now approaching their 50s, are leaving big-paying city jobs and city slime and crime and embracing lower paychecks and more free time with higher-quality country life. City people are buying second homes within weekend commuting range. Retirees continue moving to areas of greatest natural beauty and recreation, now including many with harsh winters—a counter-trend reflecting sun belt price dismay.

The interstate highway system is complete. With many companies now operating in edge cities, workers can live in real country and have a 20- or 30-minute commute to these new "office cities." Big money has noticed: large tracts of rural land in the path of growth are being grabbed by speculators. Each year more farm lands become subdivisions, shopping centers, office parks, airports, and roads. This creates diminishing supply.

The city-to-country migration is enabled by technology. In *Megatrends 2000* John Naisbitt and Patricia Aburdene state:

> Quality-of-life rural areas are as technologically linked to urban centers as are other cities. This megatrend of the next millennium is laying the groundwork for the decline of cities.

Always the most desirable property goes first. My advice is to find and buy your ideal country property as soon as possible, even though you may not intend or be able to move there for several years. If you must make payments, they will probably be less painful with city job income. And moving to your country home after it is paid for will greatly increase your security and peace of mind.

All current factors point to an increasing demand for a diminishing supply of country land. The condition of increasing demand and diminishing supply *always* drives prices up. The message is clear—buy your country land as soon as you can.

Essential country equipment #1: the horse

The original 4 X 4. Model shown comes with 4-speeds, runs on renewable fuels. Models suitable for child drivers are available. Can often be held for ransom from teenagers.

JAMES DAVID SMILLIE
Morning, 1892. Aquatint.

4
Who are you?

*Development of character
consists solely in moving toward self-sufficiency.*

QUENTIN CRISP

ost of us feel pretty confident that we know who we are. In fact
we proudly disclose ourselves to the world—to total
strangers we meet in stores, bars, and especially at parties.
Less willingly we reveal all (well, nearly all) to employment
agencies and the I.R.S. Extended city living dampens such
enthusiasm. In the city world of crime and incessant,
aggressive marketing we retreat behind security doors and
answering machines. From a state of willingly proclaiming ourselves
to all who ask, we evolve to using defensive screening techniques.
"Who are you with?" "How do you know her?" "What is your business
with him?" "I'm very busy; is this important?"

Knowing who we are and acknowledging the truth, if only to ourselves, is of critical value in determining which country conditions will make us happiest. People who move from city to country generally fall into definable groups, rather like subspecies. For some, moving from city to country is like mutating—for others, simply reverting to type. I don't particularly like labels but in this case using them will be helpful to our quest.

Categories of those in the ongoing city-to-country migration, in no particular order, are back-to-the-landers/homesteaders, boomer burn-outs/urban refugees, concerned parents, environmentalists, retirees, cashing-outers, and survivalists. Regardless of whether you identify with one, none, or all, the fact that you are reading this book means that you are looking to improve the quality of your life.

Back-to-the-landers/homesteaders

The so-called back-to-the-land movement is correctly named only in that all of our common ancestors once lived on the land. If Eve and the serpent had not gotten together on the apple thing we all might still be living in the original garden. Talk about overcrowding!

Some writers lump everybody who moves from city to country into this category. This is a gross generalization and contributes to identity crises, a big enough problem already. True BTTLs (who may or may not be rock 'n' rollers) are those who were born in the country, moved to the bright lights to seek fun, fame, and fortune, burned out on dealing with city conditions, remembered how much cleaner, greener, and saner country life was, and moved back—typically either to their growing-up place or another like it.

Those who desperately want to belong to this group but were born and reared in a city are hereby allowed membership by ancestral exemption, the grandfather clause for BTTLs. Reach back as far as necessary.

Back-to-the-landers and homesteaders lead very similar lifestyles once they are on the land. Homesteading is a self-reliant way of life on the land. There is tremendous satisfaction and security to be derived from producing home-grown food, wood fuel, and building and maintaining buildings and support systems.

It is not possible to be entirely self-sufficient and still live a high-quality life—such an effort quickly becomes long-hour drudgery. It does make sense, however, to become self-reliant. We can use current technology to enjoy long-term, secure, lower-cost living largely independent of public systems. A wind or photovoltaic system with generator backup can provide independence from the electric company. A ram pump will supply gravity-fed water. Freezers and canners can extend homegrown food availability year-round. An energy-efficient house, owner-built and maintained, can keep us winter-warm with only solar gain, a stove, and (homegrown) wood for heat. We can even cook with wood—new wood-burning kitchen stoves are available. All of these things and more are possible right now.

One factor against being totally self-sufficient is that most of us want to use as many labor-saving devices as we can afford. My father taught me to make firewood with an axe and a crosscut saw; trust me when I say that a chainsaw is more humane. Young Abe Lincoln was not the only one who quickly tired of working wood with a double-bitted axe.

As with rearing children, there is one area—home food production—where the results are worth almost any effort. Growing food takes more time than earning dollars and buying it. But the quality of homegrown food far surpasses the best food in the best stores of the best food-growing regions in the country. Homegrown vegetables and fruits are fresher, more nutritious, and safe from chemical residue. Eating poisoned food is courting an early demise—we might as well take up do-it-yourself bungee jumping. Home gardeners can look their potatoes in the eyes and feel good about what they see there.

Homesteading with modern tools and technology can be a very high quality lifestyle. Becoming self-reliant and independent from "the system" are worthwhile and enriching goals. Our body, our family, and our planet benefit.

Boomer burn-outs/urban refugees

Solitude is impracticable, and society fatal.
We must keep our head in the one and our hands in the other.
The conditions are met, if we keep our independence,
yet do not lose our sympathy.

RALPH WALDO EMERSON

City sickness, city blight—whatever the term used, the condition has become an obvious plague. Traffic congestion, smog, crime, noise pollution, insensitivity, high taxes, and high prices are symptoms of city disease. Urban burn-outs are seeking meaningful lives away from it all.

Urban refugees are moving *to* the country as well as *away from* the city. Often unequipped with country skills, many move to fringe areas and small towns rather than real country. Why not? After all, small towns are what cities used to be before too many people went there.

America's baby-boomers have met middle age—and they are not ecstatic about the introduction, never mind the relationship. Today's boomers are talking about health, longevity, ecology, and sustainability. They are thinking less about corporate ladders and more about fruit-picking ladders. They are reconsidering family, community, safety, security, and meaning of life. In the aftermath of mass layoffs many have redefined their work ethic. Working to live is accepted—living to work is passé. Many of the 76 million boomers have boarded the wagon train leaving metropolis for the boondocks.

This group's collective profile is: married, above-average education, affluent, zero-to-two children, homeowner, long-distance commuter, 60-hour work weeks, fantasizer of better quality life with more time to spend with family. Those couples who have ever thought, "We just had sex, so it must be Saturday," may fit into this group.

Concerned parents

Overcrowded classrooms, plummeting academic standards, drug dealers, guns, graffiti, and other lawlessness pervade city schools in all but the very nicest areas. Many parents who seriously address the formidable challenge of child rearing are taking their progeny out of city schools. Many move to selected rural areas with small class sizes, high scholastic standards, and total intolerance of hoodlumism. (Take note: the introduction to rural school discipline can be a shocking experience for ex-city kids accustomed to unruly classrooms.)

If you fit into this category, be aware that many rural school boards have budget challenges as serious as their city counterparts. Also, not all country communities place a premium on education. Identify several areas you like, then contact school principals with questions regarding class sizes, curriculum, gifted and special education programs, percentage of dropouts, and percentage of graduates who go on to college. Query county clerks on voter response to school bonds and taxes. Shorten your list, then visit schools and observe the attitudes of teachers and students. Don't be put off by modest physical facilities; although few one-room schools still exist, they often do a superior job of educating up to high school level. No wonder—by the time students reach the eighth grade, they've already heard the material seven times!

Small-town schools often have big-time spirit. Among the schools represented in the 1994 Rose Parade was the award-winning high school marching band of Pipestone, Minnesota, town population 4,500. One-third of the entire high school student body was in the band.

Living outside of town means students ride school buses, as I did my last three years of high school. It was a novel experience—out of 26 riders, only two of us were boys, I the oldest. The girls schemed for the privilege of sitting with us. Two boys trying to be fair to 24 girls was an awesome—and rewarding—challenge.

Environmentalists

Seventy-six percent of all Americans
describe themselves as environmentalists.
There is precious little else
about which we so thoroughly agree.

JOEL GARREAU
EDGE CITY

Conservationists, ecologists, environmentalists, Greens—however we label ourselves—constitute the surging swell of citizens who understand that Spaceship Earth is suffering from bad management. We are informed people who believe in taking greater responsibility for our conduct, who understand that we are in fact "all in this together."

Those in this group cite cities as inefficient and wasteful of energy resources, generators of greenhouse gasses, acid rain, toxic waste, and enormous accumulations of garbage. Some remain in the city to try to effect change from within. Many move to the country to lead simpler lives more in tune with the wisdom of natural laws.

This group has the greatest age spread, the highest idealism, and perhaps the greatest potential for rural life disaster. If you identify most strongly with this group, I recommend you spend substantial time vacationing in your chosen area before moving. Rent or caretake a place for a year. Learn country skills. Spend time with farm families, perhaps with alternative communities. And *do not expect to change the attitudes of the natives*. Show what you believe by actions, not words. You will find similar souls who have preceded you.

Retirees

Once the gold encircles the wrist (what—they don't do that anymore?) and the long-dreamed-about check appears in the mailbox, there is the challenge of what to do between naps. There is also the freedom to live wherever that check will cover expenses. Retirees have been moving to the country for decades. The usual scenario here is: sell the city house for big bucks, buy a place in a gentler clime for about one-third as much money and with low taxes, then fish, golf, garden, and entertain city friends who come to vacation rent-free in the country.

Retirement communities typically grow in areas with mild winters, good medical facilities, fishing lakes, and golf courses. Graying areas also grow a high number of service businesses—providing jobs for younger folks.

Now, however, many retirees are breaking the sunbelt syndrome, finding lower prices, less crowding, prettier scenery, and more satisfying lifestyles in areas of moderate-to-cold winters. These include the rural areas of southwest Missouri, northwest Arkansas, western Virginia, western North Carolina, northern Georgia, eastern Tennessee, parts of Nevada, much of Oregon, around Coeur d'Alene in Idaho, Washington County of Utah, southern Indiana, and yes, even selected areas of the Northeast. This is a short list—many other areas of moderate-to-cold winters are attracting this group.

Cashing outers

Faith Popcorn says that cashing out to the country

is a dream as old as America itself: give me a piece of land to call my own, a little town where everyone knows my name. It's a dream we are dreaming with a new heart-and-gut-felt urgency. More than the romance of the country, it's a promise of safety, of comfort, and of old-fashioned values.

Members of this group often buy or create bed and breakfast inns. They run small-town newspapers, make goat-milk ice cream, raise sheep, or operate fishing resorts. They write newsletters, make pottery, and build furniture. They may work harder than they did for the corporate cats, but they don't commute, they don't lug bulging briefcases back and forth, and they make their own decisions.

Survivalists

Those who fit this label are moving to the country because they believe that city sickness signals the start of the meltdown of social order and is leading to increasing anarchy.

Alvin Toffler wrote in *Future Shock* that "Great cities are paralyzed by strikes, power failures, riots." The New York garbage collectors strike, the 1965 Watts riots, the 1992 L.A. riots, and the 1994 L.A. earthquake were examples of near paralysis that illustrated the dependence and vulnerability of city citizens when systems break down. It is at such times that the social condition of a place is magnified and clarified. In the first 30 minutes of the 1977 New York power blackout looters had stolen $150 million in goods.

Survivalists cite growing lawlessness, political corruption, and the fragility of food, water, and utility systems as road maps to chaos. They fear that when city systems collapse there will be an enormous exodus to the country, so many heavily arm themselves to ward off the masses they believe will stream to their well-stocked country homes demanding food and shelter.

If these are your views then concentrate your search in very-low-population areas far from cities and highways. These places usually have low land prices, which will save money for a self-contained power system, perimeter security system, fortified house, and weaponry.

Pop quiz

So now, do you know who you are? Did you quickly identify with one of the above groups or, more likely, did you find something of yourself in two or more? That's fine, of course. You pass. What this chapter is about is getting you thinking about your basic and vital motivations, your needs and your wants.

Once you move from city to sanity, in addition to any of the above you may find yourself labeled urban dropout, urban flighter, rat race escapee, or new American pioneer. The diversity of names simply proves that the wagon train is composed of many unique travelers. The common quest is a higher-quality life. You are in good company.

Final thought

Country living is conducive to fresh thinking about values. Donald McCaig, in *An American Homeplace*, quotes Scott Nearing: "The only thing more cowardly than a million dollars is two million dollars." Nearing lived his words: he and wife Helen refused inheritances and, when they left Vermont for less-crowded Maine, they sold their homestead for only the value of the cash and labor they had invested in it, one-fourth of its market value. That says a lot for who *they* were.

5
Do you have what it takes

to live a simple, high-quality country life,
and—characteristics of those who transplant well

Men are born to succeed, not to fail.
HENRY DAVID THOREAU

n *You Can't Grow Tomatoes in Central Park: The Urban Dropouts Guide to Rural Relocation*, Frank Ruegg and Paul Bianchina report that the 42 dropouts responding to their survey agreed on two success factors: perseverance and a positive attitude. The survey also found that 27 of the respondents, as children, "dreamed about living in a special, less densely-populated spot." That jolted me—I had forgotten that, as a young teenager, I often fantasized about owning and living in a special rural place.

In my experience, those who have triumphantly transplanted themselves are independent types who are not concerned with approval ratings. They are self-directed. And while often gregarious, they treasure peace, quiet, and privacy.

Surprisingly, most who move to country are not seriously concerned about making a living. Most move with at least a small savings account to back them, easy to accomplish when selling inflated city houses and buying low-priced country places. Most overcome any financial obstacles and, in three to five years, are making as much as before while enjoying lower overhead.

The following listing of human characteristics is appropriate to many matters more mundane than finding our ideal country place. But here, regarding this essential enterprise, they are critical and worthy of review. As greater minds than mine have expounded on these things, this chapter consists primarily of quotes.

A dream

You've got to create a dream. You've got to uphold the dream.
If you can't, go back to the factory or go back to the desk.

Eric Burdon

Yes, I know this is redundant. But I believe that the importance of dreams cannot be overstated.

Passion

The essential conditions of everything you do
must be choice, love, passion.

Nadia Boulanger

A plan

The journey of ten thousand miles begins with a single phone call.

CONFUCIUS BELL

Hopefully you will have a plan by the time you finish this book. Perhaps you already do. Making a plan is simply gathering information, investigating possibilities, and choosing alternatives. The more information, the sounder the resulting plan.

Positive focusing

Keeping your mind on the goal and moving toward the goal
is the essence of positive focusing.
All the rest is fun, but not essential.
Unless, of course, you consider fun to be essential.

PETER McWILLIAMS

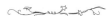

Positive thinking by itself rarely gets us what we want except positive thoughts. Positive focusing helps move us toward our goal, even if we have negative thoughts about it. Together, positive thinking and positive focusing help move us happily to our goal.

Open-mindedness

Minds are like parachutes. They only function when open.

JAMES DEWAR

The only means of strengthening one's intellect
is to make up one's mind about nothing—
to let the mind be a thoroughfare for all thoughts.

JOHN KEATS

Where there is an open mind, there will always be a frontier.

CHARLES F. KETTERING

The beautiful souls are they that are
universal, open, and ready for all things.
MICHEL DE MONTAIGNE

The quality of open-mindedness is essential to learning. Never fear to be open to new ideas. Nothing new or useful ever results from a closed mind. Specifically, consider *all* the country, not just those areas to which you presently feel drawn. Once in your new place, let your brain be like a sponge.

Persistence

Writing is easy.
All you do is stare at a blank sheet of paper
until drops of blood form on your forehead.
GENE FOWLER

Stay with it until you get what you want. Few have said it as well as cool Calvin Coolidge:

> Nothing in the world can take the place of persistence. Talent will not; nothing is more common than unsuccessful men with talent. Genius will not; unrewarded genius is almost a proverb. Education alone will not; the world is full of educated derelicts. Persistence and determination alone are omnipotent.

Here's one by Lucretius that will make a picture: "The drops of rain make a hole in the stone not by violence, but by oft falling."

Ability to make decisions

When you have to make a choice and
don't make it, that is in itself a choice.
WILLIAM JAMES

By picking up this book you've already made a decision. We'll get back to this one later, when we need it most.

Willingness to take a chance

*Be bold—and mighty forces
will come to your aid.*
BASIL KING

Willingness to take a chance derives from passion and confidence—knowing that we're ready because we've accumulated adequate information. This book provides the recipe for the ideal country place. That will contribute to your confidence level. Add passion and stir.

Essential country skills #87 and #93

Instructions for Skill #87—Chasing bears away: Always keep the pointed end of the spear in the bear's face. Tell the bear to go away. If the bear slaps the spear out of your hands, pick up the spear and again point it at the bear's face. Repeat this procedure as long as necessary to impress the bear with your sincerity. Some bears are stubborn and require prolonged training.

Instructions for Skill #93—Shooting birds for dinner: Point the gun at a bird and pull the trigger. If the bird keeps flying, repeat the procedure. Continue shooting birds until you have as many birds as people coming to dinner. Have an alternate menu.

Tolerance

Truth resides in every human heart, and one has to search for it there,
and to be guided by truth as one sees it.
But no one has a right to coerce others to act according to his own view of truth.

MOHANDAS K. GANDHI

We are all full of weakness and errors, let us mutually pardon each other
our follies—it is the first law of nature.

VOLTAIRE

Let us forget such words, and all they mean, as
Hatred, Bitterness and Rancor, Greed, Intolerance, Bigotry.
Let us renew our faith and pledge to Man, his right to be Himself, and free.

EDNA ST. VINCENT MILLAY

Essential country skill #4—milking a cow

Instructions: The cow is the large animal with horns. The milk comes out of the cow's milk nozzles as illustrated. Place a milk bucket under the nozzles. Grasp one or two nozzles and squeeze. If milk does not come out squeeze harder. If the cow kicks, you are squeezing too hard or should trim your fingernails. Apologize to the cow and pick up the bucket. Squeeze with a top-to-bottom action. Squeezing with other actions may cause the milk to flow upward instead of downward—this will annoy the cow. Continue squeezing a few thousand times until the milk bucket is full. Thank the cow and go make some ice cream.

Note: When buying a cow the most important consideration is the nozzle-to-hand fit. Whenever you see a cow, squeeze her nozzles. Keep searching and squeezing until you find a good fit.

ANGUS MACDONALL

Remarkable view for a city tenement, 1924.

6
Besides being important, what do you really want?

*The great question . . . which I have not been able to answer,
despite my thirty years of research into the feminine soul, is
'What does a woman want?'*

SIGMUND FREUD

You have to know what you want to get.

GERTRUDE STEIN

Blissful dream fantasy

ne more time. This time let it all hang out. Treat yourself to a fantasy.
Imagine that you are living where you wish, with whom you desire,
doing the work about which you are most passionate, enjoying
your favorite activities. Now save those delicious thoughts by writing
them down. We will use them later.

As a teenager, I was impressed by Louis Bromfield's *Pleasant Valley*
and *Malabar Farm*. In 1939, with German invasion imminent, Bromfield
had left France and returned to Ohio, to the valley of his youth. There he
created Malabar Farm, his dream place, which became the most famous

experimental farm in America. Earlier he had written *The Farm,* a fictionalized family biography, which proved to be a forecasting of Malabar. His writings at Malabar were strong with a love of the land, a gut-felt romance, and a longing to create his version of Utopia.

What I wanted was a piece of land
which I could love passionately,
which I could spend the rest of my life
in cultivating, cherishing and improving,
which I might leave together, perhaps,
with my own feeling for it, to my children
who might in time leave it to their children,
a piece of land upon which I might leave
the mark of my character, my ingenuity,
my intelligence, my sense of beauty . . .

LOUIS BROMFIELD
PLEASANT VALLEY

Bromfield's writings seeded my dream of one day owning a self-sufficient home place with hills and fields and trees, and a stream running through it all. For many years my dream was forgotten as I served in the U.S. Army, sought an education, married, reared children, and tended a business. The dream resurfaced in a five-year plan written in 1975. In 1976 I found my dream place, a small, secluded creek valley, one of Earth's special places.

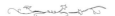

I feel that if one follows what I call one's bliss—the thing
that really gets you deep in the gut and that you
feel is your life—doors will open up. They do!

JOSEPH CAMPBELL

Purposefully creating a new life in a new place is perhaps the most significant creative thing one can do. Everything we create is the result of all that we are, and creating a new life is intensely, lovingly personal. Everyone has a dream of their ideal place. If your dream is clear to you, you have your goal. If your dream of an ideal place is fuzzy, the following questions will help you begin to bring it into focus.

Are you seeking a permanent, temporary, or a second home?

This is a fundamental question. If you are seeking a permanent home you have the luxury to ignore investment considerations. But do be concerned about growth direction, as nothing can so annihilate peace and quiet as nearby development.

If you need a temporary home, you will do well to buy where values are rising, so that you can make maximum profit when you sell. The optimum location is where rapid growth is imminent. Read Jack Lessinger's book, *Regions Of Opportunity: A Bold New Strategy For Real Estate Investment With Forecasts To The Year 2010.* If you must be able to sell quickly when the time comes, buy something that is in high demand. Not too big, not too small, and within a short distance of school, shopping, and highway. Try for assumable financing and high loan-to-sale price ratio—invest as little cash as possible. Sellers are more likely to make an assumable loan than institutional lenders.

A second home, used for long weekends and vacations, often eventually becomes more desirable than the primary residence. It would be wise to treat the search for a second home as if it were for a permanent home, as it may turn out to be. If you want a second home that may become a permanent home, then do not compromise—look for your ideal place. Spending enjoyable holidays and vacations at a second home is seductive—you may soon find that life is better there than "back home." Welcome to the country.

Wants and needs

*Modern man lives under the illusion
that he knows what he wants,
while he actually wants
what he is supposed to want.*

ERICH FROMM
ESCAPE FROM FREEDOM

What are your true needs and wants, your hot buttons—what turns you on? Do you want to grow crops, garden, landscape, conduct a business, or farm commercially? Find a traditional school for your children? Have your fishing boat tied up to a dock in front of the house? Ski out the back door? Hunt and trap? Park your plane on your own landing strip near your house? Answers to these questions will begin to shape your requirements. *Write them down.*

How much land do you want?

This decision not only has a dollar value—in many ways it affects quality of life. One of the reasons most of us move to the country is to experience openness and quiet not possible with close neighbors. Larger parcels create more privacy—our activities remain only ours unless we choose to share them. Later, if children or grandchildren are drawn to join us living on the land, a larger acreage will allow each a measure of privacy.

Securing a high level of privacy derives from two qualities: location and size of acreage. Other than climate, location is the only factor that cannot be changed about a piece of land. Area population change is inevitable but we can go a long way toward ensuring stable tranquillity by choosing a home place with attention to certain factors.

Desirability of place is a double-edged sword—if we find an area highly desirable, others will find it so also. The result can be a phenomenon, or disease, sometimes indelicately called "Californication." There are two solutions: choose a place that has a feature others find objectionable (economically depressed, poor accessibility, remoteness, occasional flooding); or get there first and buy enough land to buffer the inevitable invasion. Note: when the invasion comes, taxes will rise.

Beyond privacy, there are other considerations for owning more land than needed for personal use. We presently own 130 acres but use only about five on a regular basis other than for cutting firewood. We feel good about the remaining land being protected in its natural state, the trees helping to ameliorate global warming, all vegetation protecting the watershed and providing a home to a multitude of flora and fauna, the natural world essentially untouched. And there is deep pleasure gained from walking on and observing one's own land, knowing that it is safeguarded and will not be damaged during our lifetime. Or just sitting on a rock and *absorbing*. It is a better church than any building.

Wendell Berry carries it further:

> If we are to be properly humble in our use of the world, we need places that we do not use at all. We need the experience of leaving something alone. We need places that we forbear to change, or influence by our presence, or impose on even by our understanding; places that we accept as influences upon us, not the other way around, that we enter with the sense, the pleasure, of having nothing to do there; places that we must enter in a kind of cultural nakedness, without comforts or tools, to submit rather than to conquer. We need what other ages would have called sacred groves. . . . We need wilderness as a standard of civilization and as a cultural model. . . . Only if we know how the land was can we tell how it *is*.

The how-much-land decision must be a very personal choice for each of us, but the following is offered as a guide:

- Space for house and other buildings: garage, workshop, barn, other outbuildings
- Space for activities for yourself and your animals: crops, pastures, gardens, orchard, woodlot, pond, landscaping, leisure activities
- Extra acres to ensure the desired degree of privacy and quiet
- Land for natural, undisturbed space

Jed Clampett: *Pearl, what d'ya think? Think I oughta move?*
Cousin Pearl: *Jed, how can ya even ask? Look around ya.*
Yer eight miles from yer nearest neighbor. Yor overrun with
skunks, possums, coyotes, bobcats. Ya use kerosene lamps
fer light and ya cook on a wood stove summer and winter.
Yer drinkin' homemade moonshine and washin' with
homemade lye soap. And yor bathroom is fifty feet
from the house and you ask "should I move?"
Jed: *I reckon yor right.*
A man'd be a dang fool to leave all this!
THE BEVERLY HILLBILLIES

If decisions were a choice between alternatives,
decisions would come easy.
Decision is the selection and formulation of alternatives.

KENNETH BURKE

TOWARDS A BETTER LIFE

Part II
Criteria and considerations

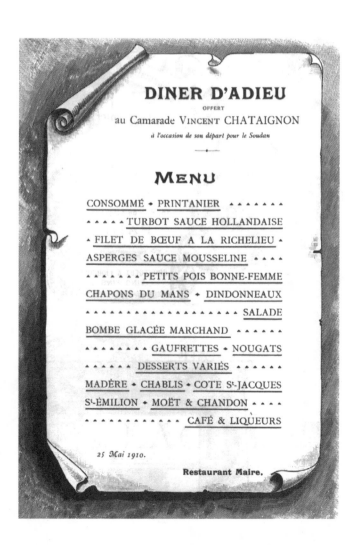

DINER D'ADIEU
OFFERT
au Camarade Vincent CHATAIGNON
à l'occasion de son départ pour le Soudan

MENU

CONSOMMÉ • PRINTANIER • • • • • • •
• • • • TURBOT SAUCE HOLLANDAISE
• FILET DE BŒUF A LA RICHELIEU •
ASPERGES SAUCE MOUSSELINE • • • •
• • • • • • PETITS POIS BONNE-FEMME
CHAPONS DU MANS • DINDONNEAUX
• • • • • • • • • • • SALADE
BOMBE GLACÉE MARCHAND • • • • •
• • • • • • • GAUFRETTES • NOUGATS
• • • • DESSERTS VARIÉS • • • • •
MADÈRE • CHABLIS • COTE Sᵗ-JACQUES
Sᵗ-ÉMILION • MOËT & CHANDON • • • •
• • • • • • CAFÉ & LIQUEURS

25 Mai 1910.

Restaurant Maire.

7
On developing a criteria list

It is a funny thing about life . . .
If you refuse to accept anything but the best,
you very often get it.
SOMERSET MAUGHAM

elocation from city to country can be a sublime success or a descent into hell. I know many who love it and many who have left it. In my experience, those who carefully looked before they leaped have not only lasted but flourished. Making a criteria list is writing a personal ticket to a successful trip.

Our purpose in developing and considering complete criteria is first to clarify values, interests, wants, and needs. We began that process in chapter 4—*Who are you?* Second, to become aware of conditions, both positive and negative, and available options. Third, by application, to lead you to your ideal country home place.

The method presented in this book is to develop a criteria worksheet, which will include all important considerations of moving from an urban to a rural home place. The worksheet is an evolving plan that will emerge as each subject is explored and your wants and needs become clarified. After the worksheet is completed you will use it to write your criteria list.

Your criteria list will be a personal preference profile. If you develop your list carefully and use it to find your ideal country home, I am confident that it will raise the quality of your life.

Following is a list I wrote in the mid-1970s as part of a five-year plan to leave city life in northern California for country life—somewhere.

My criteria for an ideal permanent home place—the place where the heavy furniture stays

1. Four seasons but milder winters than those I grew up with (in Wisconsin)
2. An area of hills and valleys
3. Primarily wooded
4. Clean air
5. Clean flowing water
6. Land prices low enough to allow purchase of at least 40 acres
7. Low population density
8. Low property taxes
9. Background bureaucracy—minimal local regulations re: zoning, building codes, permits, etc., to maximize personal freedom
10. Within one hour of a city with a four-year college or university
11. At least twenty miles away from railroads, major highways, and cities, and not contiguous to national forests—to minimize chances of development or eminent domain proceedings
12. I don't care if there is a house or not

I applied my criteria to the contiguous 48 states, narrowed my list to seven states, did further research, decided on one area, and told a large number of real estate agents in that area exactly what I wanted and when I would arrive to look. I drove nearly 2,000 miles to the area and spent the next two weeks looking at dozens of properties in a band about 60 miles wide and more than 100 miles long.

How did it work out? Wonderful! I got everything I wanted except #10, but, with one exception about which I will write later, everything else is so great that I have no regrets. In fact, because some areas are growing so rapidly, I'm glad I landed further out in the boondocks than I planned. Our nearest four-year college city is Springfield, Missouri, nearly two hours away. Had I uncompromisingly bought land within one hour of Springfield, I might now find my tranquillity destroyed by the growth of Branson, predicted by many to become the country music center of America. If bumper-to-bumper summer traffic is a good indicator, it already is. We hillbillies don't go near the place during tourist season unless we entertain visitors who insist on the experience.

The author taking his mother to Branson

CRITERIA WORKSHEET

Lifestyle/preferred activities _____

Climate _____

Topography: Flat   Rolling   Hills   Mountains _____

Soil: Garden quality 1/4 acre minimum   Cropland _____

Trees: Hardwoods   Softwoods   Firewood   Lumber _____

Vegetation: Lawn   Pasture _____ acres   Other _____

Acreage, minimum/maximum _____

Work _____

Farming _____

Air quality _____

Water: Rainfall quantity _____   Well   Spring   Stream   River   Lake

Water delivery system: Gravity Electric pump & pressure tank Other _____

Waste system: Public Septic tank Composting toilet Outhouse Other _____

Health considerations _____

Community _____

Demographics _____

Transportation _____

Taxes _____

Services _____

Electricity: At house   On property   Available   Independent system _____

Telephone: Clear reception for modem _____

Radio/TV reception: Important   Not important   Satellite dish _____

House: Yes, size _____ Age _____ No ___ Don't care _____

Outbuildings: Garage   Workshop   Barn   Machinery shed Other _____

Prices: Total max. $ _____ $ _____ /acre. Financing _____

Notes _____

You will have noticed that my list did not include an income source. My 5-year plan extrapolated my real estate investment equities into a totally reasonable financial formula for supporting an idyllic country life. Alas, divorce and recession later required major adjustments. As Pansy Penner said: "Just about the time you think you can make both ends meet, somebody moves the ends." Oh well, we all need to learn humility—some of us, ahem, more than others.

With the 20-20 vision of hindsight, I realize how many criteria I did not think of back in 1976, and how lucky I was to find a place that, for instance, continues to have clean water and soil and is far upwind and upstream from toxic pollution.

Eleven keys to successful city-to-country migration

1. Verify that you truly wish to live in the country
2. Determine who you are and what you want to do
3. Identify the characteristics of your ideal property
4. Locate regions that have the climatic, topographic, demographic, economic, and other characteristics that fit your wants and needs
5. Narrow your list down to two or three to investigate
6. Determine your ideal area
7. Look at all appropriate properties in your ideal area, measure them against your criteria, and choose the best one
8. Obtain a fair-price contract on your chosen property, with adequate protection to allow withdrawal if you discover a challenge that is larger than you can live with
9. Satisfy yourself, through inspections and investigations, that the property has no hidden flaws, and you will be able to do with it as you wish
10. Close the sale and take possession
11. Enjoy living on your country property. If you took care of the first ten steps and have an income, this one is a natural

Marilyn and Tom Ross, in *Country Bound!*, offer seven yardsticks for measuring an area's quality of life. They include: cost of living, crime, weather (climate), health care, environment (pollution), leisure (culture, arts, recreation, attitude, and entertainment), and infrastructure (education, transportation). The authors of the many where's-the-best-place books also listed in the bibliography use essentially the same criteria as the Rosses. In this book we will consider all of these and more.

The criteria worksheet includes the subjects we will be considering. Make a copy and use it to make notes as you continue to read part II. Look at the notes you have made thus far and transfer your priorities to the worksheet.

A final thought. While the purpose of this book is to help you find your ideal country home, a certain reality must be faced—namely, that perfection is, well, impossible. As expressed by Peter McWilliams in *You Can't Afford the Luxury of a Negative Thought*, "You can have anything you want—you just can't have everything you want."

But we can try. What a wonderful challenge. Onward!

*Our requirements were: isolation enough to avoid
the hustling and jostling of the city and its suburbs;
a minimum of fertile soil on which to grow our food;
abundant fresh water; a woodlot to provide our fuel.*

HELEN & SCOTT NEARING
CONTINUING THE GOOD LIFE

GABRIELLE DE VEAUX CLEMENTS
1883. Etching.

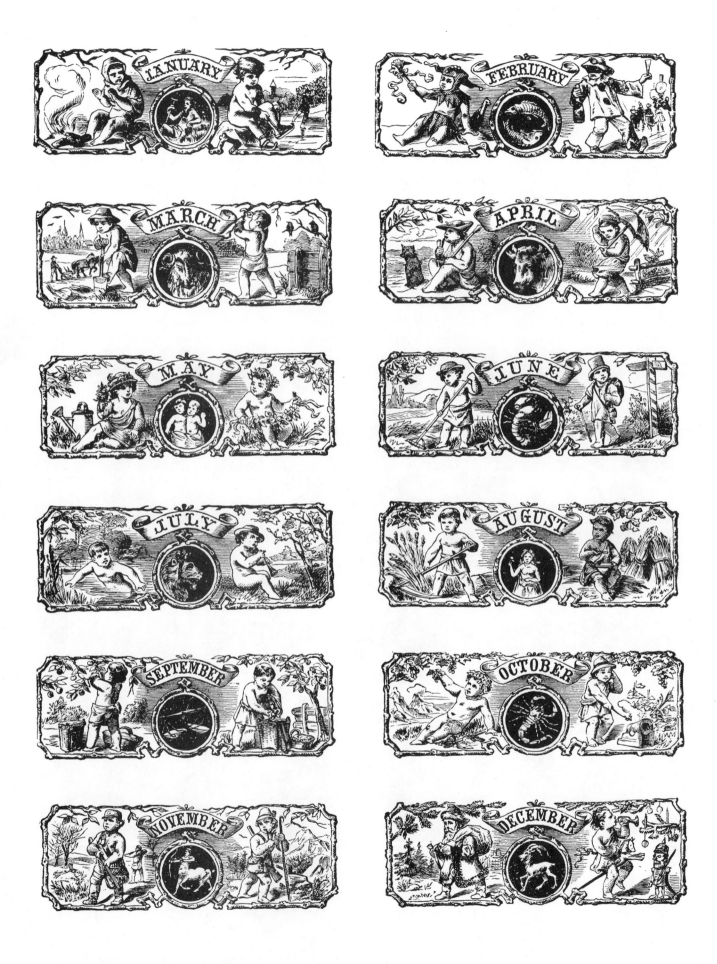

8
Lifestyle

A man who has spent much time and money
in dreary restaurants moodily chewing
filet of sole on the special luncheon
is bound to become unmanageable
when he discovers that he can
produce the main fish course directly,
at the edge of his own pasture,
by a bit of trickery on a fine morning.

E.B. WHITE
ONE MAN'S MEAT

ifestyle is the things we do, which comes from our needs, our values, and the influence of our place. In chapter 4—*Who are you?*, we began to explore needs and values. First on our criteria list is preferred activities. *What* we wish to do may dictate *where* we do it. Gardening in the desert, skiing on the plains, and golfing on a mountain peak are unreasonable expectations.

Country lifestyle is the result of needs, habits, values, the land's influence, the size of the place, the tools and the skills we have.

In the country we get our exercise preparing soil, planting, tending animals, harvesting crops, making firewood, building stone walls, and walking. In the city exercise is accomplished at "fitness centers" where the fitness seekers pay for the privilege of using machines to work muscles. What a waste. Why *hasn't* someone developed a way to convert all that running, climbing, pedaling, and lifting into electricity? Maybe public utilities should own those places and pay exercisers for expending their calories to generate Btus.

The fact that you are considering moving to the country means that you *want* to change at least some of your activities. The ideal life includes doing those things we most enjoy. Being in control. Having maximum free choice and maximum independence.

Besides your vocation, what do you do?

List all of your activities for the last year. Add any that you really want to do that you don't do now. Circle those that are especially important to you. You will want to make sure those activities are all available or possible in your new spot.

Here is a list of place-related activities to bump your brain: swimming, fishing, floating, boating, water skiing; hunting, trapping; snow skiing, ice skating, making snowpeople, having white Christmases; golfing; attending the symphony, concerts, music shows, plays, opera, ballet, baseball, football, basketball; hang gliding; bird watching; bee keeping. Some activities may be practiced nearly anywhere but climate, topography, raw materials, or local conditions may make them more enjoyable in certain places. These include gardening, hiking, horse-back riding, running, woodworking, nature photography, and camping.

To thine own self be true

One ridge to the north of us lived a lady who brought a fur opera jacket with her when she and her husband moved from the city. The nearest opera house is five hours from our area—in good weather. Each year she took the jacket out of its protective case, shook it and aired it and brushed it. But only once did she and her husband make the ten-hour round trip to attend the opera. Just before they moved, in the midst of explaining why they were leaving, she showed me the coat and spoke of how important the opera was to her. She explained that their modest budget did not allow the expense of a long drive, overnight accommodations, meals, and tickets.

If part of you will die if you can't go to the opera, major league ballgame, symphony, or ballet, then your ideal place will be within easy driving distance to the opera house, the stadium, or the theater.

Habits are easier to alter than passions. Old habits follow us, hold hands with our shadow, wake up with us each morning. But they do change and we are often the better for it. Fresh opportunity creates new habits according to values deep or values learned. Moving to the country, to space and calmness, provides conditions for growth. We can leave the old and embrace the new, or we can retain the best of the old, reach for the best of the new, meld the two and let place and values forge a natural result.

There is a difference between living in the country and living on the land. The former simply implies residence. The latter means gaining sustenance from the soil, the woods, the waters, being a part of the place and letting the place become part of us. (Sometimes our language is inscrutable: how did living *on* the land come to mean the same as living *off* the land?)

Homesteading

A noun, homestead is a home and the adjoining land. A verb, homestead is to settle on a property and to gain sustenance from it. In this country the concept evolved from the Pilgrims' early subsistence patches. The phrase came into public usage with the Homestead Act of 1862, which gave 160 acres of public land to any adult who could live on it for five years. By 1900 about 600,000 had said yes. Considering conditions in the late 1800s, today's option of buying land may be easier.

Some feel that homesteading is synonymous with family farming. It once may have been but in current usage it is not. Homesteading implies that substantial sustenance comes from one's land. Many modern family farmers grow cash crops only, then buy their food at the supermarket. Use of the word nowadays is pretty loose—anyone who moves from city to country and grows a garden is in peril of being labeled a homesteader. There are worse things. It's a great tradition and can be a high-quality lifestyle.

In *The Owner-Built Homestead* Barbara and Ken Kern offer:
> Reduced to its simplest terms, a homestead is an ecosystem in which humans evolve in mutual association and coexistence with plants, animals, and other life forces. In this cohabitation the various components of the homestead germinate, develop, and mature at varying rates for varying purposes, all interdependent and individually supportive of life therein.

Most modern homesteaders have these things in common: they believe that life is better in the country; they believe that self-sufficiency is a right goal; they believe that humans are destroying Earth; and they want to make the transition from being part of the problem to being part of the solution. Modern homesteaders striving for self-sufficiency are working environmentalists, not only committed to being part of the solution, but living their truth. They walk their talk. They are value fueled.

Self-reliance

There is a time in every man's education when he arrives at the conviction that envy is ignorance; that imitation is suicide; that he must take himself for better, for worse, as his portion; that though the wide universe is full of good, no kernel of nourishing corn can come to him but through his toil bestowed on that plot of ground which is given him to till. The power which resides in him is new in nature, and none but he knows what that is which he can do, nor does he know, until he has tried.

RALPH WALDO EMERSON
SELF RELIANCE

Self reliance. There is a resonance to it—it evokes security, holds hands with words like home and harvest and wood heat. It implies working with, instead of against nature.

It can indeed provide security. Available information and technology allow substantial self-control of one's basic needs. Wind or photovoltaic generation of electricity now allows use of a full array of tools and appliances independent of an electric company. Good soil and an adequate growing season can produce a large percentage of a family's food needs. With a tight house and a wood stove, a woodlot can provide heat. "Five Acres and Independence" has evolved from a book title to a dream, a challenge, a rallying cry, a reality.

Yes, five good acres is enough. My parents, brother, sister, and I ate very well from a bountiful one acre until we moved to our farm. But more land provides cropland, firewood, wild game if you want it, less chance of bothering your neighbors or your neighbors bothering you, and a condition to allow part of the world to heal itself.

*I often think today of what a difference it would make
if children believed they were contributing
to a family's survival and happiness.
In the transformation from a rural to an urban society,
children are robbed of the opportunity
to do genuinely responsible work.*

Dwight D. Eisenhower

Having it all

The ideal life includes access to what we value. It is now reasonably possible to live in a rural place, surrounded by nature, and use and enjoy the latest creations of technology. More easily than ever, we can have the peace of the country and the products of the city. We can live, work, and grow our food in the midst of nature using space-age tools, and access knowledge and entertainment at will through the magic of technology.

We have portable culture. With tapes and CDs we have the world's finest music. With satellite antennas we can receive news and programming from around the globe. After a dinner of home-grown food we can watch the latest movie, then take a safe moon-and-starlit walk in a parklike setting on our own property.

Reflections

For each of us our individual life is our most creative endeavor. Rooted in the soil of our genetic heritage, shaped by our experiences, nourished by our values, directed by our dreams, we choose from all and make ourselves as best we can.

We create our lifestyle, changing it to fit our experiences. Knowledge, experience, and success give us the courage to evolve, to grow beyond yesterday. We take ourselves with us no matter where we go, but moving to a new place allows reevaluation of our values. Our lifestyle, as a reflection of our evolving values, must often change for us to grow. For some, city activities become vague country memories. For others, rural barriers to social and cultural activities can be intolerable.

Where you decide to plant yourself will come partly from how you want to live each day. Living in a small town allows you to walk to the coffee shop to compare

sage observations with your cronies. Living just outside of town probably dictates a bicycle or car trip. Living in the boonies means sipping coffee on the front porch with yourself, your partner, or your cat or dog for company.

Old bad habits are easier to break in the country. New habits, true to your values, will give you greater pleasure. They will also make you healthier.

So now, after lifestyle on your criteria worksheet, write those activities you wish to keep and new ones you wish to adopt. Your ideal spot will have appropriate weather for, enough space for, and will be close enough to places allowing those activities.

You don't get to choose how you're going to die.
Or when.
You can decide how you're going to live now.

JOAN BAEZ

9
Choose your climate

*The first day of spring was once the time
for taking the young virgins into the fields,
there in dalliance to set an example
in fertility for Nature to follow.
Now we just set the clock an hour ahead
and change the oil in the crankcase.*

E.B. WHITE

Climate is predictable weather patterns

limate is the general state of atmospheric conditions over a long
period of time—a composite of averages and extremes during a
number of years. Weather is the expression of day-to-day conditions. In other words, climate is a large amount of weather averaged
out. Climate affects patterns of vegetation and water resources, and
affects every human endeavor. Increasing evidence shows that
human impact on the environment is causing changes in climate.

The following maps show average conditions over many years.
Conditions for any given year will differ significantly from long-term
averages. Sharp changes may occur in short distances, particularly in
mountainous areas, due to differences in altitude, slope of terrain, type of soil,
vegetation cover, bodies of water, air drainage, and human activity.

The value of weather

The main value of weather is conversation. As "Kin" Hubbard pointed out, "Don't knock the weather; nine tenths of the people couldn't start a conversation if it didn't change once in a while."

We humans are fascinated by anything that we can't control. Actually, we're embarrassed by our failure. That's why there are so many weather jokes. (City slicker: "Think it'll rain?" Farmer: "Always has.")

So-called perfect climate isn't. It's predictable, it's boring, it's expensive to live where it occurs. Seasons bring continual change and delight the senses. Cold is refreshing. Gardeners know that many plants need a cold dormancy period before they produce—like politicians between elections. That's why apples grow better up north.

Nonetheless, some folks prefer dependable warmth. My mother and father, who grew up in Wisconsin and northern Michigan, now live in Arizona. They're both in their 80s and have evolved from snowbirds to roadrunners, though at their age there's not much running going on. They love the warm winters. But what an awful spot to garden! Their place is a tiny oasis in the desert but the oven-like summer heat challenges even my mother's formidable gardening skills.

Many others who seek predictable comfort without effort have moved to the sub-tropical climate of the Sun Belt. But Florida in summer is awfully hot and humid, and southern California has so many problems it is losing natives as fast as it is gaining immigrants.

Climate is important for much more than just the quality of temperature comfort. If your greatest passion is skiing then your ideal home will be in or near a snow area. If gardening is your highest priority you will choose a climate with a long growing season and ample rainfall.

In praise of seasons

Interest in the changing seasons is a much happier state of mind than being hopelessly in love with spring.

GEORGE SANTAYANA

When I visualize four seasons I think of a rainy warming spring, grasses appearing, flowers exploding into view, the burgeoning, multi-green panorama of budding trees, birds building nests, spotted fawns on wobbly legs; a summer of waking to sunlight, lushly clothed trees, heat, thunderstorms, occasional humidity, meals straight from the garden, straw hats, the smell of new-mown grass, sitting in the porch swing until 9 P.M., sleeping with just a sheet; a glorious autumn, my favorite season, with vines, shrubs, and trees offering yellows, oranges, and reds, nature's big palette, each day a new color mix, cool days and cooler nights; then a winter of resting plants, gray, somber days, my beard full of frost after the mailbox walk, and of course snow, although in our part of the world it *usually* lasts for only a few days; and then, finally, impatience for spring to begin again.

Like the seasons of human life, the seasons of weather move us, invigorate us, and inspire us to taste of life to the fullest. Four seasons show off nature. Those who refuse winter give up the glory of spring and autumn. Changing temperatures are elixirs for human vigor. The energy of the cycling natural world makes boredom an unlikely condition.

Preference may simply be conditioning. I grew up in Wisconsin. If you grew up, say, in Florida or southern California, you may have different feelings. And feelings are always correct. So visualize *your* ideal climatic conditions.

We decided in favor of the north-east, for various reasons.
Aesthetically, we enjoy the procession of the seasons.
In any other part of the country we would have missed
the perpetual surprises and delights to which
New England weather treats its devotees:
the snow piled high in winter and the
black and white coloring from December to March;
the long lingering spring with its hesitant burgeoning into green;
the gorgeous burst of hot summer beauty combined with cool nights;
and the crisp snap of autumn with its sudden flare of color
in the most beautiful of all the seasons.
The land that has four well-defined seasons
cannot lack beauty, or pall with monotony.

HELEN & SCOTT NEARING
LIVING THE GOOD LIFE

Climate considerations

Almost anything about a piece of land can be changed except the climate and, usually, the topography, although bulldozer operators working for determined developers sometimes make even large hills disappear. For us more sensitive types, topography pretty much stays intact.

Climate and topography are wedded together, in fact shape each other. A billion or so years of rain and freezing turns rock into soil. A flat terrain becomes hills and hollows. Birds drop seeds, trees and grasses grow and cause water to linger where it falls before it begins its insistent decline. Hills cause warm wind currents to rise, dropping their gift of water as they meet higher, cooler air. Evaporation reloads the water machine and the cycle continues.

In truth, man can change the weather. If we cut down enough trees we can create a desert; some feel that if we grow enough trees, we can reclaim arid regions. There is reason to believe that the Sahara desert was once the Sahara forest. Archeological evidence proves the Sahara had extensive settlement during prehistoric times. Much of its land is fertile—only 20 percent of Saharan soil is sand. But natural regeneration is thwarted by overgrazing and wood gathering. Scientists now fear further desertification will occur in both Africa and South America where tropical rain forests are being systematically destroyed. According to Worldwatch Institute's *State of the World 1994*, Earth's forests cover 24 percent less land than in 1700 and just between 1980 and 1990 decreased by an area twice the size of Texas. Most scientists agree that forest destruction contributes to the global warming condition.

United States climate

Most of the 48 contiguous states have substantial seasonal climate variability. Coastal areas, moderated by the oceans or large lakes, have less variability. The eastern U.S. is humid, with annual precipitation averaging about 40 inches. The northwestern coast receives more than 100 inches per year but the rest of the west is mostly semi-arid, with 10 to 20 inches per year.

The 48 states have been divided into four major climatic regions, shown below. *Cool* areas experience a wide range of temperatures, from -30 degrees to 100+ degrees. These areas typically have cold winters and hot summers with winds year-round, generally out of the northwest and the southeast. *Temperate* denotes an equal distribution of overheated and underheated periods, with seasonal winds from the northwest and south along with periods of high humidity and large

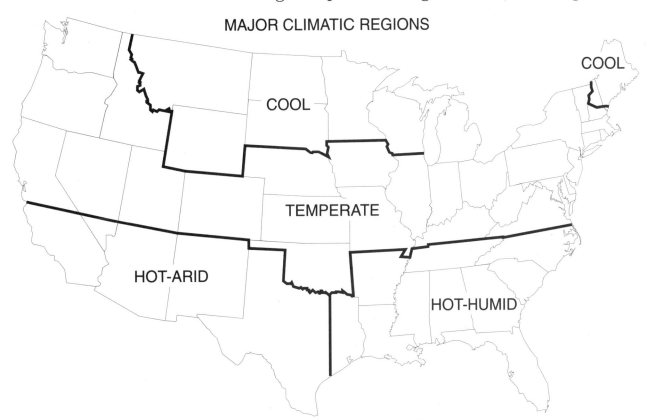

MAJOR CLIMATIC REGIONS

COOL

COOL

TEMPERATE

HOT-ARID

HOT-HUMID

amounts of precipitation in the east but much less in the west, except in the far northwest. *Hot-Arid* is a region of clear, dry atmosphere, extended periods of overheating, and large daily temperature range. Wind is usually along an east-west axis with variations between day and evening. *Hot-Humid* is a region of high temperatures and consistent vapor pressure. Wind velocities and direction vary throughout the year, with velocities of up to 120 miles per hour accompanying hurricanes, which usually come from the east-southeast.

Climate has a profound influence on human experience. With the exception of love, weather has arguably appeared in more songs than any other subject. Well, okay, old songs. As I don't mind dating myself, I'll let words from songs introduce most of the various features of weather, which with seasonal occurrence we call climate.

"Everything's coming up roses for you and for me . . ."

If your activity criteria includes gardening, you'll need a climate that cooperates. All ornamental and food plants have natural climatic preferences: citrus thrives in the south and apples do best in the north; if you must have fresh mangoes or die, you will not move to Maine. Growing tomatoes is a far greater challenge in Alaska than in Tennessee.

Pick the climate zone where you can grow what you most want to look at and to eat fresh. The Northwest, with lots of rain and cool temperatures, is lush with rhododendrons and ferns. Much of the lower Midwest has a six-month growing season, from mid-April to mid-October, which allows growing a wide variety of fruits and vegetables.

The United States Department of Agriculture developed plant hardiness zones based on average minimum temperatures. These zones are often referred to by nurseries and gardening books where plants are classified according to their ability to survive cold.

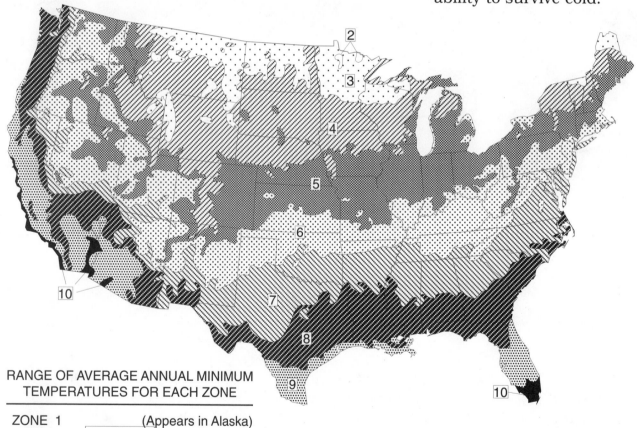

RANGE OF AVERAGE ANNUAL MINIMUM TEMPERATURES FOR EACH ZONE

ZONE 1		(Appears in Alaska)
ZONE 2		-50° to -40°
ZONE 3		-40° to -30°
ZONE 4		-30° to -20°
ZONE 5		-20° to -10°
ZONE 6		-10° to 0°
ZONE 7		0° to 10°
ZONE 8		10° to 20°
ZONE 9		20° to 30°
ZONE 10		30° to 40°

USDA Plant Hardiness Zone Map

Shows the lowest temperatures that can be expected each year. These temperatures are referred to as "average annual minimum temperatures" and are based on the lowest temperatures recorded for each of the years 1974 to 1986.

The minimum temperature often determines whether a plant will survive in a given spot. The problems faced by southern gardeners are often the opposite of those in the north. Southerners are unable to grow some plants common in northern landscapes because of too much heat or too little winter cold. Azaleas won't make it in hot, dry Arizona.

Whether garden plants will thrive, or whether they will grow to maturity and fruit depends in great part on the length of the growing season, for most garden plants the period between the last spring freeze and the first fall freeze. A long growing season may allow two crops of certain vegetables, for instance brassica and various salad plants. A growing season can be too long—constant heat and warmth precludes growing certain plants, although botanists regularly introduce new varieties tolerant of diverse conditions.

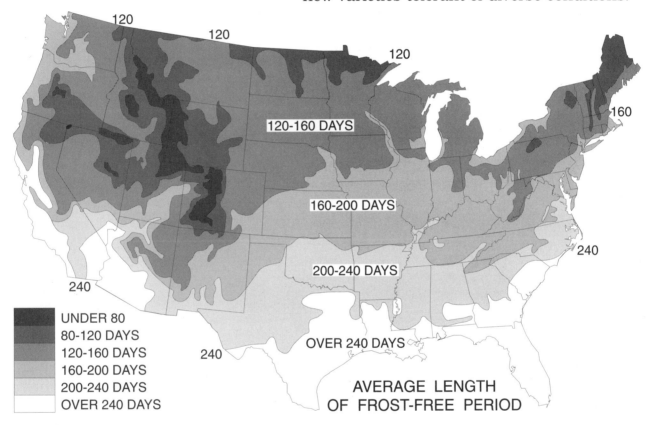

UNDER 80
80-120 DAYS
120-160 DAYS
160-200 DAYS
200-240 DAYS
OVER 240 DAYS

AVERAGE LENGTH
OF FROST-FREE PERIOD

Microclimates

Small areas on the sunny or shady, upwind or downwind side of a hill or mountain, protected valleys, and other spots often exhibit climatic conditions substantially different than those in the surrounding area. Water warms and cools more slowly than land masses, so areas near large bodies of water tend to exhibit more stable climatic conditions. These microclimatic areas are sought by those who wish to raise certain crops which might be damaged by late frost, or which thrive on certain temperatures, air-movement patterns, or precipitation. Well-known microclimates include New York's Finger Lakes region below Lake Ontario and California's Napa Valley. Microclimates abound in mountainous areas.

"It's too darn hot. . ."

*It was so hot here that I found there was nothing left for it
but to take off my flesh and sit in my bones.*

SYDNEY SMITH

The retiree flight from northeast states to Florida
is propelled by the lure of escaping cold, windy,
snowy winters. Once there, many find the sultry
summers unbearable. Snowbirds from Montana
spend winters in Arizona, then flee north before
the summer sun starts sizzling. Unless your
ideal home is *two* homes, a compromise is in order.

MEAN ANNUAL NUMBER OF DAYS
WITH MAXIMUM TEMPERATURE 90°F AND ABOVE
Data source: U.S. Dept. of Commerce Nat'l Oceanic & Atmospheric Administration
(After H. McKinley Conway, Jr., and Linda L. Liston, "The Weather Handbook.")

Note:
Sharp changes in number of days
90° and above may occur within
short distances due to differences in
altitude, slope of land, type of soil, vegetative
cover, bodies of water, air drainage, etc.

"Baby, it's cold outside," and "Let it snow, let it snow, let it snow."

In the range of inorganic nature, I doubt if any object can be found more perfectly beautiful than a fresh, deep snowdrift, seen under warm light.

JOHN RUSKIN

Cold and snow are not constant companions but they often hold hands. To me, cold without some snow is rather like eating bad pizza without wine or beer.

Winter heaven is awakening to a fresh snow, walking in a white wonderland, taking pictures for Christmas cards, following animal tracks, and seeing the world perfectly clean. Skiing and ice skating are optional. An evening in front of a crackling fire is the perfect end to an exhilarating day.

While a foot of fresh snow is a skier's paradise, it is bad news to someone who has to drive to work. Even with snowblowers, getting out to a cleared road can be a major challenge. If you want to live in snow country and must commute to work, you will want to have short, flat access to a county road. County road crews typically are out plowing the roads first thing in the morning. And employers in snow country are aware of how road conditions affect commuters.

The map at the top of the next page shows where the cheeks are rosy, the skiing is great, and Christmas is guaranteed to be white.

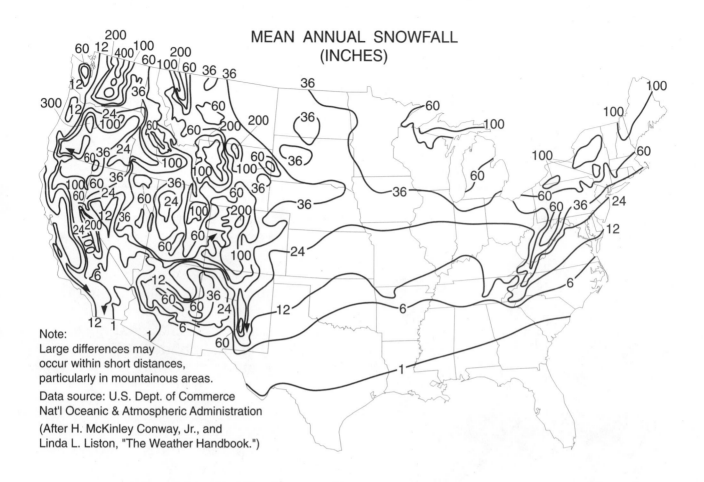

MEAN ANNUAL SNOWFALL
(INCHES)

Note:
Large differences may
occur within short distances,
particularly in mountainous areas.

Data source: U.S. Dept. of Commerce
Nat'l Oceanic & Atmospheric Administration

(After H. McKinley Conway, Jr., and
Linda L. Liston, "The Weather Handbook.")

The effect of elevation (altitude)

Temperature in the atmosphere drops with increasing elevation. Some writers state that the rate of decrease is 3.3 degrees Fahrenheit per 1,000 feet. Others say one degree Fahrenheit for every 250 feet. Take your pick.

"The iceman cometh"

Yeah, I know, it's a play. We don't think too much about ice unless we ice skate, or unless we find ourselves suddenly lying on it looking up at the sky, or unless our car slides into a ditch.

If you choose an area with four distinct seasons but have not lived with ice, practice driving in a large, empty parking lot covered with hard snow or ice.

Accelerate, brake, and turn increasingly smaller figure-eights until you know what to expect and how to handle it. Plan ahead—it's like driving a boat. Expect other drivers to make mistakes. They will.

"I'm singing in the rain. . ."

When it rains we'll laugh at the weather.

LORENZ HART

MOUNTAIN GREENERY, 1926

Precipitation usually equates to available water. In many populated areas water demand exceeds the supply. That condition is worsening. Water has always been valued—it now is fast becoming a high-priced commodity. We would do well to put ourselves where precipitation and groundwater are dependably abundant.

As shown on the following map, precipitation differences can be great within short distances, most dramatically in the Northwest. In Washington, depending on which side of the Cascade Range you are on, you may receive a stingy six inches or an awesome 100-plus inches of rainfall.

Desert or deluge, take your pick.

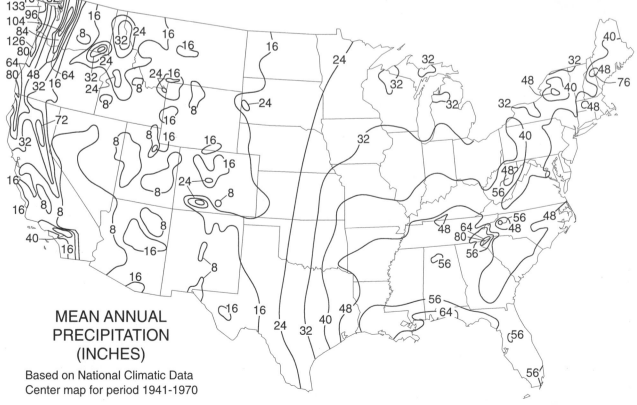

MEAN ANNUAL PRECIPITATION (INCHES)

Based on National Climatic Data Center map for period 1941-1970

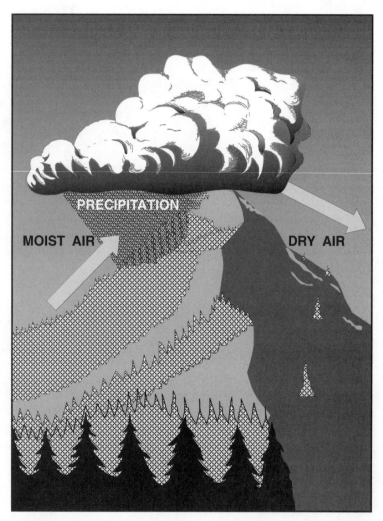

The reason that mountains collect rain on their windward side is the orographic effect—the rain shadow of a mountain—shown in the drawing at left. Warm, moisture-laden air currents are forced upward by mountains; as they rise they collide with cooler air, which precipitates the moisture. Once past the peak, the now-dry air slides down the leeward slope, evaporating ground moisture, which makes the moisture difference between the west and east sides even more dramatic, as illustrated by the lush growth on the west slope and the relative lack of tree growth on the east slope.

"I just finished drying off from my shower and I'm already dripping with sweat."

What men call gallantry, and gods adultery,
is much more common where the climate's sultry.

LORD BYRON

Well, that's not from a song (although singing and showers do go well together), but we've all heard the expression, especially if we have friends living in Florida or what is often called the deep south.

Humidity is water suspended in air, like fog. It's not much of a nuisance except when high humidity combines with high temperatures. High relative humidity is uncomfortable, energy draining, and may be detrimental to some health conditions. Either high or low humidity may feel uncomfortable. Dry desert air dries one's skin and nasal passages. High humidity thwarts perspiration and intensifies heat discomfort.

MEAN RELATIVE HUMIDITY (%), JANUARY

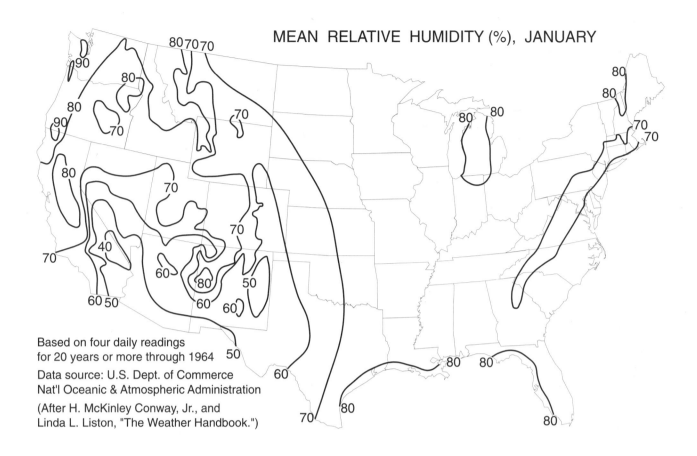

Based on four daily readings
for 20 years or more through 1964

Data source: U.S. Dept. of Commerce
Nat'l Oceanic & Atmospheric Administration

(After H. McKinley Conway, Jr., and
Linda L. Liston, "The Weather Handbook.")

MEAN RELATIVE HUMIDITY (%), JULY

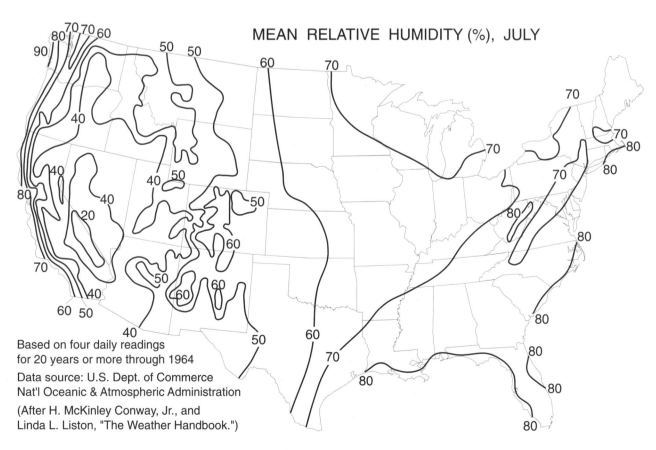

Based on four daily readings
for 20 years or more through 1964

Data source: U.S. Dept. of Commerce
Nat'l Oceanic & Atmospheric Administration

(After H. McKinley Conway, Jr., and
Linda L. Liston, "The Weather Handbook.")

"I'll huff and I'll puff, and I'll blow your house down."

Okay, that's also not from a song. It's from a nursery rhyme, but it should be from a song. Why *hasn't* someone written a musical about the three swine architects? Miss Piggy is the obvious choice for narrator and Jack Nicholson would make a great huffer. I wonder if he can sing.

The January and July wind maps on the facing page are produced from ground data gathered at local weather stations, most often airports. The direction of the arrows indicates the prevailing wind direction during those two months, indicative of both winter and summer conditions. At first glance, these maps seem to indicate that U.S. winds have little order and are in fact rather helter skelter.

While local low-level winds may come from many different directions depending on constantly changing atmospheric conditions, the prevailing winds and weather movements in the U.S. generally move from west to east. This is shown in the map below—Major Climatological Storm Tracks.

These maps are useful not only for understanding weather movement but also for determining the potential for acid rain and other airborne pollution for a given site. They are also useful for planning the placement of buildings, gardens, landscaping, and windbreaks.

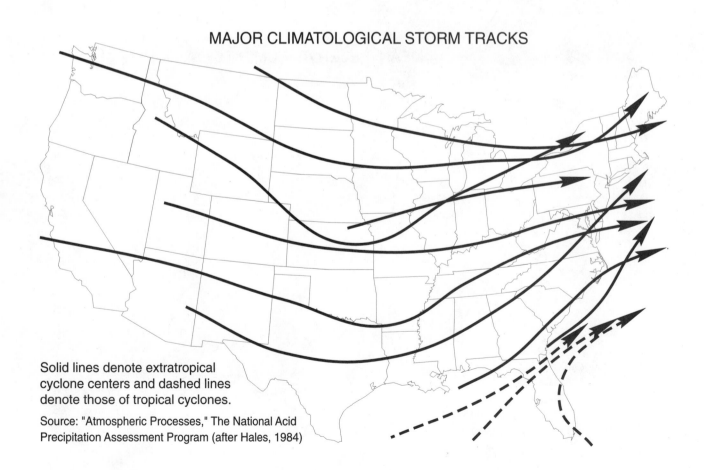

MAJOR CLIMATOLOGICAL STORM TRACKS

Solid lines denote extratropical cyclone centers and dashed lines denote those of tropical cyclones.

Source: "Atmospheric Processes," The National Acid Precipitation Assessment Program (after Hales, 1984)

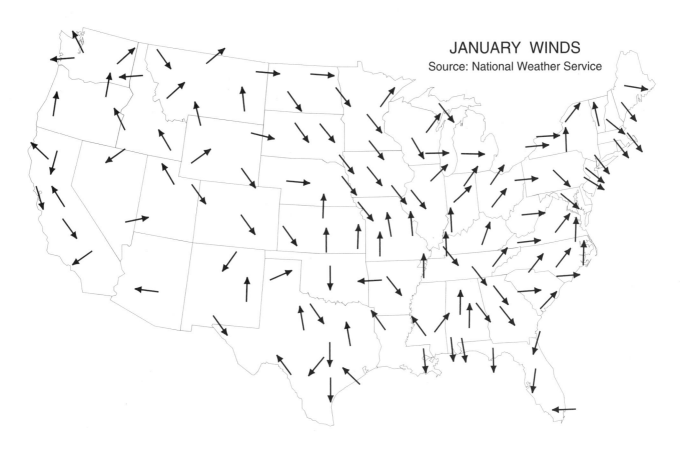

JANUARY WINDS
Source: National Weather Service

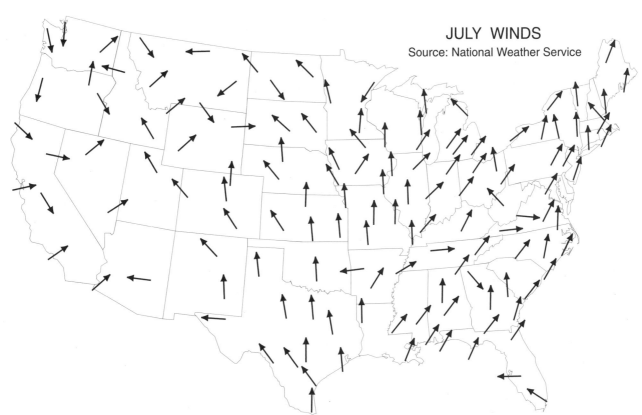

JULY WINDS
Source: National Weather Service

"Don't know why there's no sun up in the sky . . . stormy weather . . ."

Thunder is good, thunder is impressive;
but it is lightning that does the work.
MARK TWAIN

Smart man, Mr. Clemens. One of the advantages of summer thunderstorms is that lightning affixes nitrogen to rain drops and down they come to fertilize our tomatoes and corn. That's why lawns become greener after a good, rollicking thunderstorm. I love 'em. I sit on the front porch and applaud the performance. Jupiter was believed by the Romans to be the god in charge of the sky and the weather. It's a pure pleasure to watch his trainees flexing their thunder muscles.

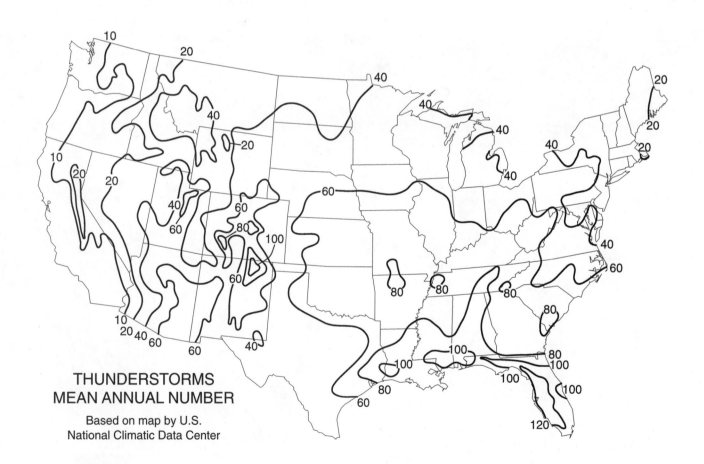

THUNDERSTORMS
MEAN ANNUAL NUMBER

Based on map by U.S.
National Climatic Data Center

Too much water too fast

The top news story of 1993 was The Great Flood that battered the Midwest—approximately ten million acres of lakes where there had been homes, roads, towns, and farmland. The floods of 1889, 1937, and 1973 killed 2,100, 250, and 23 respectively. The 1993 flood killed *only* 26 people because of abundant warnings, evacuation plans, lack of flash floods, and a massive levee and dam system. Thousands of people had to leave their homes and many had no homes to return to—many buildings were beyond repair and were broken up and carried to a landfill. Some people rebuilt, some to new building codes that require elevated residences. Government cost estimates rose in one week from 500-million to eight-billion dollars in damages.

All this in spite of billions of (taxpayer) dollars spent by the Corps of Engineers constructing an elaborate flood-control network, including 7,000 miles of levees. Are we or are we not the arrogant species? Perhaps one day even bureaucrats will concede that nature is in charge.

Nature bats last.

BUMPER STICKER

All waterways are subject to flooding—generally, the larger the watershed, the greater the possibility. Our little stream floods about twice each year. Its watershed, over 2,000 acres, is heavily wooded so most water slowly soaks into the ground to recharge the several springs which provide steady year-round flow.

But occasionally we get a sustained heavy rain, say four inches in 24 hours, the ground stops absorbing, and the creek rises within a few hours to raging river status. At our road crossing, it has expanded from its usual 15-foot width and 12-inch depth to over 100 feet wide and four feet in depth. And the water moves—*fast*. The house is nicely sited, about 200 feet back and about 15 feet higher than the stream at normal flow, so there is no danger. But the several days the stream takes to normalize is inconvenient unless we are both on the house side with our usual full stock of supplies. Chris and I remember well the night she returned from a rainy day in the city and found the crossing impossible to safely ford. We shouted our frustrations to each other over the roar of the torrent before she went off to stay with a neighbor.

A natural condition—a human challenge. I envision a pond with a road atop a dam with a very large underflow capability.

Too little water too long

Some climatological bureaucrat decreed that no rain for up to two weeks is a dry spell; anything longer is a drought. In that case there's a whole lot of droughting going on. Really serious droughts seem to occur at 20- to 22-year intervals in the western U.S. Our most famous drought area, the so-called Dust Bowl, covers an area of about 150,000 square miles, including the Oklahoma and Texas panhandles and adjacent parts of Colorado, New Mexico, and Kansas, an area of light soil, annual rainfall of about 15 inches, and high winds. The dust condition is exacerbated by tilling for crops and the resultant destruction of grasses and other root systems to anchor the soil. The Dust Bowl does not qualify as an area for ideal home places.

Drifts of soil piled up by dust-bowl winds against a farmer's barn, Liberal, Kansas, 1936

Too much air too fast

Sounds like the description of a political speech. Midwesterners think Californians are in imminent danger of falling into the ocean from earthquakes whereas Californians envision Midwesterners being demolished by tornadoes. And everyone but those living there is convinced that Floridians and others living on the Gulf and east coasts will all eventually be blown away with hurricanes.

Tornadoes, also known as twisters or cyclones, are often associated with severe thunderstorms. They typically leave a path of destruction less than 200 feet wide and average 5 to 15 miles in length. Most occur in spring and early summer in the central southern U.S., later across more northerly regions. Of the nation's yearly total of about 1,000 tornadoes, most occur in Texas, Oklahoma, and Kansas.

Contrary to the belief of Californians, we in tornado country do not run for our basements at every thunderstorm. Weather forecasts in these areas dependably include tornado alerts and, since tornadoes occur most frequently during the middle and late afternoon, they are rarely a surprise. Harold Brooks, a meteorologist with the National Severe Storms Laboratory points out that, while the Tri-State Tornado of 1925 killed 700 people, a similar 1989 twister killed no one. The warning system works.

Students at the University of Oklahoma get their thrills by chasing tornadoes. They haven't caught any yet but they are doing their darndest. All in the name of science, of course.

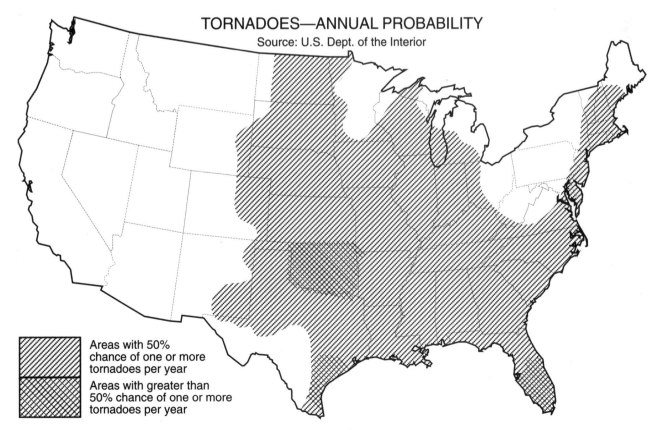

TORNADOES—ANNUAL PROBABILITY
Source: U.S. Dept. of the Interior

Areas with 50% chance of one or more tornadoes per year

Areas with greater than 50% chance of one or more tornadoes per year

The Richelieu Apartments, Pass Christian, Mississippi, before and after Hurricane Camille, 1969

"Shake, rattle, and roll"

Philosopher-historian Will Durant said that civilization exists by geological consent and is subject to change without notice. Those who have lived through strong earthquakes are most likely to concur.

Earthquakes are not part of climate but, as natural phenomena, acts of God, they fit here best. I have survived earthquakes in Japan and in both northern and southern California including the 6.6 L.A. quake January 17, 1994 which rousted me out of bed at 4:31 a.m. I have visited L.A. at better times. Like the guy said, I can't explain it, you had to be there. That quake killed 60 and created the most expensive natural disaster in the history of the U.S.A.

Thirty-seven states have a significant danger from earthquakes, including the Northwest, New England, and the Midwest.

The danger from earthquakes exists primarily in and close to cities; in sparsely populated rural areas earthquakes are of less danger because of the nature of, or absence of structures. In the L.A. quake the greatest loss was from fire, damage to freeway overpasses, large concrete parking structures, masonry facades, multiple-story buildings (one three-story building collapsed down to two stories, killing 16), and homes built on the edge of cliffs or sides of unstable hills. Worldwide, earthquake damages include landslides and dam collapses.

Single-story homes are usually damaged to a dangerous degree only when they are near the quake's epicenter. Nevertheless, the prudent person will not choose to live in an area of high seismic risk. As we have the entire country to choose from, there is no need to consider such a location.

Collapsed freeway overpass, L.A. earthquake, January 17, 1994—magnitude 6.6

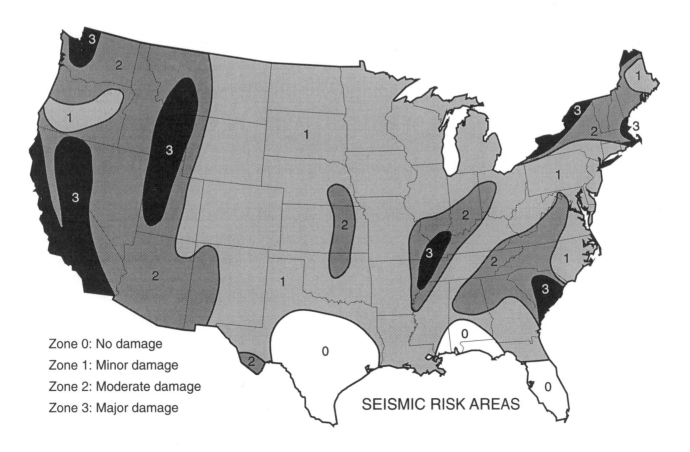

Zone 0: No damage

Zone 1: Minor damage

Zone 2: Moderate damage

Zone 3: Major damage

SEISMIC RISK AREAS

The bottom lines

Climate can be a substantial factor contributing to quality of life. It regulates our activities and brain waves. It affects our moods. It also makes decisions that we must live with. You can fight city hall far more easily than the weather. Outside activities are often dictated by weather conditions. But inside our houses, with today's technology we can live in any climate in reasonable-cost comfort while remaining true to environmental sanity. Pick a climate that will allow you to perform your preferred activities, grow the food and ornamental plants you wish, provide health, interest, and vigor, and give you the sights you like to see. Now make notes about your climatic preferences on your criteria worksheet.

Resources

The best source of climatic data and maps for country, states, and cities is the National Climatic Data Center, Federal Building, 37 Battery Park Avenue, Asheville, NC 28801-2733. (Phone: 704-259-0682) It has data from 300 primary weather stations and 1,063 cooperative stations. Publications are available for each location at very low cost.

The World Almanac (1993, p. 185) contains monthly normal temperatures and precipitation, based on the 30-year period 1951-1980, and Annual Climatological Data for 83 cities.

National Earthquake Information Service
U.S. Geological Survey
Box 25046, Federal Center
Denver, CO 80225
303-273-8477
State seismicity maps are available for nearly all states, for $1.50 to $3.10 each.

The way I see it,
if you want the rainbow,
you gotta put up with the rain.
Dolly Parton

WILLIAM HENRY JACKSON
Palace Butte Park, Gallatin Mountains, Montana Territory

10
Land characteristics

Topography, soil, and vegetation

The hills are alive with the sound of music,
With songs they have sung for a thousand years.
The hills fill my heart with the sound of music,
My heart wants to sing ev'ry song it hears.
OSCAR HAMMERSTEIN II

The hills are alive—and it's pretty frightening.
BARBRA STREISAND
A HAPPENING IN CENTRAL PARK, 1967

The topography, soil, and vegetation of a place have a major influence on lifestyle. In our area, socializing is affected by distance—of roads, not straight-line. The roads of hills-and-hollows terrain cause 45-minute drives to visit friends only a couple miles away as the crow flies. In nice weather the alternative is to walk—up and down wooded hills, fording streams, occasionally using old logging roads. It is pleasant going during the daytime, but even with flashlights walking home in the dark through face-slapping branches is some less wonderful. After heavy rains, it is common for bridges in narrow valleys to become impassable, necessitating even longer drives.

There may be a psychic connection between people and place. Others and I have marveled at the high incidence of us Capricorns in the Ozarks. We speculate that the heavily vegetated, rugged hill country is simply natural terrain for goats, who

delight in climbing and will seemingly eat anything. We try to have annual Capricorn parties, although January road conditions are the most challenging of the year.

The ideal country home place has at minimum enough good soil for a garden and orchard, a woodlot, and sufficient vegetation to avoid erosion of sloping land and to provide a pleasing view. All these items are factors of topography.

Americans can choose to live in terrain that is mountainous, hilly, flat, coastal, desert, or plains. Choices continue with ridgetops, valleys, hollows, bottomland, and upland. Then we have forests, grasses, cropland, mixed vegetation, even swamps. Each of these land characteristics has advantages and disadvantages. Each has its own character and each shapes the character of the characters who live there. This influence of topography on humans is illustrated by the words that define those who live in certain places: swamp rat, desert rat, hillbilly, flat-lander, mountaineer, woodsman, etc.

Topography 101

As the outside of the earth cooled down, cracks developed which created the giant plates that comprise the present mantle, the solid stuff we walk on and that underlies the seas. The swirling gasses settled down to a pattern, separated into layers, an atmosphere developed, water fell, hit the rock and began wearing on it. The plates, floating on the hot inner magma, slowly moved. Where they pushed into each other, edges lifted and became mountains. A few billion years of plate bumping, rain falling, frost cracking and heaving, rivers forming, and Earth began to look like the neat place we see today. (We know all this because Cecil B. deMille was there to film it.) Up to this point we are talking about geology, which is sort of the underlayment of topography, which is on top, which is why—ahem—it is called top-ography.

The action of rain, wind, freezing, and the glaciers created soil from rock. Depending on the rock it came from, soil is composed of percentages of various minerals. When plants die and decay they become humus, which becomes food for the next generation of plants. Depending on the incidence of temperature, moisture, type of soil, wind, sun angle, and other things, unique plants grow in different places.

A quick topographic trip—from sea to shining sea

Areas that have similar physiography often have similar geology, hydrology, and climate. The following map shows the physiographic regions and provinces of the contiguous states. A brief explanation of each numbered region follows.

1. Superior Upland—Hilly area of erosional topography on ancient crystalline rocks.
2. Continental Shelf—Shallow, sloping submarine plain of sedimentation.
3. Coastal Plain—Low, hilly to nearly flat terraced plains on soft sediments. The east coast is like the edge of a broken jigsaw puzzle, with continuous inlets, bays, and sounds. The coastal plain extends from Long Island south to and around Florida including the Gulf coast to Mexico. With an average width of about 150 miles this is approximately ten percent of the land.
4. Piedmont Province—Gentle to rough, hilly terrain on belted crystalline rocks becoming more hilly toward mountains. 300 to 1,000 feet in elevation, a transition to the Appalachian Mountains. The east edge of the Piedmont is an escarpment down which rivers tumble in falls to the plain.
5. Blue Ridge Province—Mountains of crystalline rock 3,000 to 6,000 feet high, mostly rounded summits.
6. Valley and Ridge Province—Long mountain ridges and valleys eroded on strong and weak folded rock strata.
7. St. Lawrence Valley (look in upper New York)—Rolling lowland with local rock hills.

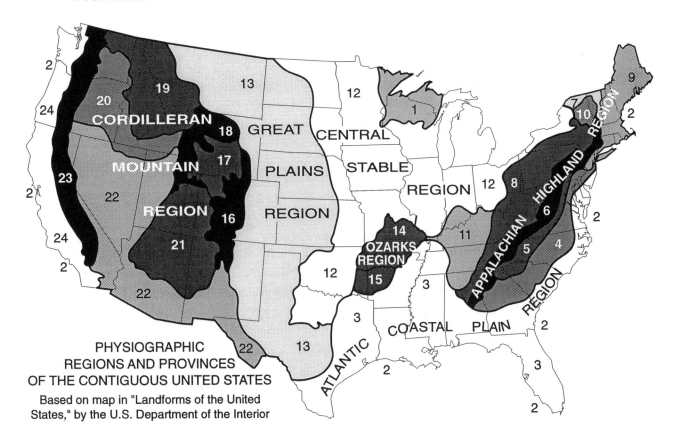

PHYSIOGRAPHIC REGIONS AND PROVINCES OF THE CONTIGUOUS UNITED STATES

Based on map in "Landforms of the United States," by the U.S. Department of the Interior

8. Appalachian Plateaus—Generally steep-sided plateaus on sandstone bedrock, 3,000 to 5,000 feet high on the east side, declining gradually to the west. The Appalachians, a system of mountains, protrude northeast to southwest, paralleling the coast from above Maine all the way to Alabama.

Note: The East has mountains in more states than the West: the White is in New Hampshire, the Green in Vermont, Maine, and Connecticut; New York is pushed up twice with the Catskills and the Adirondacks; Pennsylvania, Maryland, and the Virginias share the Alleghenies; Virginia also has the Blue Ridge which lifts the west end of North Carolina and enters Georgia; the Great Smoky Mountains *are* southeastern Tennessee; the Cumberland Plateau starts in northern Alabama, goes across Tennessee and up into Kentucky.

9. New England Province—Rolling hilly erosional topography on crystalline rocks in southeastern part to high mountainous country in central and northern parts.

10. Adirondack Province—Subdued mountains on ancient crystalline rocks rising to over 5,000 feet.

11. Interior Low Plateaus—Low plateaus on stratified rocks. Includes diverse Kentucky, with mountain coal in the east (Appalachian Plateau), flat-to-rolling farming country in the middle, the Bluegrass region along the Ohio River, a rolling coal and farming area in the north bulge.

12. Central Lowland—Mostly low rolling landscape and nearly level plains. Most of area is covered by a veneer of glacial deposits, including ancient lake beds and hilly lake-dotted moraines. Includes the Lower Peninsula of Michigan, with 11,000 natural lakes shaped by glaciers; Minnesota, where glaciers ground out 15,291 lakes, one for every 18 citizens; and Dairyland Wisconsin (14,000 lakes), a mix of glacial hills and rolling hayfields, the better soil southeast, hills southwest, woods and cranberry bogs north in the Superior Upland. Northwest Missouri is a plains region, the northeast nearly flat. The glaciers stopped at the Missouri River. Northern Missouri, Iowa, and Illinois are the land of megafarms. In some places the topsoil is many feet deep.

13. Great Plains—Broad river plains and low plateaus on weak stratified sedimentary rocks. Rises toward Rocky Mountains, at some places to altitudes over 6,000 feet. From North Dakota the Great Plains sweep southward, interrupted by the Bad Lands and Black Hills of southern and southwestern South Dakota. The plains—grassland, buffalo land—extend down through Nebraska, Kansas, through the panhandle of Oklahoma to Texas. Texas has high plains in the northwest extending down through vast prairie and plains, some hills, to the Gulf coast in the Atlantic Coastal Plain Region.

14. Ozark Plateau—High, hilly landscape on stratified rocks. The Ozark Plateau—the oldest exposed land in America—the only major highland between the Appalachians and the Rockies—creates southern Missouri and

northwest Arkansas. Hills and hollows covered with oaks, hickories, short-leafed pine, cedar, dogwood, redbud. Rocky. Springs, streams, reservoirs. The best soil is in the bottoms.

15. Ouachita Province—Ridges and valleys eroded on upturned folded strata.

16. Southern Rocky Mountains—Complex mountains rising to over 14,000 feet. Includes Colorado, with the highest average elevation in the U.S.—1,000 peaks higher than 10,000 feet. Eastern Colorado is Great Plains, western is Colorado Plateau—the Rockies go down the middle.

17. Wyoming Basin—Elevated plains and plateaus on sedimentary strata.

18. Middle Rocky Mountains—Complex mountains with many intermontane basins and plains.

19. Northern Rocky Mountains—Rugged mountains with narrow intermontane basins. Includes most of Idaho, the rugged Bitterroot Range in the north and the wide, arid Snake River valley across the south, the eastern part of the Columbia Plateau.

20. Columbia Plateau—High rolling plateaus underlain by extensive lava flows; trenched by canyons.

21. Colorado Plateau—High plateaus on stratified rocks cut by deep canyons.

22. Basin and Range Province—Mostly isolated ranges separated by wide desert plains. Many lakes, ancient lake beds, and alluvial fans. The Wasatch Range splits Utah, with Plateau land east, and west the Great Basin, third largest interior drainage region in the world—continues to the alpine Sierra Nevadas of western Nevada and eastern California.

23. Cascade-Sierra Nevada Mountains—Sierras in southern part are high mountains eroded from crystalline rocks. Cascades in northern part are high volcanic mountains.

24. Pacific Border Province—Mostly very young steep mountains; includes extensive river plains in California portion. In the northwest the Cascade

Range starts in northern California, defines western Oregon and divides wet, western Washington, lush with Douglas fir, hemlock, cedar, and spruce, from the dry, sagebrush east of the Columbia Plateau. The Coast Range dominates far western Oregon, more hilly than mountainous along the ocean. Between the Coast Range and the Cascades is the fertile Willamette River valley, up to 50 miles wide. The leading lumber state, Oregon contains vast forests of ponderosa pine, Sitka spruce, and hemlock. Western Oregon is wet; the south-east is semi-arid high plain.

Soil quality

So long as one feeds on food from unhealthy soil,
the spirit will lack the stamina to free itself
from the prison of the body.

RUDOLF STEINER

Soil serves as an anchorage for plants and as their nutrient reservoir. So soil quality is highly important if you want to garden or live amongst growing things, like trees, bushes, and grasses. Gardens can be built from scratch but it's a huge amount of work. Even rocky soil can be fertile and grow great trees but digging holes for new fruit, nut, and shade trees might be a job for a backhoe. Unless you intend to farm, you only need really good soil for a garden, perhaps a quarter acre. Unlike the climate and politicians, soil can be improved. As Charles Long says in *Life After The City,*

> Don't look for good garden soil on an agricultural map. Gardens are little pockets of soil that will take some special treatment regardless of what the rest of the country is like.

If you want to grow field crops or have a small farm operation get plenty of qualified local advice on the soil you are considering. Check with the people at the extension office or the soil conservation department.

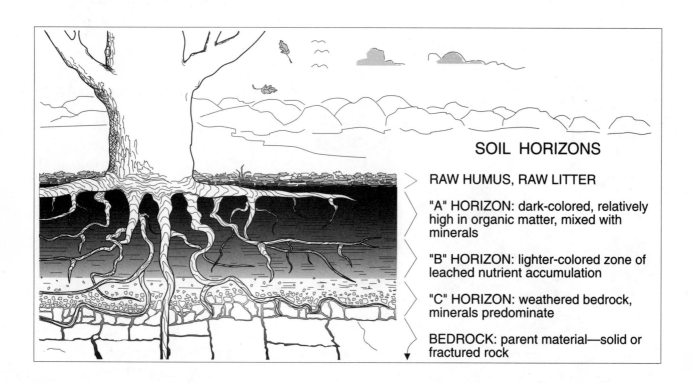

SOIL HORIZONS

RAW HUMUS, RAW LITTER

"A" HORIZON: dark-colored, relatively high in organic matter, mixed with minerals

"B" HORIZON: lighter-colored zone of leached nutrient accumulation

"C" HORIZON: weathered bedrock, minerals predominate

BEDROCK: parent material—solid or fractured rock

Soil is a complex natural material formed from disintegrated rock, which includes decomposed minerals. Other than minerals, nutrients for plants derive from decaying organic matter acted upon by soil microorganisms. Dark soil is generally more fertile than light-colored soil, the darkness deriving from humus, decomposing vegetative matter. Soils are classified according to the percentages they contain of clay, sand, silt, or humus. Loams, which have about equal percentages of sand, silt, and clay, have ideal texture and are typically the most fertile.

In the moist southeastern U.S. soil is often thick clay. The predominant red color is caused by the presence of iron particles. Similar soil is found along the northwest coast. In drier areas of the country where weathering has been less intense surface soil contains little clay. In moist mountainous regions such as the Appalachians or Ozarks most hillsides are covered with colluvium—loose, weathered rock debris. The Rockies are similar but drier, so loose deposits are thinner.

The northern part of the country contains areas of glacial deposits. Glacial action extended down to Long Island, northern Pennsylvania, the Ohio and Missouri rivers, and Puget Sound lowland. In hilly New England, deposits are stony. In the central region, glacial deposits are overlaid with wind-blown silt—loess. These areas contain some of the best agricultural land in the world but the fine soil is highly subject to wind and water erosion. It runs deep, so farmers have wasted much of it to erosion. In other areas the best soil is often found in bottom lands where flooding and runoff from hillsides have deposited fine soil particles.

The acidity or alkalinity of soil determines to a large extent what can be grown in it. A pH scale is used to express both acidity and alkalinity in soil; pH values range from 0 to 14, with 7 being neutral. Less than 7 indicates acidity, more than 7 shows alkalinity. Most common garden crops do well in the mid-range, from 6.5 to 7.5. A soil that is too acid can be corrected by adding lime, alkalinity may be reduced with sulfur, but highly alkaline soil is useless. Soil that is highly alkaline often has a white, crusty look and supports little or no vegetation. A high percentage of organic matter, the goal of organic gardeners, seems to broaden the pH range in which a given plant will thrive.

Before soil tests, farmers judged the pH level of soil by tasting it. Considering the things farmers have been putting into and onto soil in the last few decades, I would not recommend tasting soil. A soil test is most accurate but you can estimate the acidity of soil by observing plants that thrive there. Acidic but usable soil is indicated by ferns, azaleas, rhododendrons, blueberries, strawberries, dandelions, and plantain—the low plant in lawns with broad, strong-veined leaves that my grandmother used to make a poultice to draw infection after I cut my five-year-old foot on a piece of glass. A knowledgeable herbalist friend used the same treatment on my 50-year-old toe where a rattlesnake nailed me. It still works. (The plantain, not the rattlesnake.) Never call it a weed again.

Hydrangeas are tolerant of a wide range of soil acidity or alkalinity but have the quality of reacting like litmus paper, the flowers being red in alkaline soil and blue in acidic soil. The reason is that the trace element aluminum, which makes them blue, is not available to the roots in alkaline conditions.

Tall, lush growth of a wide variety of plants generally indicates that soil structure, fertility, and pH level are appropriate for gardening.

You can test soil for texture by moistening some and rubbing it between your fingers. Clay feels and looks slippery. A gritty feeling indicates high sand content. Silt almost feels greasy but has less of the sticky, plastic feel of clay.

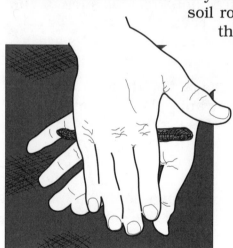

Soil texture can also be examined by the procedure shown here. First squeeze a moist handful. It should form a lump, what is called a cast. Roll the cast between your hands to form a soil rope. Lastly, work the end of the rope under your thumb, trying to make it thin, thinner than the dough strips on top of grandma's apple pie. Too much sand and the rope will crumble. Too much clay and the strip will shape easily. Something in between has a good mixture of sand, silt, and clay—it is called loam—the preferred soil texture for gardening and farming.

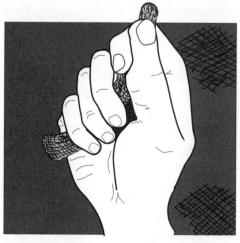

Soil problems

Inadequate drainage

Good drainage is necessary for plant health, roadways, building foundations, human bladders, basement drains, and septic tank leach fields. Land that retains large puddles for days after a rain breeds mosquitoes. Plant indicators of soil that is generally too wet for most fruit trees and vegetables include curly dock, horsetail, cattails, rushes, wiregrass, and willows. Unless drainage problems can easily be corrected, such property should not be considered as a growing site.

Erosion

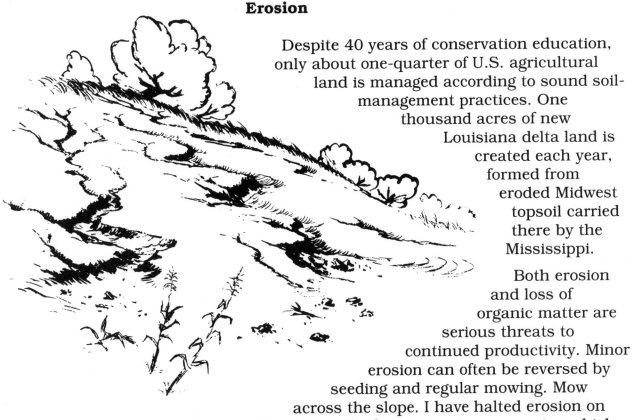

Despite 40 years of conservation education, only about one-quarter of U.S. agricultural land is managed according to sound soil-management practices. One thousand acres of new Louisiana delta land is created each year, formed from eroded Midwest topsoil carried there by the Mississippi.

Both erosion and loss of organic matter are serious threats to continued productivity. Minor erosion can often be reversed by seeding and regular mowing. Mow across the slope. I have halted erosion on the five or so sloping acres around our home by frequent summer mowing which has thickened the grass stand, raised the humus level, and stopped runoff in all but the heaviest rains. A certain indicator that more rainfall is being absorbed is the increased flow from a small spring below "the back yard," a field of about two acres.

Severe erosion can be stopped, even reversed, but the process can be costly and time consuming. If the land price is very good it may be worth considering. Consult with the local extension agent and conservation office on what it will take to correct the condition.

After you move to your land, to avoid creating erosion channels on dirt roadways, get into the habit of always driving slightly to one side of previous wheel tracks. Encourage visitors to do the same.

Chemical contamination

Land that has been farmed may be contaminated with herbicides, pesticides, and the salts and residues of chemical fertilizers. Potatoes, tomatoes, corn, beans, carrots, and other crops commonly receive chemical fertilizers and pesticides. If you are unable to obtain reliable crop and soil treatment history by talking to the owner and neighbors, soil tests will reveal the condition of the soil. It is safest to consider farm land guilty until proven innocent.

WINSLOW HOMER
Lumbering in Winter. 1871.

Vegetation

Plants respond to moisture, sunlight, soil types, and growing seasons. The primary visual difference between the arid West and the moist East and Northwest is the quality and quantity of vegetation. Much of the Southwest is cactus or chaparral. Western mountainous areas typically have trees on the west side, where most of the limited rain falls. Valleys often have the best soil and the best vegetation. The plains area was once famous for grass but farmers have destroyed most native grasses to plant grain crops. From eastern Oklahoma to the Atlantic, most states have substantial forests, although in farming country only scattered woodlots remain. Each state map in this book shows wooded percentages. Countrywide, less than five percent of the virgin forests remain.

I would rather have land with an overabundance of vegetation than a small amount. Land can be cleared if necessary but trees take decades to mature, and trees, shrubs, and grasses all contribute to soil fertility and water absorption. As the following shows, in addition to contributing to the scenery you look at each day, the vegetation on your land may contribute many valuable products.

Building materials and fuel

In a recent poll of 1,000 people, 29 percent said their ideal home was a log home in the woods. There are many areas with more than adequate trees with which to

Thomas Lincoln's cabin, Farmington, IL, c. 1886

build a home. States with enough trees suitable for logs that log home companies thrive there include Washington, Oregon, California, Montana, Minnesota, Wisconsin, Michigan, Missouri, Arkansas, Tennessee, North Carolina, Pennsylvania, New York, Vermont, and Maine. I'm sure I've missed some and I do apologize. Altogether, some 500 log house companies offer homes made of local trees. In addition to the great Northwest forests, large forested tracts still exist in most of the eastern half of the states. If a log house is not your thing, local sawmills will convert logs into rough-sawn or milled lumber to your specifications, often at very reasonable rates. And many home sawmill designs are available that allow homesteaders to make lumber.

The best trees for firewood are the hardwoods—and in my opinion the best of the best is oak, found throughout the northeast quarter of the country and south to northern Mississippi, Alabama, and Georgia. The following ecoregion map shows major forest types and areas.

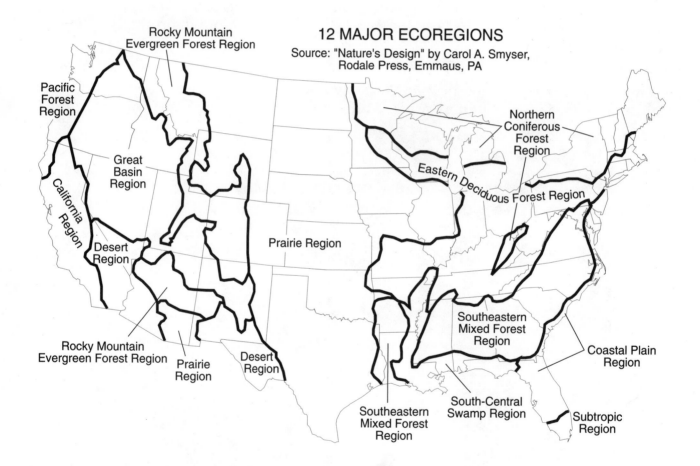

12 MAJOR ECOREGIONS
Source: "Nature's Design" by Carol A. Smyser, Rodale Press, Emmaus, PA

Food from woods and fields

Just about any area that has trees grows some kind of nut tree. The south is justly famous for its pecans. The Midwest and northern areas have black walnuts. On our place, although we have some fine old black walnut trees, the favorite for eating is the meat of the butternut, a smaller tree which grows along the stream. The natives call it white walnut. The shell is more elliptical and the meat is

sweeter than a black walnut. The light brown wood is softer than black walnut and carves nicely.

Maple trees are beautiful in all seasons, glorious in autumn, make great furniture, and provide sap for syrup and sugar. I have no personal experience with sugaring but if you settle in the Northeast you will likely have neighbors who can teach you how to tap trees and cook the sap down.

Natural fruit in our part of the Ozarks includes berries, grapes, persimmons, and pawpaws, sort of a wild banana. Our favorite is mulberries from a big old tree behind the house. Besides its fruit it gives us entertainment—we enjoy watching the red squirrels use hanging tricks to reach the ripest berries out at the ends of limbs, while crows angrily complain from the top of the tree.

Wild mushrooms, gathered with the knowledge to choose the correct ones, are a special treat. Morels, chanterelles, and coral mushrooms are all popular in our area.

Essential country skill #101 —using a pig to discover mushrooms. Instructions: Buy a trained pig and follow him.

House sites

Think carefully about whether you wish to build a home. An old, existing house will almost always be sitting on the best building site on the property, creating the dilemma of whether to keep it as is, remodel, tear it down, or move it.

Land without a house will need to have at least one good building site unless you intend to live in a cave. Then the land will need a good cave—or a good cave site where you can build a cave. The ideal building site has enough semi-flat land for not only a house, but garden, orchard, and outbuildings such as garage, workshop, and barn.

Perfectly flat land is actually a negative as it inhibits drainage. This may create a wet basement or unstable foundation condition. Unless you use a composting toilet, you will probably need a septic tank, which uses a leach field system to drain waste water. Sloping land is much more likely to drain well. Land that slopes more than slightly should be inspected for stability, as certain conditions create creep, or slide areas, often too unstable for houses without expensive foundations.

The best house site faces south to receive sun for light, gardening, and solar heating. A slight slope to the southeast is ideal, as it warms quickly in the morning. North-facing slopes are cool in summer but cold and possibly wet in winter, plus a garden might have to be away from the house, out in the sunlight. West-facing homes may cook in the hot afternoon sun.

Access roads

Access challenges occur with roads on north-facing slopes that ice up in the winter, then don't get enough sun to thaw; ill-drained roadways that develop deep muddy ruts; and stream crossings that flood. Any of these conditions warrant buying a four-wheel-drive vehicle—your life will be ever so much easier. In hilly areas with serious winters, unless you have a four-wheel-drive vehicle with a winch on the front and unlimited time and energy to fight your way up a steep ice-covered road, you will want to give consideration to the cost of building and maintaining a good, year-round access road to your dream property.

The price we pay for our secluded valley setting is a north-slope road that drops over 300 feet in four-tenths of a mile, then crosses a stream that sometimes floods. The worst condition occurs when snow melts during the day, freezes that night, then new snow falls on top of the ice, insulating it from daytime warmth. One Christmas season we were isolated for over a week while this condition persisted. Then we got an ice storm. The road was so slippery it could not be walked on at all. Visiting friends were directed into a neighbor's flat field up at the top, then we all carried their luggage (and gift case of wine) down through crusty snow in hillside woods to the point where our four-wheel-drive truck had been able to ascend. We had a great visit—it was one of those memorable occasions appreciated all the more for the outrageous conditions. The wine only helped.

House site with excellent water, no garden spot, and expensive access road

You too may find a place that is your ideal in every way but access conditions. If you need not get out to a job, then the only major consideration is what to do in case of a medical emergency. In our case, though it would be slow, there is an old logging road on a south-facing slope that leads to the top of the north ridge, with negotiable woods between it and an old ridge road, which eventually leads to a county road. In case of extreme emergency, there is a helicopter at a hospital 25 miles away but only minutes away by air.

One advantage of our difficult access road is protection from unannounced visits. Because of the slow, steep descent and the landform, we can hear gravel crunching under tires for at least ten minutes before the vehicle comes into view across the stream—plenty of time to become prepared for "surprise!" visitors.

Scenic beauty

One of the biggest bonuses of country life is being amidst natural beauty—for many of us a primary motivation for living here. Someone has even coined a term—terrain therapy—as a name for the healing that occurs when we look at natural scenes. Being in a place of natural beauty helps to overcome depression and improve various aspects of our health. It is now believed that the immune system is strengthened by the positive emotions produced by looking at the natural world.

Climate and scenery typically go together—dry and warm-to-hot usually dictates desert, mild often means southern coastal, etc. The climate you embrace may prescribe the scenery you enjoy. The exception is four diverse seasons with cold winters—at Christmastime you could find yourself skiing white powder in the West, icesailing the frozen blue topping of a Northeast lake, or deciphering the puzzle of bird and animal tracks in a fresh Midwest woodland snow.

Now, on your criteria worksheet, write your landform, soil, and vegetation preferences.

Resources

The National Atlas of the United States of America contains 765 maps and charts. It is out of print but can be found in many libraries.

The United States Geological Survey produces thousands of new and revised topographic maps each year. Free indexes are available for all states from Earth Science Information Centers. For the location of your nearest ESIC, call 800-USA-MAPS.

For general information on all available maps and map services contact:
National Cartographic Information Center
U.S. Geological Survey
507 National Center
Reston, VA 22092
703-860-6045

Soil maps are available from:
U.S. Soil Conservation Service
U.S. Department of Agriculture
P.O. Box 2890
Washington, D.C. 20013
202-205-0027

Soil information and maps are also available from state conservation offices, local university extension services (sometimes called agricultural extension service, or just "extension office"), and county land conservation offices.

In wildness is the preservation of the world.

HENRY DAVID THOREAU

11
The cost
of living

rofessor and author Jack Lessinger uses the name Caring Conserver to describe a type of modern American:

> Caring Conservers have found a way to deal with overconsumption by the most astonishing feat of social alchemy. . . . [they] *change their sense of values*—by consensus. Faced with the necessity of buying less of what they prefer, people change what they prefer. . . . Caring Conservers don't turn grudgingly to their substitutes. *They adore them.*

Sounds like Faith Popcorn's concept of "Small Indulgences," in *The Popcorn Report*.

Planning a move to the country is an excellent time to consider a cost-of-living adjustment. The reasons for moving to the country speak to values, how we relate to the condition of our self and our family, and to the social, economic, and political conditions of our country. In the next chapter we explore options for making a living. Lowering the cost of living makes earning a living simpler. It also may allow us to pursue interests long repressed. This is a good time to weigh the pros and cons of working at home, which we also consider in the next chapter. One of the cons is uncertainty of income, a condition tolerated more easily from a position of modest needs.

Country costs less . . .

Real estate

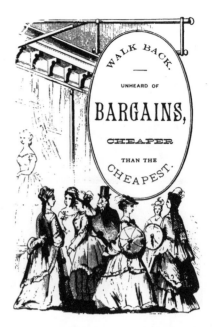

For the price of a city lot you can buy from one to forty acres, depending on the region—but note the entry about Rocky Mountain states below. Land prices range from about $200 to $2,000 per acre, depending on area, soil quality, water, and size of parcel. Because of lower labor costs, rural houses are often less expensive. This is good if you wish to build, but expect materials to cost as much, possibly more, because of trucking costs. Some old farms are priced according to the number of acres, with very little value given to the old buildings. You can save money if you are willing and able to take a deficient older house and bring it up to modern standards. Property taxes are less in the country, as is the number of services provided.

Food

Gardening is one of the great country living experiences. By growing a substantial part of your food you can save money, be healthier, and gain a lot of satisfaction. But if you plan to buy all your food, be aware that grocery prices are often higher (and quality lower) in remote rural areas, where products incur higher trucking costs.

Clothing

Clothing costs are lower mostly because we wear simpler cloth in the country. Working at home will especially save on wardrobe costs—the effect of designer suits is lost when all the people you see are in blue jeans and T-shirts.

Vehicle purchase and maintenance

This item can go either way. If you will work at home you probably won't need a late model car. If you commute or operate a home business that requires substantial travel, your needs will be greater. If you have high school-age children, expect to put on plenty of miles taking them to school functions.

The best single vehicle for the country is a pickup truck. If you need four-wheel-drive, expect to pay a premium. How often you need to buy a new vehicle depends on miles driven.

1911
Packard Eighteen
Landaulet

Farmers removed the rumble seat. Voilà—the first pickup truck!

Gravel and dirt roads are hard on tires and suspension systems. Air filters, oil, and oil filters need to be changed more often because of the dust. Country values contribute to the tendency to drive a vehicle longer—this saves on purchase costs but adds maintenance costs.

Vehicle insurance

Car insurance is substantially less than in the city where the high rate of thefts and repair costs drives premiums up. Pickup truck insurance may be even less than for a passenger car if you buy property in an agricultural state—such states often have special insurance rules for farm vehicles used within a certain mileage radius of your home.

Utilities

Private water systems are safer and less costly to operate than buying water from a municipal system. Some city people we know spend $100 per month on bottled water—it will cost far less than that to pump from your own well for household needs *and* garden irrigation.

There is generally no trash pickup in the country and that's a blessing. Rather than sending it "away" to a landfill we can compost all vegetable garbage, sort for recycling most paper, metal, plastic, and glass, and return batteries, appliances, and other dead items to where they may be recycled. In our county the volunteer fire departments bolster their operating budgets through the sale of recyclable materials and are happy to accept appropriate items.

If you heat with wood cut from your own woodlot you can save hundreds of dollars on your yearly heating costs.

Furniture

Country homes are usually furnished more casually than city homes. In many areas, craftspeople make furniture from local woods. Buying directly cuts out the cost of all the wholesale and marketing middlepeople. In our area there are auctions every weekend throughout the summer where furniture may be purchased for reasonable prices.

Contract labor

Rural wages are lower than in the city. Plumbers, electricians, carpenters, painters, and others may charge half or less of city wages. This is a regional factor and also depends on how far out you are from the city. The other side of the coin is that if you hire yourself out you also receive less.

Recreation/entertainment

Rather than spectator activities, country recreation tends toward personal activities: hunting, fishing and other water sports, hiking, and sightseeing. Cable TV is often unavailable but satellite antennas are becoming good buys. Entertainment costs will be higher if you make frequent visits to the city, for gas, meals, tickets, and overnight lodging.

In our neck of the woods, summer socializing runs heavily to community pot-lucks and volleyball or croquet, then making music. Wintertime features dinner and just plain talkin' or an occasional party, often a benefit.

Dancing a Jig

Mostly we prefer to stay home. Some of our finest summer evenings are spent sitting in the porch swing, counting trees and watching the grass grow. What with the state of the world, a body needs to dissipate tension.

... but sometimes country costs more

Real estate

Beware: many trendy rural places are fast becoming *expensive*, both in real estate prices and living costs. In addition to the entertainment figures mentioned earlier, California migrants with more impatience and home equity money than common sense have caused prices to quickly climb in Washington, Oregon, Montana, Wyoming, Idaho, Nevada, Arizona, New Mexico, and Colorado. One relocation service advises Californians to change vehicle license plates before visiting— locals hate Californians that much. Real estate agents love 'em.

Utilities

Electric costs are somewhat higher in sparsely populated areas where it takes more poles and wire to serve fewer customers. Electric air-conditioning costs are therefore higher. Electric heating is inefficient and most expensive of all systems, to be avoided if possible.

Your monthly telephone bill may be larger. Until you become established in your new community most of your calls are likely to be out of your local calling area.

Regarding service: both electric and rural phone service are subject to greater interruption from weather conditions. Private-line phone service taken for granted in the city may be unavailable in some rural areas and very expensive in others. This is an especially important factor if you plan to run a home business.

Bottom lines

It generally costs less money to live in the country than in the city. How much less depends on how much you pay for your property and how independent you become. Making firewood and gardening are the first steps to lowering personal and environmental costs. Investing in solar heating, photovoltaic or wind electric generation equipment, and energy-efficiency upgrades to your house can further lower monthly costs dramatically while also helping to heal the planet.

Five agribusiness mega-corporations control the American food supply. One third of our nation's food is produced by the largest one percent of agribusiness farms. Buying supermarket food means supporting agribusiness. Agribusiness runs on fossil fuel. Supporting agribusiness means spending up to twelve calories of fossil fuel for every calorie of corn used in breakfast cereal. Using such wasteful quantities of fossil fuel creates huge health and cleanup costs due to air and water poisoning, not to mention the enormous diplomatic and military costs of maintaining the flow of oil. (Yes—that is the real reason we insisted that Saddam Hussein leave Kuwait.)

The true cost of living will always include the economic, health, and cleanup costs to our environment and our communities. We can express and implement our values not only by how we spend our money but how we avoid the necessity for money and how we conduct ourselves in our homes, on our land, and in our community. Buying locally will help keep our community economy healthy.

The *Statistical Abstract of the United States* is published annually by the U.S. Bureau of the Census. It includes a cost-of-living index. It is available from the U.S. Government Printing Office, Washington, DC 20401.

We have been urged to "think globally, act locally." In *Sex, Economy, Freedom & Community* Wendell Berry offers this perspective:

> If we could think locally, we would take far better care of things than we do now. The right local questions and answers will be the right global ones. The Amish question 'What will this do to our community?' tends toward the right answer for the world. . . . In order to make ecological good sense for the planet, you must make ecological good sense locally. You *can't* act locally by thinking globally. No one can make ecological good sense for the planet. Everyone can make ecological good sense locally, if the affection, the scale, the knowledge, the tools, and the skills are right.

Got no check books, got no banks.
Still I'd like to express my thanks—
I got the sun in the mornin'
and the moon at night.

IRVING BERLIN

Essential country equipment #3—the pig

The pig is the original breakfast food production unit. This is the high-cholesterol model. Pigs make good companions but can be an embarrassment at formal dinners as they are unable to hold a wine glass.

JACOB FAIRDEALER

SELLS

TEA AND COFFEE,

WHEN DUTY FREE,

AT A REDUCTION—NOT AN INCREASE.

Anti-Tea-and-Coffee-Corner Man.

HATCHET & GIMLET'S

FASHIONABLE

HARDWARE STORE.

Gold Coffee Pots. | Silver Skittels.
Parlour Cooking Stoves.

FELT & PLUSH,

CHARACTERISTIC HATTERS,

AND DEALERS IN

PERSUASIVE ROCKY MOUNTAIN BEAVERS,

NOBBY CASTORS,

Indian Skull Caps, &c.

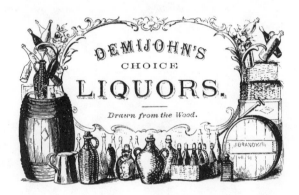

DEMIJOHN'S

CHOICE

LIQUORS.

Drawn from the Wood.

BREVES & SEMIBREVES,

JOBBERS IN

DULCET SYMPHONIES,

JEWS-HARPS AND BASS DRUMS.

Reference:—BOSTON JUBILEE.

BULLOCK & CLEAVER,

DEALERS IN

NUTRITIOUS MEATS,

DAINTY GAME,

SAVORY PISCATORIAL TIDBITS.

CHOICE CUTS FOR ALL.

SNEEZER'S

INCOMPARABLE

ODOROUS SNUFFS,

SEGARS,

DELICIOUS FINE CUTS, ETC.

One Price for all Sexes and Colours.

MORTAR BLUEPILL,

Graduate of the College of Pharmacy,

PRACTICAL PHARMACEUTIST,

PRESCRIPTIONS CAREFULLY COMPOUNDED.

12
Making
a living

*I would live all my life
in nonchalance and insouciance,
were it not for making a living,
which is rather a nouciance.*

OGDEN NASH

We Americans, in the land of the free and the home of the brave, descendants of men and women who paid for our freedom with their lives, lemminglike, allow our employers to dictate where we will live. The modern American, designating money as the overriding consideration, willingly uproots children from school and family from community to go where the company dictates that one must go to do its work. Until the layoff. The good of the company becomes the downfall of the family and the community. Social scientists now believe that the high incidence of mental illness in the U.S. is tied to the loss of that sense of belonging to a community that results from following jobs.

Wendell Berry has considered the ramifications of how and where we work. In *The Unsettling of America* he offers this:

> What is new is the *guise* of the evil: a limitless technology, dependent upon a limitless morality, which is to say upon no morality at all. How did such a possibility become thinkable? It seems to me that it is implicit in the modern separation of life and work. It is implicit in the assumption that we can live entirely apart from our way of making a living. . . . If human values are removed from production, how can they be preserved in consumption? How can we value our lives if we devalue them in making a living? If we do not live where we work, and when we work, we are wasting our lives, and our work too.

It seems so obvious that the most fulfilling life comes from living *and working* in one's ideal place. A vocation is most sane and fulfilling if it is performed in one's community, is useful to the community, and uses local resources at a level that can be sustained without hurting the land or the people. As with most human activities, if it is good for the community it is good for the nation and ultimately good for the world.

Your ideal country home place may not immediately appear to have an opportunity for you to make a living. The lowest-priced property is often located in economically depressed areas where jobs are few, wages are low, and prices paid for locally-produced products are modest. Intentionally lowering one's "standard of living," which is defined by each of us according to our experience, may be an upsetting process, especially for those who have always lived in cities and have no memory of the quality of a simpler life. In fact, such a lowering can be a great contribution to personal growth.

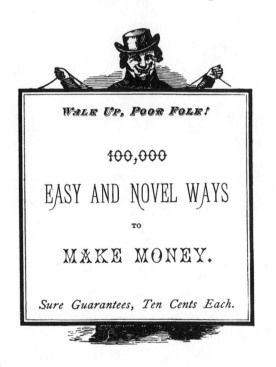

WALK UP, POOR FOLK!

100,000

EASY AND NOVEL WAYS

TO

MAKE MONEY.

Sure Guarantees, Ten Cents Each.

Talking to a variety of people living in an area may reveal work or business opportunities not readily apparent. If you have several skills or are adaptable, talk to people who would like to do business with you if you settle there. Bankers, insurance people, store keepers, and chambers of commerce can get you started. Living the ideal life includes working at something you enjoy. Use this time to consider and find your ideal work.

If finding immediate employment is a criterion, your ideal place may be near a known job market. If your skill is vital, like nursing or automotive repair, you should have little trouble finding work almost anywhere. If your skill is in reasonable demand you can concentrate your search in rural areas near edge cities, where employment opportunities and wages are better than in the country.

Other options are to teach yourself a new business, take an existing business to the country, or buy one once you get there. This is a good time to consider not only living where you most want to be but doing what gives you the most satisfaction. That said, we will devote most of this chapter to identifying existing work opportunities.

Where are the jobs?

In the past, the greatest employment opportunities were in metropolitan areas. Modern industry follows tax incentives, local inducements, low land costs, and low wages. Company headquarters and production facilities have moved to the fringe outside the suburbs, within easy commuting distance to true country. And commuting to work in a town or small city is a sight different than commuting to New York or Los Angeles.

In *Rural and Small Town America,* Fuguitt, Brown, and Beale relate population movement to jobs:

> Much of the recent transition in rural and nonmetropolitan America is intertwined with changes in industry.

Predominantly, industry chases low wages but there are other factors. States with right-to-work laws are pulling jobs from unionized areas because of union manning requirements, job classifications, advancement procedures, and task definitions. There appears to be a backlash by professionals against steel, concrete, and glass surrounded by blaring traffic. Many high-tech firms are moving to rural areas because of the demand by managers and engineers for attractive living areas. CEOs and board chairmen have decided to take their businesses where people want to live—and where they and their families want to live.

The trend of big business to move to rural areas is well-established and shows no sign of reversing. All this is good news for the would-be country dweller.

*What's money? A man is a success if he gets up in the morning
and goes to bed at night and in between does what he wants to do.*

Bob Dylan

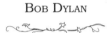

As early as the late 1960s, government tabulations showed that manufacturing employment was growing more rapidly in the countryside than in metropolitan areas. Metro area bureaucrats noticed also, took action to capture those new tax bases, and petitioned the government to allow them to expand their areas. This is one reason why today's so-called metropolitan areas include large areas not even remotely metropolitan in nature. As examples, Kansas City and St. Louis metropolitan areas each now include ten counties, many of which are decidedly rural. G. Scott Thomas (see Sources at end of this chapter) points out that the metropolitan designation has been given by the federal government to such places as Grand Forks, North Dakota, Casper, Wyoming, and Enid, Oklahoma.

In *The New Corporate Frontier: The Big Move to Small Town, USA,* CEO/author David A. Heenan says:

> What we are seeing unfold is the selective preference for penturbia, particularly for those medium- and small-sized communities capable of providing the career opportunities and social amenities normally associated with big cities and suburbs. The most favored frontier towns are often linked to a major university, a state capital, a research park, or a similar institution that tends to provide the diversity and cultural spark sought by young professionals.

The primary place of American jobs has become edge cities, those places defined by Joel Garreau as out by the suburbs, where developers have created shopping malls and office parks. Garreau says there are more than 200 new edge cities, already holding two-thirds of all American office facilities. 80 percent of these new centers have emerged in the last twenty years. One of Garreau's qualifying criteria for edge cities is that they have more jobs than bedrooms. The expected pattern was for city dwellers to commute out of town to the jobs. Instead, city slickers have become clod kickers and commute *in* to the jobs from country homes.

There has been a substantial shift of manufacturing to rural and small-town areas. About 700 of our 2,400 nonmetropolitan counties power their economies with manufacturing.

In years past, corporations left the towns where they started and moved to big cities. After World War II, they started moving to the cleaner air, lower costs, and golf courses of the suburbs. These days, states Heenan, they're headed back to the hinterland. He feels that the U.S. could emerge as "the first postindustrial country without important cities." He feels that the perceived need for a big city environment was always exaggerated anyway.

New York City, often referred to as the barometer of the nation, exemplifies the move outward. In 1960, 27 percent of the Fortune 500 industrial companies lived there; in 1970, 23 percent; in 1980, 16 percent; and in 1990, only 9 percent. Other large U.S. cities reflect a similar trend. Almost half of Chicago's 44 Fortune 500 companies are not in town but out in the suburbs.

Big business guru Peter Drucker predicts that the city of the future will be occupied by headquarters of major companies with much of the clerical, accounting, and administration staff located in the suburbs or even thousands of miles away from major urban centers.

Examples of companies located in or near rural areas

The following examples of companies in low-population-density areas are presented here to give you specific places where jobs may be available. If one of these towns is in your area of interest you may wish to write the company human resources department to determine employment potential.

L.L. Bean, the $600 million mail-order empire, is run from Freeport, Maine, population 7,000. Wal-Mart is headquartered in Bentonville, Arkansas, (11,257). With a name like Smuckers, you might know that the jam and jelly king is in the country—Orrville, Ohio, where 7,700 people think the name is beautiful. Corning, New York (12,000) is home to Corning Glass Works. Silkscreening is the business of Bacova Guild, Ltd., located in Bacova, Virginia. It does almost $17 million a year in this town of—50! Gerber Products is in Fremont, Michigan (3,875). Ben & Jerry's Homemade is swirled in Waterbury, Vermont (1,702).

Maytag, the $3 billion appliance maker is headquartered in Newton, Iowa, (14,800). The fastest growing supermarket in the country is Food Lion, based in Salisbury, North Carolina (25,000). Tiny Springdale, Arkansas, is home to Tyson Foods, the nation's largest chicken processor. The Andersen Window Company people call Bayport, Minnesota, home (3,205). Weaver Popcorn Company ($70-plus million sales) is in Van Buren, Indiana (935).

Johns-Manville located its international headquarters twenty miles outside of Denver; Kodak and IBM built new plants ten miles further out. Dow Chemical headquarters are in Midland, Michigan. Phillips Petroleum is in Bartlesville, Oklahoma. Toolmaker Adamus Carbide Corporation left its Kenilworth, New Jersey, home for the open space, reasonable wages, and hard-working people of Oak Ridge, Tennessee.

In "California in the Rearview Mirror," *Newsweek* (7-19-93) reported that in five years Coeur d'Alene, Idaho, and surrounding Kootenai County have nabbed 2,000 California jobs in fields as diverse as swimwear and computer software.

The big story of 1985 was the GM announcement that it would build its $3 billion Saturn plant in Spring Hill, Tennessee (1,275). Disappointing locals, GM imported most of the workers, but the payroll created many new jobs in the community.

Not only American companies are creating jobs outside of cities. History professor Jon C. Teaford, in *Cities of The Heartland*, reports that Japanese automakers invested in America's heartland during the 1980s, but they studiously avoided locating their facilities in major urban areas.

> Instead, they chose to build their factories in corn fields outside of Marysville, Ohio, Lafayette, Indiana, and Bloomington, Illinois. The Japanese clearly preferred areas where labor unions were weak, where the population was rock-rib Republican, and where the workers would be overwhelmingly white. This they found in the rural Midwest.

States bidding for payrolls

Payrolls have become auction items for states wooing big companies to their non-urban areas. In 1991, Toyota decided to build an assembly plant in Georgetown, Kentucky, after the state had contributed $300 million. In 1992, South Carolina offered $130 million to snare a BMW plant.

Intel, the computer chip giant, announced in April 1993 that it was building a $1 billion, 1,000-employee plant in New Mexico, despite an ardent courtship by California. Rio Rancho used a $114 million tax-incentive package to get the deal. The Albuquerque suburb is a classic example of the new edge cities—in 1970 Rio Rancho's population was 2,000; in 1992 it was 38,000.

The *Wall Street Journal* (11-24-93) reported that Alabama promised over $300 million in various incentives to outbid North Carolina and become the site of the first U.S. Mercedes-Benz car plant. Somehow I doubt that M-B will follow Henry Ford's philosophy and pay employees enough to purchase the product they make. Besides the state package, I'm betting they moved there primarily for low wages.

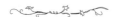

Industrial plants and other nonfarm businesses do not bring utopia to the countryside any more than they have to the cities. If they lack competition for labor force, they may be exploitative—offering low wages and benefits.

CALVIN BEALE

Beware of boom towns

In *Places Rated Almanac*, Richard Boyer and David Savageau point out that in a boom town there are

> rising personal incomes, which ensure real estate appreciation; expanding personal employment opportunities; improved infrastructures; somewhat lower violent crime; increasing amenities; and high-quality health care and education. On the other hand, the disadvantages of living in a boom town include rising costs of living; increased property crime rates; environmental pollution; and, maybe worst of all, noticeable loss of personal discretionary time.

By the way, *Places Rated Almanac* provides an excellent example of the peril of making and depending on economic predictions. The book, published in 1987, predicted that the Los Angeles-Long Beach area would create the greatest number of new jobs in the country, 407,770. Then the Cold War ended, defense cutbacks were announced, and southern California entered its most difficult economic time in memory. In November 1993 southern California's unemployment was at 9.5 percent, the nation's worst.

Boom towns can even more quickly become bust towns, especially if most jobs are dependent on one or two commodities or companies. Wyoming's oil and coal industries yo-yo the state economy. The West Virginia coal area boomed during the 1974 oil shortage and headed back down as soon as it ended. Oil-influenced Texas has more empty bank-owned houses than any other state.

Any area that is dependent upon infinite supplies of a finite material is on thin economic ice. The mining and logging towns of the West are almost a cliché in this regard. The states in the Rockies notably have boomed from mining operations, and busted when the ore ran out. Jim Robbins, in *Last Refuge*:

> If a town loses a sawmill or mine with one hundred workers, and it is the largest employer, the shutdown can be devastating. On the other hand, if there are ten small businesses, each with ten employees, the economy is more resilient and the power of any one company is reduced.

Our world is changing quickly. Don't trust your economic future to one company. The shoe factory or television assembly plant that you depend on for wages to buy groceries may move to Mexico. South of the border is not the only danger—much shoe and clothing production has moved to Asia.

One-horse towns are fine (and far superior to no-horse towns) but be skeptical of one-industry towns. The ideal home is in an area with a diversified economy.

Home workers and home businesses

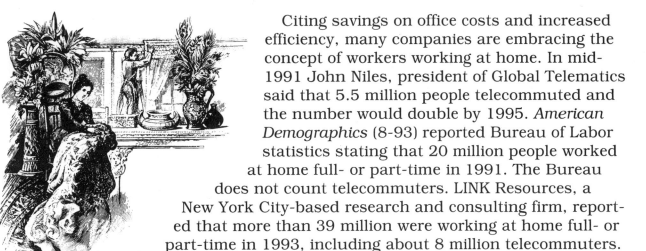

Citing savings on office costs and increased efficiency, many companies are embracing the concept of workers working at home. In mid-1991 John Niles, president of Global Telematics said that 5.5 million people telecommuted and the number would double by 1995. *American Demographics* (8-93) reported Bureau of Labor statistics stating that 20 million people worked at home full- or part-time in 1991. The Bureau does not count telecommuters. LINK Resources, a New York City-based research and consulting firm, reported that more than 39 million were working at home full- or part-time in 1993, including about 8 million telecommuters.

Linked by telephones, fax machines,
Federal Express, and computers,
a new breed of information worker
is reorganizing the landscape of America.
Free to live almost anywhere,
more and more individuals are deciding
to live in small cities and towns and rural areas.

JOHN NAISBITT AND PATRICIA ABURDENE
MEGATRENDS 2000

With computers, fax-modems, and overnight mail delivery, many workers can now operate from almost anywhere. Visionaries see fiber-optics creating connections between home offices and head offices. Virtual workplace already exists—VeriFone, the company that makes those little terminals that merchants use to verify credit card purchases, is based in Redwood City, California. All 1,500 workers have laptops or personal computers hooked up to Internet. Not only do the staff perform their duties at home—the chief information officer works from his home in New Mexico.

Cottage industry is growing. Many companies now employ home workers to craft marketable products. My wife and I for years have bought clothing from Deva, a rural company that uses home workers to cut and sew the patterns.

Over ten million self-employed Americans operate their businesses from their homes. The number is growing. In *Age Wave*, Ken Dychtwald states:

> It is predicted that by the year 2000, over 20 percent of the work force will go to work without leaving home.

If you are one of us who think of a J-O-B as a Journey Of the Broke, perhaps

you will use this time as a transition to self-employment. If you start your own business, you enter the realm of entrepreneurs, we who have maximum control over our working conditions and hours. Many of us daily exhibit our belief in the inalienable right to work 12 to 16 hours per day. But they are *our* hours, doing what *we* want, for *our* benefit.

The vital factors for success are your level of knowledge, your focus, and your persistence. Most people who succeed have a passion for what they do and they obtain and keep a very high level of knowledge about their field.

If you anticipate working with computers, don't take rural electric or telephone service for granted. Electrical outages from storms are fairly common in rural areas with long, hard-to-maintain rights-of-way. Telephone line static, which affects modem and fax transmission, is more common in the country. If the fault is old, frayed lines the company may be willing to replace them. Our phone company replaced nearly a half mile of phone lines for us. Noninterruptible power sources are a good investment for computer users.

Working in the boonies with computers has spawned a new term: electronic cottage, and the acronym ACW—Another Computer in the Woods. Having both a computer *and* an outhouse is an anomaly certain to impress your city friends and relatives. Perhaps one day the ultimate country chic will be to have a computer *in* the outhouse; well, that may be, ahem, carrying it too far. Then again, some of the world's greatest thoughts were conceived during morning sits.

Explore, and explore. . . .
Make yourself necessary to the world,
and mankind will give you bread.
RALPH WALDO EMERSON

If you plan on taking a business to the country, check out the competition and consider local conditions. Our nearest neighbor had experience on drill rigs so he bought a drilling outfit and set up a well-drilling business. Unfortunately for him there are two established drillers in the area who are well known and respected, one full-time and the other a farmer who drills part-time. Both know the local geology and usually hit water. After about a year of too few clients and too many dry holes my neighbor pulled up for the last time and sold out.

Rather than finding a job, you can buy one. The current *American Treasures*, a United National Real Estate special catalog, lists operating and potential bed & breakfasts, resorts, even an old operating grist mill and resort complete with cabins, campground, and canoes.

By working faithfully eight hours a day,
you may eventually get to be a boss
and work twelve hours a day.

ROBERT FROST

If you can't find a job or buy one, then make one. Invent something. Take my idea of generating electricity at fitness centers and make a living and save oil at the same time. Invent a more efficient solar distiller to make fresh water from salt water, so coastal communities can stop stealing other people's water. Create a job barter system for everyone in your bioregion. Design a kitchen stove that operates with the flu heat of a wood furnace. Figure out uses for the mountains of old tires. Make a homemade paper maker that will use local plant fibers. Perfect a process for melting used plastics and molding roofing shingles.

Some of our friends' successful home businesses include medicinal herbs, exotic animals, wreaths, paintings, specialty seeds, sculpture, and wooden jewelry. Here are some other ideas for country home businesses: home schools, pottery, furniture making and repair, bed & breakfast, auto repair, tire repair and sales, welding, horseshoeing, taxidermy, weaving, firewood, fish farming, chimney cleaning, secretarial services, desktop publishing, chainsaw repair, sign painting, woodcarving, recycling center, photography, mail-order sales, split-rail fencing, child care, campground, appliance repair, silk screening, market gardening, cider making, wild berry winemaking, food co-operative.

Again, living the ideal life includes working at something you enjoy—at home. Try to use this time of transition to consider what you really want to do. Use the lower cost of country living to give you the slack to develop your ideal work. On your criteria worksheet write the work conditions you want, unless you are considering farming as your work. In that case, read the next chapter before listing your work criteria.

Resources and recommended reading

Many of the "place rating" books listed in the bibliography include employment considerations. Retirement books acknowledge and respond to the fact that most retired folks need to supplement social security and pensions.

- Brabec, Barbara. *Homemade Money: The Definitive Guide to Success in a Homebased Business.* Third Edition. White Hall, VA: Betterway Publications, 1989. Includes a substantial resource directory.

- Germer, Jerry. *Country Careers: Successful Ways to Live and Work in the Country.* New York: John Wiley & Sons, 1993.

- Naisbitt, John and Patricia Aburdene, *Megatrends 2000, Ten New Directions for the 1990's.* New York: William Morrow and Co., 1990.

- Ross, Tom & Marilyn. *Country Bound!* Buena Vista, CO: Communication Creativity, 1992.

- G. Scott Thomas, *Where To Make Money: A Rating Guide To Opportunities in America's Metro Areas,* Buffalo, NY: Prometheus Books, 1993. Rates 73 metro areas, many of which are accessible from rural areas via a 30-minute commute.

United National Real Estate, *American Treasures.* 4700 Belleview, Suite 200, PO Box 11400, Kansas City, MO 64112-0400. 800-999-1020. Lists historic houses, bed & breakfasts, and other rural business properties.

Don't go around saying the world owes you a living;
the world owes you nothing; it was here first.
MARK TWAIN

He worked like hell in the country
so he could live in the city,
where he worked like hell
so he could live in the country.
DON MARQUIS

Money often costs too much.
RALPH WALDO EMERSON

You probably thought that
this depicts beer brewing as
a potential career. Actually it
is the author congratulating
himself for having finished
this chapter

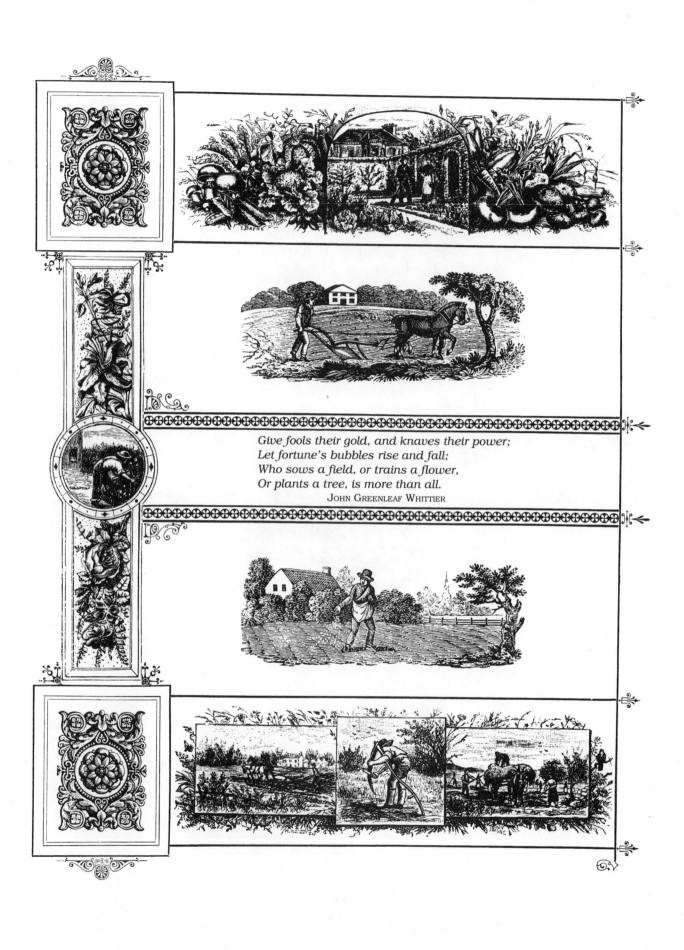

Give fools their gold, and knaves their power;
Let fortune's bubbles rise and fall;
Who sows a field, or trains a flower,
Or plants a tree, is more than all.
      JOHN GREENLEAF WHITTIER

13
Farming

Those who labor in the earth are the chosen people of God,
if He ever had a chosen people, whose breasts He has made
His peculiar deposit for substantial and genuine virtue.
It is the focus in which He keeps alive that sacred fire,
which otherwise might escape from the face of the earth.

THOMAS JEFFERSON

ood family farmers are among the most admirable of people. Few other lifestyles are so honest with nature—few other lifestyles are so complete. To choose farming is to commit to hard work and challenging conditions; to do it well requires an abundance of man's most admirable qualities. It is an ideal condition for family life.

Or so it was until politicians, bureaucrats, and college professors collusively decided they knew best. Jefferson was prescient but incomplete with his warning: "Were we directed from Washington when to sow, and when to reap, we should soon want bread." While most of today's so-called bread is not worth eating, what the direction from Washington has cost us is thousands of our family farms.

As an ex-farmer's son who has observed the wrenching stories of farm foreclosures, suicides, and killings caused largely by oppressive governmental interference in farm people's lives, I caution you against farming if what you envision requires you to borrow money, use large machinery, compete with agribusiness, or be involved in any government program. Hopefully, the media coverage of broke and broken farm families has provided adequate warning to those who contemplate farming. I am reminded of the story of the old farmer who had just won $10 million in the state lottery. A reporter asked him what he was going to do now that he was rich. The farmer replied that he guessed he'd "just keep on farming 'til I go broke."

Contrariwise, as an organic gardener and advocate who observes a swelling demand for chemical-free food I am optimistic that small-scale food producers and specialty products producers can make a decent living and enjoy high-quality lives with their families. If they follow a sound plan, produce multiple high-demand products for nearby markets, and stay clear of government subsidy programs there is every reason to believe that they can do well.

Subsidy programs are seductive and counter-productive. A farmer's acceptance of such programs inevitably leads to dependence, loss of freedom, and loss of pride and dignity. That cost is too high.

Mid-sized farms have become an endangered species. (Too bad they are not as protected as, say, the spotted owl.) Today's farmer can either be a small-farm operator or compete with the big boys: agribusiness, industrial agriculture, corporate food production. The odds are against a mid-sized farmer with modest financial resources—say a mere millionaire. Operating on a level above small-scale farming requires substantial dollars—few mid-sized farms produce sufficient earnings to bridge the years of weather or market disaster. In most cases, investment capital receives a higher return from a simple savings account than from farming. College agriculture professors, machinery sellers, chemical company representatives, bankers, and politicians are prone to give lengthy encouraging advice to mid-sized farm operators, but such farming is a much tougher life to live than talk to give. (It is not my intent to offend— if I have omitted any qualifying group, I do apologize.)

There are 3,141 counties in the United States. Of our approximately 2,400 nonmetropolitan counties, about 700 are primarily agricultural. Farming operations range from immense agribusiness operations to very small herb, vegetable, floriculture, and specialty enterprises. To define this range in modern farms, rural sociologists have created a new term—two-tier farming—which relates to scale. It is as important to consider farming from the perspective of personal time commitment.

Full-time versus part-time farming

Farmers are now members
of a capital-intensive industry
that values good bookwork more than backwork.
So several times a year almost every farmer
must seek operating credit
from the college fellow in the white shirt and tie
—in effect, asking financial permission
to work hard on his own land.

ANDREW H. MALCOLM

Full-time farming on a large scale requires a huge financial investment in land and equipment. It means hard work for long hours, often seven days per week. It requires knowledge of soil, crops, farm skills, planning, marketing, and financial management. It means dealing with high land costs, high equipment costs, volatile interest rates, too little rain, too much rain, late freezes, early freezes,

THOMAS GAINSBOROUGH
Landscape with Cows. Etching.

government programs, and market conditions manipulated by a few huge agribusiness food companies. On the latter, Senator Lloyd Bentsen noted in 1991:

> Currently, a rancher in Texas gets 53 cents a pound for his lambs, while we pay $6.99 a pound for leg of lamb at the grocery store.

Part-time, small-scale farming is, ah, a growing trend. The Census Bureau reported in late 1984 that there were 637,000 farms of less than fifty acres, an increase of 17 percent in four years. There are even more today. Part-time farmers typically work at primary jobs in nearby areas and tend their crops and livestock evenings and weekends. The rewards are often seen as quality of life rather than just dollars— healthy exercise, high-quality food, and an opportunity to instill traditional values in children.

Agribusiness and family farms today

Agribusiness is owned by investors who see land as something to be mined for dividends, ignoring all consequential results, expecting and planning for the day when the land will be mined out, and expecting taxpayers, through government programs, to ensure their continued profits. In spite of efficiency claims made for huge acreages farmed with large machinery, such farming is not only wasteful but threatens the food supply of future generations. The Land Institute's Wes Jackson is one of those who point out that agribusiness consumes more calories in fossil fuels than it produces in food. Taxpayers underwrite agribusiness owners' profits not only by subsidizing oil prices, but by paying for price support programs, footing the health costs of food tainted by pesticide residue, and dealing with waters polluted by farm chemicals. And agribusiness owners are the prime beneficiaries of land-grant college research.

Family farming once was a self-sufficient lifestyle of feeding the family and providing surplus to nearby communities. Today's "successful" so-called family farm is a specialized business, highly capital- and energy-intensive. It concentrates on the production of one or two market crops, uses machinery to the

fullest extent on large fields, and depends on borrowed money for the purchase of equipment, seeds, fertilizer, and pesticides to maximize yields on expensive land. Increasingly, the family that owns the farm lives in a nearby town, to save the wife commuting time to her job. Two-thirds of U.S. farmers live in cities or towns.

Today's successful family farmers typically grew up on their farms, love the land they inherited, and continue farming in spite of the many adversities and modest income. A typical midwestern farmer might have a capital investment in land and equipment of $1.5 million, and sell crops worth

$300,000. Net income—depending on production costs, weather, market demand, and other factors—might be $30,000 or less. That's a two percent return on capital investment. It has to be a labor of love—they sure aren't getting paid.

Osha Gray Davidson states that while off-farm employment was once a stop-gap to survive tough times, today most family farmers have jobs. About one-half of all U.S. farm families now derive more income from nonfarm sources than from the sale of farm products. Average 1990 farm household income was $39,367, with $5,742 from farm operations and $33,625 from other sources, primarily off-farm jobs.

Regenerative farming

Good regenerative farmers, practicing what is sometimes called sustainable agriculture, share much with organic gardeners. They care about the quality of their products. They love their land and work to improve it. Regenerative farming is practiced by farmers who take responsibility for their actions, who are sensitive to the environment, who know that land is a national treasure. They rotate crops, use chemical fertilizers sparingly or not at all, protect against erosion, and strive always to improve fertility. They are becoming more appreciated by society as a whole, which is becoming educated to the value of food grown without chemicals.

Sustainability is defined as actions that meet the needs of the present generation without compromising the needs of future generations. Soil erosion epitomizes the need for sustainability.

> Globally, crop lands damaged between 1950 and 1990 by moderate to extreme soil erosion total an area equal to China and India combined. Yet to feed the world's projected population, output must triple in the next 50 years, according to the U.N. Development Program.

(Robin Wright, "Learning to Give as Much as We Take From Earth," *Los Angeles Times*, January 18, 1994) Wright's article reports that while population is growing, the supply of food and good water is diminishing.

Small can be beautiful

Small-scale farming, easily confused with part-time farming, can be a viable *full-time* occupation. Organic fruits and vegetables, sheep and goats, flowers, ornamental shrubs, and exotic animals are suitable for modest-sized operations. A retired professor from Tuskegee Institute has developed a plan for farming on 10 to 200 acres. In his book listed below, Booker T. Whatley gives complete instructions. Key issues: buy land close to a city so that subscribers to your Clientele Membership Club will drive to your farm to pick their own produce; grow multiple high-value crops or animals that clients demand; by-pass all middlemen; and adhere to a sound, year-round plan. Whatley warns that his plan is not for everyone.

> You've got to be a good manager to operate one of these farms. You've got to be a good planner and you've got to think for yourself.

Informed consumers are demanding and paying for organically-grown produce. Wendell Berry notes:

> There is a rapidly increasing number of consumers who wish to buy food that is nutritionally whole and uncontaminated by pesticides and other toxic chemical residues. And these people would prefer not to pay the exorbitant food prices required by long-distance transportation, processing, packaging, and advertising, all of which result from 'agribusiness' control of food.

The Food Marketing Institute agrees—they found that three-fourths of all shoppers have a major concern about chemical residues in food.

If you intend to grow food crops or animals, buy land that is not poisoned with the residue of chemical fertilizers, herbicides, and pesticides. Some constituents of these products may persist in the soil decades after their application. Organic certification programs require soil tests to prove that the land is free of chemicals.

If you choose this route, educate yourself well. Visit successful pick-your-own operations. Check out local farmers' markets and food co-ops. County extension agents may be a good source of information. The Cooperative Extension Service of the U.S. Department of Agriculture was established in 1914 to apply the results of agricultural research done in U.S. land-grant colleges. Operating through state and county extension agents, it helps U.S. farmers to learn and use new techniques. (After observing the farm failures of the last few decades, and deservedly catching a lot of heat, they are becoming more responsive to small farmers.) Home-demonstration agents supply information and advice on food-preserving and cooking techniques and on farm economics. The 4-H programs train young people in agricultural, food-processing, and management techniques.

Alas, Big Brother has gotten into the organic act. BB involvement started with the National Organic Foods Production Act of 1990. In 1991 the USDA appointed a National Organic Standards Board charged with defining what is and isn't organic. Now we even have a new farmer: The Transitional Farmer, who is not yet certifiable but is presumably headed in that direction. Inasmuch as it is the close collaboration of our federal government, agribusiness, and land grant colleges that has created our present poisonous food situation, consumers will have to be very careful with claims of organic compliance. I suspect that federal standards will be more lax than state and local standards already developed. Should you choose to become a certified organic food producer, I recommend that you contact the local organic growers association in the area in which you will farm. They will know what is happening on the federal level and how it relates to local conditions.

Increasing numbers of farmers and city refugees are embracing specialty farming. While the scale of operations is usually small, rewards can be high from growing and raising exotic salad plants, premium fruits and vegetables, and animals such as llamas and ostriches.

Once considered a classic, this model is no longer in favor.

Farmland prices

According to the U.S. Department of Agriculture, on January 1, 1993 the average value of U.S. farmland and buildings was $700 an acre, 15 percent below the record high of $823 in 1982. Rhode Island has the most expensive farmland in the country ($4,894 per acre), and Wyoming has the least expensive ($149 per acre). Average area prices, in order, were Northeast ($1,753), Southeast ($1,235), Corn Belt ($1,193), Pacific ($1,190), Appalachia ($1,129), Lake States ($950), Delta States ($802), Southern Plains ($480), Northern Plains ($462), and Mountain ($295).

Farmland includes cropland, pasture, orchard, and woodland. Cropland prices are typically higher than prices for woodland. Demand for farmland for nonagricultural uses is highest in coastal regions.

Perhaps the USDA does not consider growing grapes to be an agricultural use. California's Napa Valley vineyard land will now set you back $40,000—per acre.

Keeping the right to farm

46 states have right-to-farm laws to protect farmers from being taxed out of existence by intruding development. Some places actually pay farmers for development rights, so the landowner can realize value gain but still keep farming.

If you are considering producing food as your work, then note appropriate needs on your criteria worksheet in the areas of soil quality, acreage, farming choices, water quantity, and market demographics.

Resources

Office for Small-Scale Agriculture
901 D Street, SW
Room 328 Aerospace Building
Washington, DC 20250-2200
202-401-1805
Provides information on growing crops and raising animals.

Alternative Farming Systems Information Center
National Agricultural Library, Room 304
10301 Baltimore Boulevard
Beltsville, MD 20705-2351
301-504-5724; FAX 301-504-6409
Source for scientific or popular literature on all types of alternative farming practices. For free bibliography of *Part-time Farming, Small Farms and Farming in the United States,* ask for QB 93-64.

Recommended reading

- Berry, Wendell. *The Unsettling of America: Culture & Agriculture.* San Francisco: Sierra Club Books, 1977.

- Davidson, Osha Gray. *Broken Heartland: The Rise of America's Rural Ghetto.* New York: The Free Press, 1990.

- McCaig, Donald. *An American Homeplace.* New York: Crown Publishers, 1992.

- Whatley, Booker T. *Booker T. Whatley's Handbook on How to Make $100,000 Farming 25 Acres.* Emmaus, PA: Regenerative Agriculture Association, 1987.

14
Air

She [mother] *took us out in the yard one day and asked us*
if we knew the price of eggs, of apples, of bananas.
Then she asked us to put a price on clean air,
the sunshine, the song of birds—
and we were stunned.

RALPH NADER

ir, the most essential element for life. Once dependably clean, alas, unpolluted air can no longer be taken for granted. Many of our homes and offices have unhealthful air. Numerous modern buildings have what has become known as "sick building syndrome." Fungi and bacteria in ventilation ducts and gases produced by man-made materials in tight buildings with inadequate fresh air intake may only cause headaches, sore throats, and shortness of breath. If the fresh-air intake of a sealed building is close to the cooling tower of another, the fine mist, called drift, may cause bacterial infections as serious as Legionnaires' disease.

In certain natural areas the air can actually improve health and alertness. Tony Hiss reports that experiments have shown that

> . . . unscented air, if it contains a certain quantity of small-air ions—clusters of molecules with a negative electrical charge—can also have the effect of a drug, lowering the amount of serotonin in the midbrain; high levels of serotonin are associated with sleepiness. . . . mountains, forests, and streams . . . naturally have an abundance of small-air ions.

Forests are clean-air factories. Natural areas produce carbon dioxide from decaying vegetation. Living trees utilize carbon dioxide and sunlight through the miracle of photosynthesis to create growth and oxygen. Fortunate are the humans who live in a forest.

Best-quality air is immediately downwind from where natural conditions cleanse air and create oxygen. There are exceptions to that. The west coast receives prevailing winds coming in off the ocean, clean air. But because of the hills surrounding the Los Angeles basin, heavy pollution from factories and vehicles lingers, creating very unhealthful air conditions.

After traveling across the Pacific, west-coast air is clean until it encounters industrial and vehicular pollution. Midwest air is a combination of winds down from Canada and up off the Gulf of Mexico, in addition to the prevailing westerlies from the Great Plains, primarily agricultural land. Most of the wind path is sparsely populated and relatively clean. The eastern states, especially east of industrial centers, have relatively poor air quality.

All parts of the country downwind from factories and cities have polluted air. Some areas have such bad air that the American Lung Association is suing the U.S. Environmental Protection Agency for not enforcing standards of the Clean Air Act (4-29-94, National Public Radio). The EPA sometimes seems more sensitive to commercial entities than common citizens. Don't depend on bureaucrats to ensure your clean air.

Finding a place with existing healthful air conditions is of prime importance. Study the wind and storm maps and become aware of pollution sources for your preferred areas.

Make air quality notes on your criteria worksheet. Also read chapter 28—*Toxic pollution.*

Resources and recommended reading

- Hiss, Tony. *The Experience of Place.* New York: Alfred A. Knopf, 1990.

- Hall, Bob and Mary Lee Kerr. *1991-1992 Green Index: A State-By-State Guide to the Nation's Environmental Health.* Washington D.C.: Island Press, 1991.

EPA Emergency Planning and Community Right-To-Know Hotline: 800-535-0202. They report on local pollution rates, in addition to contaminated landfills, toxic waste sites, and polluted lakes and beaches.

CHARLES ALVAH WALKER
Pastoral Landscape, 1894. Monotype.

15
Water

Man is a complex being:
he makes deserts bloom—and lakes die.
GIL STERN

After air, the most essential item

ithout it life would cease—with an abundance of it life flourishes. Earth's water system is a perfect design. No new water is being made—it is simply recycled. The water we drink today may have been drunk by Confucius 2,500 years ago. Too bad wisdom is not transmitted as easily.

Quantity

Water is the most valuable and indispensable resource of any land. Abundant healthful water is a prime ingredient of the ideal life. Each of us each day minimally needs about 75 gallons for drinking, cooking, bathing, and cleaning.

Irrigation of garden and landscape can increase water requirements enormously. A stream or pond is an excellent source of irrigation water, which need not be free of bacteria. Such a system will require a pump, pressure tank, and piping separate from the household system to avoid contamination of the latter.

Almost two percent of the total area of the U.S. is covered with water. The country averages 29 inches annual precipitation (based on a 77-year record) but excepting the coastal area of the Pacific Northwest, the western half of the country is generally dry and the eastern half is generally wet. Many western states are using groundwater faster than it is being replenished and face serious regional water shortages. In 1980 five western states—California, Texas, Idaho, Kansas, and Nebraska—used nearly 55 percent of the total volume of groundwater used in the U.S. In these and other western states the groundwater levels are sinking. In the central and eastern states groundwater levels are still at about the same levels as they were in the early part of the century.

The following groundwater map shows major U.S. aquifers, defined as capable of yielding 50 gallons per minute or more to wells. Depths to water vary, of course. In addition to areas indicated, wells along river basins generally are recharged by the river water migrating outward. While drawing this map I consulted two different maps published by the U.S. Geological Survey—each showed the same general patterns but indicated substantially different specific boundaries. Therefore I suggest that you use this map only as an indicator of general groundwater distribution.

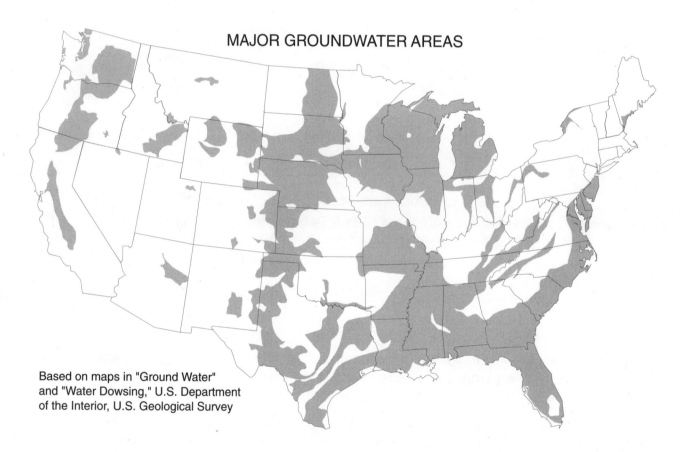

MAJOR GROUNDWATER AREAS

Based on maps in "Ground Water" and "Water Dowsing," U.S. Department of the Interior, U.S. Geological Survey

Living where naturally occurring water is inadequate for the population is living in direct conflict with the laws of nature. In truth there is no shortage of water—there are simply places with a surplus of people. As Henry Miller said:

> The world is not to be put in order, the world is order. It is for us to put ourselves in unison with this order.

A modern insanity is that the largest consumer of energy in California is the system of pumps that move water. Thousands of miles of aqueducts traverse the state, requiring continual pumping. The California broccoli consumed in Cincinnati is a product of both water and oil.

Rainfall and groundwater distribution do not always correlate, as can be seen by comparing the precipitation map in Chapter 9—*Climate* with the groundwater map here. In fact, the rainiest part of the country, along the Oregon and Washington coastline, shows relatively little groundwater.

Effective precipitation and effective moisture

Total annual precipitation alone is an insufficient measure of moisture available at the earth's surface, as it does not take into account the manner in which it is distributed throughout the year. In many areas agricultural activities are geared to precipitation patterns—any deviation of which may result in reduced or failed crops.

The significance of seasonal distribution relates to the concept of precipitation or moisture effectiveness. A considerable amount of moisture is returned to the atmosphere by evaporation and transpiration, as depicted in the drawing of the hydrologic cycle on page 108. These two factors are directly influenced by the temperature at which precipitation occurs. When precipitation occurs as snow no moisture is available until spring melt, which may result in excessive runoff and loss of water.

Effective moisture is that portion of total precipitation that becomes available for plant growth. Effective moisture is determined by calculating the *potential evapotranspiration,* the amount of water that could be evaporated and transpired under conditions of optimal soil moisture and the normal amount of heat energy sent down by the sun. Various formulas have been devised to calculate effective

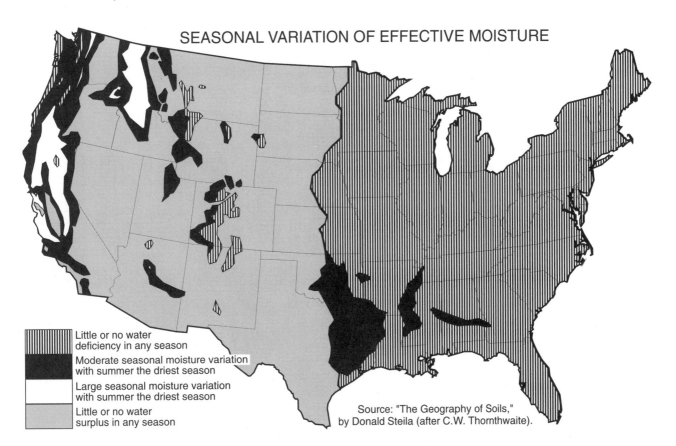

SEASONAL VARIATION OF EFFECTIVE MOISTURE

Little or no water deficiency in any season

Moderate seasonal moisture variation with summer the driest season

Large seasonal moisture variation with summer the driest season

Little or no water surplus in any season

Source: "The Geography of Soils," by Donald Steila (after C.W. Thornthwaite).

moisture. Fortunately, there are people who just love to measure and calculate such things so you and I can simply look at this map and say, aha!, there's the place to grow things—like vegetables and hay and trees and stuff—that won't require constant irrigation. Or, aha!, there's the place to be for summer fun without rain showers to wilt my hairdo. If having a bad hair day is a biggie trauma for you, studying this map, the precipitation map, and the humidity map will help you find your best potential area and save you needless suffering.

By looking at the previous map we can see where adequate moisture is almost always available, where there are summer shortages, and where there is often inadequate moisture. One could quite easily predict from this map where the most and least amount of vegetation occurs. The moist eastern half of the country, for

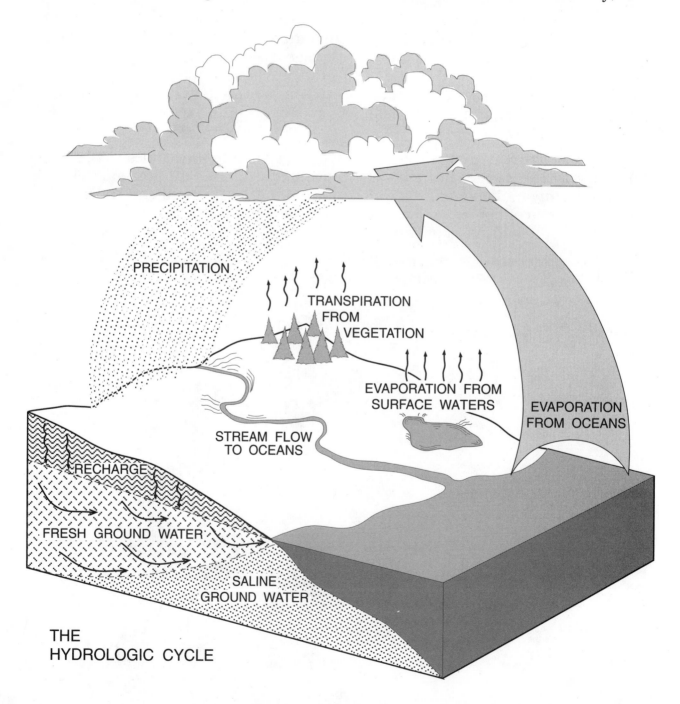

PRECIPITATION

TRANSPIRATION
FROM
VEGETATION

EVAPORATION FROM
SURFACE WATERS

EVAPORATION
FROM OCEANS

STREAM FLOW
TO OCEANS

RECHARGE

FRESH GROUND WATER

SALINE
GROUND WATER

THE
HYDROLOGIC CYCLE

instance, is much more heavily wooded than the west, with the notable exception of parts of the Northwest, especially west of the Cascade Range.

As shown in the preceeding illustration, the hydrologic cycle is elegant: water primarily evaporates from the surface of the oceans, seas, and lakes, is lifted by warm air, is moved by winds, collides with cooler air, condenses out of the sky and precipitates according to gravity—downward. Whether precipitation is rain, snow, sleet, or hail depends on temperature and air movement. Some water soaks into the ground and the rest flows to the ocean, to repeat the cycle.

The ideal home place includes an abundant supply of naturally-occurring healthful water. There are filter systems that allow you to purify polluted water, but generally they are an unnecessary expense and maintenance item. There are still areas where the groundwater is pure and the surface water allows swimming and fishing with no danger to health. While many places have insufficient natural water to maintain life, many more areas have a great excess, making them a clearly superior choice for a home place.

Country home water is most often supplied by a well with electric pump and pressure tank system. Less frequently the source is a spring. In the most fortunate cases the spring is at a higher elevation than the house and water flows into the house by gravity. Such an idyllic system is most appreciated during electric outages.

Water shortage areas

Americans use one-third of all the flowing water in the country every single day. The Mississippi is losing flow; the Colorado is being depleted yearly and no longer carries water the full length of its channel. The Ogallala aquifer, the irrigation source for the huge grain belt from South Dakota to Texas, is sinking rapidly—the water that now creates life in twenty percent of all irrigated cropland in the country may run dry in as little as 40 years. Some predict that the eight-state region it underlies will eventually have to make do with rain only. In a mere 100 years we will have emptied what was once the largest underground body of fresh water in the world. If you have flown over the area, those little green circles you see from 35,000 feet are 80-acre crop plots with center-pivot irrigation systems pumping from the Ogallala.

California's most recent drought, which ended in 1993, lasted seven years. Prior documented droughts since the 1400s have lasted 20, 40, and 60 years. (Robert Kourik, "A Grayt Way to Water," *Real Good News*, February 1994)

Michael Hudlow, director of the National Oceanic and Atmospheric Administrative office of hydrology, predicts severe U.S. water shortages in the 1990s. University of Colorado professor of natural resource law Charles Wilkinson, author of *Crossing the Next Meridian*, believes there should be an extraction tax on water. Are you ready for that?

Some say that the water wars of the past are minor compared to the water wars of the future. The west is far overbuilt for its water resources. Major and fast-

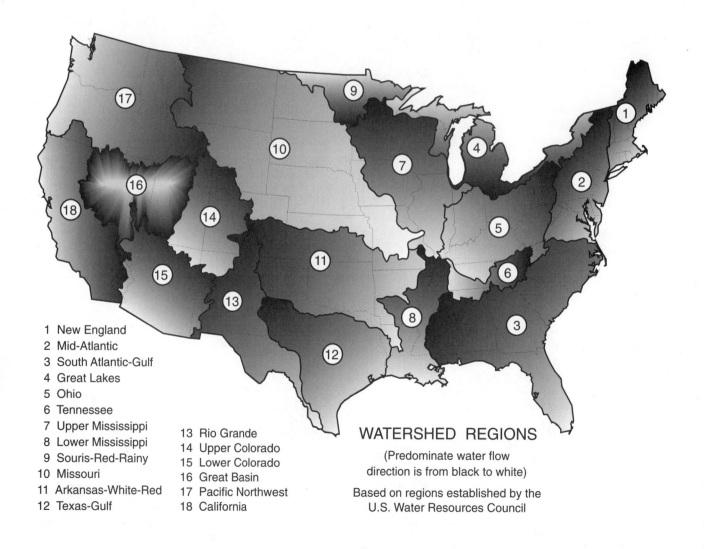

1 New England
2 Mid-Atlantic
3 South Atlantic-Gulf
4 Great Lakes
5 Ohio
6 Tennessee
7 Upper Mississippi
8 Lower Mississippi   13 Rio Grande
9 Souris-Red-Rainy   14 Upper Colorado
10 Missouri   15 Lower Colorado
11 Arkansas-White-Red   16 Great Basin
12 Texas-Gulf   17 Pacific Northwest
                          18 California

WATERSHED REGIONS

(Predominate water flow
direction is from black to white)

Based on regions established by the
U.S. Water Resources Council

growing populations live in arid areas of California, Arizona, Colorado, and Nevada, all of which covet and use the water of the Colorado River. But its flow is only two percent of the Mississippi and five percent of the Connecticut, Delaware, Hudson, and Susquehanna rivers combined, which drain about the same size area as the Colorado.

Small-acreage rural landowners in low-rainfall areas are at risk as cities go after their water. Las Vegas water officials filed water claims to an aquifer underlying 26 valleys in three rural counties north of the city. A public outcry forced them to reduce their claims. The stated moral defense was that they feared California was going to file claims first.

In *Last Refuge*, Jim Robbins shows how powerful cities take water rights from rural residents.

> In 1992, large city utilities from Denver, Las Vegas, Phoenix and elsewhere formed a Western Urban Water Coalition to lobby for more water for cities and to 'oppose uneconomic and inefficient water uses.' Which means agriculture. . . . What is taking place, essentially, is a transfer of subsidies. The developers of the sprawling western cities are shouldering out the farmers and taking over the expensive, federally-built dams in the West. And they have managed to convince Congress of the need for more subsidies. A $5 billion [that is not a typo—that's a b] concrete-lined ditch called the Central Arizona Project, which slices several hundred miles east from the Colorado River through the Sonoran Desert is a good example. Originally intended for agriculture, the water will now be used by Phoenix and Tucson.

No part of America so dramatically illustrates the arrogance and insanity of humans building cities with insufficient water as the West. Phoenix receives about eight inches of rain annually but continues to grow like a blue-spotted cancer across the desert—the blue of thousands of swimming pools. Recently surviving seven years of drought was semi-arid Los Angeles, where 12 million people depend on water pumped in from the Owens Valley, the Colorado River, and from northern California. That's right—L.A. County residents fill *their* swimming pools with water from the northern Sierras.

Reservoirs

After WWII the U.S. Army Corps of Engineers needed work so they built dams for flood control, electricity generation, and irrigation. The dams created reservoirs of high-quality water. Today, while the original purposes are usually maintained, the Corps has yielded to political pressure and allows fishing, other water sports, and land development around the lakes. Many of these sites are surrounded by beautiful scenery. The combination is irresistible and has created retirement and recreation-oriented communities.

Rapid growth has occurred along lakeshores, rivers, and smaller streams feeding into reservoirs. Private property lines begin at a federal "take line," above the high-water mark. If you consider buying property adjoining a reservoir or feeder stream, find out what restrictions are enforced on permits and construction of homes and dock facilities. In some places no new permits for docks are being issued. Also, be aware that the Corps controls lake water levels, which causes friction with homeowners and sportsmen whose activities may be adversely affected.

Water use laws

Riparian rights are the law in those states with adequate rainfall—from Minnesota to Louisiana and east. In these states each landowner may use a reasonable amount of the water on or under owned land but may not appreciably diminish flow to those downstream.

Idaho, Montana, Wyoming, Nevada, Utah, Colorado, Arizona, and New Mexico use the Colorado Doctrine of prior appropriation—first in time is first in line. Early settlers were granted the right to extract a certain amount of water; downstream landowners may have no right to use any of the water that flows across their land. If you consider land in these states you must never assume that a spring, stream, or even a river flowing over or adjacent to the land ensures that water is no

problem. It often is. Water rights are bought and sold like commodities. The city of Phoenix bought a ranch entitled to 14 percent of the underlying aquifer, now to be pumped to the city.

The remaining western states on both sides of the Colorado Doctrine group use the California Doctrine, a combination of riparian and prior application laws. California farmers with water rights, including rights to take water from the taxpayer-funded canal that moves northern California water to the L.A. area, are allowed by federal law to sell water to municipalities. In the arid and semi-arid West, water always flows—to money.

Fire protection

Unless carefully engineered, home water systems rarely have adequate pressure and flow to serve as dependable fire-fighting systems. The best country home fire

protection system is careful construction of safe electrical and heating designs, constant vigilance, smoke detectors, and a number of appropriate fire extinguishers placed in strategic locations.

Using water wisely

Few water systems are without cost to operate, maintain, and purify. Even if a water supply is unlimited and pure, it makes sense not to waste water because it takes energy to deliver it to the tap, and energy usually comes from fossil fuels, the burning of which is contributing to the destruction of our environment. The only system I know which costs essentially nothing to operate is a gravity flow system, and most such systems require treatment to ensure safety.

The EPA estimates that 37 percent of household water is used to flush toilets. A good way to save water plus the cost, maintenance, and potential problems of a septic system is to use a composting toilet. There are many models presently available.

Garden irrigation uses huge amounts of water. Water is conserved, weeds are diminished, and plants are fed by applying a thick layer of organic mulch around plants, shrubs, and trees.

Raise the cutting deck on your lawn mower. Lawns that are cut higher will not dry out so fast. Mowing at regular intervals thickens the grass stand, causing rain water to be absorbed that might otherwise run downhill. Such a program also diminishes erosion and helps to maintain the water table.

Water quantity guidelines

- Water abundance *usually* corresponds with area rainfall and snowfall.
- Wells should be tested for quantity as well as quality. Minimum recharge rates can be tested by continuous pumping during dry periods.
- Small streams may not flow year-round. Talk to area residents about stream history. If stream flow is critical to your needs, observe it at the driest time of the year.
- If a water source is on the land of another, determine that your property has a deeded easement or right-of-way for piping, canal, etc., to deliver the water.
- Never buy a property lacking a reliable year-round supply of good-quality water.

Quality

When water seeps through overlying material to the water table, particles in suspension, including micro-organisms, may be removed. How much is removed depends on the thickness and character of the overlying material. Clay, or "hardpan," provides the most effective natural filter for groundwater. Silt and sand also provide good filtration if fine enough and in thick enough layers. The bacterial quality of water improves during storage in an aquifer because conditions there are usually unfavorable for bacteria. Clarity alone does not guarantee that groundwater is safe to drink; this can only be determined by laboratory testing.

The most prudent position is that all water sources are assumed to be contaminated until proven otherwise. As a general rule, all household water should be tested before use and again at regular intervals. If the plumbing in your new home has been unused for a period, open all faucets and let the system thoroughly flush before using the water.

Good water is essential for high-quality life. It is necessary to become aware of the condition of water in the various areas you consider for your home. The following unpleasant information is included to alert you to potential problems and areas to avoid. Should you wish more information, a resource list follows. The really ugly information has been limited to Chapter 28—*Toxic pollution*.

Almost all human activities threaten water purity. For decades, manufacturers and agribusiness operators have sent criminal amounts of poisons into our waters. In 1969 the heavy oil layer on the Cuyahoga river in Cleveland caught fire and blazed out of control, horrifying the nation. A federal report declared:

> The lower Cuyahoga has no visible life, not even lower forms such as leeches and sludge worms that usually thrive on waste.

Partly as a result of the public outcry following the Cuyahoga fire, Congress created the Clean Water Act in 1972. Yet, in 1991, according to EPA reports, industrial, municipal, and military facilities knowingly discharged over 243 million pounds of toxic substances into surface waters. An additional 411 million pounds of toxins were transferred to treatment plants, which in turn transferred partially treated sewage to surface waters. And then we and our children went swimming and fishing in those waters.

Twenty-one years after the Clean Water Act was passed, the EPA listed 18,770 impaired water sites, only 529 polluted primarily by toxic point sources; most of the rest are polluted by runoff. (Michael Parfit, "Troubled Waters Run Deep," National Geographic Special Edition *Water* 1993)

Municipal water supplies often arrive from far away, affected by conditions foreign to users. A 233-mile-long aqueduct from Owens Valley helps slake L.A.'s huge thirst. New Yorkers have been advised that people with low salt tolerances shouldn't drink too much city water—the rock salt used in the Catskill mountains to keep roads ice-free is filling city reservoirs in the area.

The average American city dweller drinks water that has been filtered, chemically treated to kill bacteria, then delivered to the tap through a vast network of old, corroded pipes constructed of various materials. The EPA reported that of the nation's 660 large public water systems, 130—which provide drinking water for 32 million people—exceeded the "action level" for lead content.

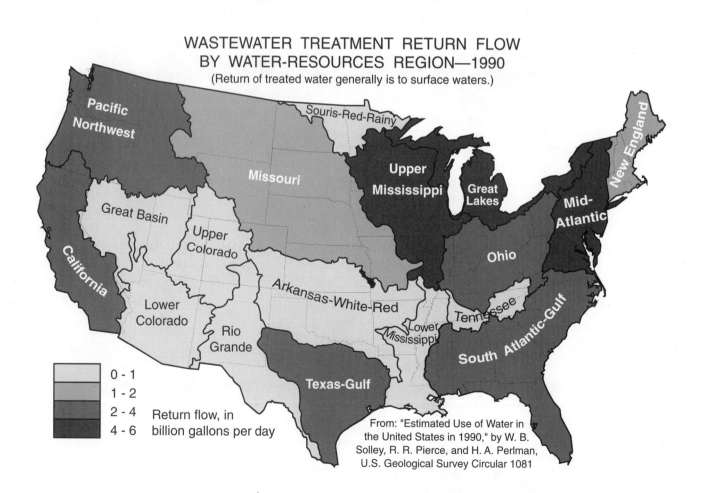

WASTEWATER TREATMENT RETURN FLOW
BY WATER-RESOURCES REGION—1990
(Return of treated water generally is to surface waters.)

0 - 1
1 - 2
2 - 4
4 - 6   Return flow, in
          billion gallons per day

From: "Estimated Use of Water in
the United States in 1990," by W. B.
Solley, R. R. Pierce, and H. A. Perlman,
U.S. Geological Survey Circular 1081

Private rural water supplies are usually wells. In areas of high agricultural chemical use they are vulnerable to contamination. Public supplies are even more vulnerable. The EPA's *National Pesticide Survey Project Summary* of 1990 found that community water systems were two and a half times more likely to register pesticides above minimum reporting limits than were private rural wells.

In *The Truth About Where You Live*, Benjamin A. Goldman writes of pesticide waste dumps, municipal landfills, toxic waste pits, injection wells, pesticide applications, mining and oil exploration sites, and septic tanks that pollute groundwater—the water that cities, small communities, and rural homeowners tap with their wells.

It's enough to make you sick. Avoid considering property near these facilities and conditions. Even private septic tanks can now be avoided by using one of the many commercially available composting toilets.

WINSLOW HOMER
"Blue-eyed girls brought pails, and dipped them in thy crystal pool."
The Story of the Fountain, 1872

Agricultural water pollution

Beware of potential well contamination from agribusiness operations. U.S. farmers apply nearly 400,000 tons of pesticides per year. Over 30 years after biologist Rachel Carson explained the danger in *Silent Spring* we continue to poison ourselves. Osha Gray Davidson reports that a 1986 EPA study found 17 different pesticides in the groundwater of 23 states. In the food basket of the nation, 58 pesticides were found in 3,000 California wells. Setterberg and Shavelson state that two-thirds of California's wells are contaminated. In "The Mississippi River Under Siege," (*Water,* National Geographic) William S. Ellis wrote that DDT continues to be found in the Mississippi although it has been banned in the U.S. for more than 20 years.

The Department of Agriculture estimates that areas of greatest potential pesticide contamination are California's San Joaquin Valley, western Texas and Oklahoma, Kansas and eastern Nebraska, the upper Midwest, western Pennsylvania, and the entire southeastern coastal plain from Florida to southern New Jersey.

Mining pollution

Avoid areas downhill or downstream from current or old mining operations. Almost every place where minerals have been extracted are now polluted. Decades of coal mining has poisoned much of Appalachia's water. Still, there are nonpolluted places. In *An American Homeplace,* Donald McCaig writes of his farm in Highland County, Virginia:

> There are several reasons our farm has clean water . . . Though the Chamber of Commerce and other forward-thinking citizens here have begged industry to come and set up shop, provide employment and paychecks, so far industry has declined this offer, preferring to ruin the water of communities with better roads. And there's never been much in Highland County worth stealing. We lack coal and other minerals, there's no oil. The best timber was taken off in the early twenties.

Wells

In rural areas, approximately 97 percent of Americans depend on underground water sources. The average depth of all domestic U.S. wells is less than 50 feet. Shallow wells are more subject to local pollution sources but even deep wells may be affected by distant pollution sources.

Wells are subject to contamination from both surface and below-ground contaminants. Pesticides, herbicides, chemical fertilizers, and industrial wastes are common sources of pollution.

The EPA has stated that there is some toxic substance in all U.S. groundwater. In light of this, it is imperative to test all household water and if necessary to consider point-of-use water purification devices.

Essential country skill #3: pumping water. Instructions: Grasp the pump handle as shown. Raise the handle. Push the handle down. Repeat until bucket is full. If the bucket does not fill, see Essential country skill #53: repairing wooden buckets.

Most wells were created by well drillers who kept a detailed log of the drilling history, the depth, the quality, and the amount of flow developed. Consult with well drillers about a well's capacity to meet your needs. County health officials or extension agents may be able to refer you to a local laboratory that tests water.

New wells are expensive. Again, local well drillers are the best source of information. Nobody can guarantee finding water but local drillers stay in business by being successful a high percentage of the time.

Springs

Some people still believe that a spring emits pure water because it has miraculously been filtered by the ground. Not usually so. Michael Parfit, a writer in *Water,* gets his water from a spring at a mountain in Montana. He always figured his water was safe, because it was "at the beginning of the flow." Then he had the water tested. The lab reported: "Too numerous to count—background bacteria."

In 1982, I had the opportunity to join a college field trip to hydrologist Tom Aley's place in southern Missouri. Tom first walked us around the surface of his land, teaching the difference between general recharge and discrete recharge, the two ways that rainwater moves down into the ground. One of the discrete recharge areas was a sinkhole caused by the collapse of a cavern ceiling, now a stagnant, scum-filled pond, with living and dead plants and various animal remains. We later climbed down into his Tumbling Creek Cave, which Tom calls Ozark Underground Laboratory. We were shown the gush of water falling from a crevice in the cave's ceiling, the beginning of the stream, water gathered from recharge

areas above, including the sinkhole. Tumbling Creek meanders along the cave floor (we admired the blind cave salamanders and avoided disturbing the bat colony) and exits a mile away at the base of a bluff, what anyone would call a spring. Almost zero filtering takes place between the recharge area and the outlet, the "spring." And we all know what accumulates under bat colonies.

Aley has performed many dye tracings, proving the recharge sources of springs to be numerous, distant, and dangerous, including abandoned dump sites full of old batteries, paint cans, and chemical containers. He explains that the greater the spring flow, the greater the probability that the collection area is large and diverse and includes such toxic recharge areas.

The point is that springs are simply outlets for underground water flows, not far from the surface, and little filtered. Rain falls on the land, finds cracks in the surface, gathers with water from other sources and makes its way into an underground stream. When it appears as a spring, it may or may not have been filtered. Until tests prove otherwise, always assume that a spring is polluted. And if you use it, have it tested annually, as conditions in the recharge system may change.

Surface water

Water for household needs is vital, but why settle for survival? Springs, streams, rivers, ponds, and lakes enhance not only the water supply but are pleasurable additions to any property. Some of our favorite times are spent sitting on our porch, listening to the unceasing sounds of our little stream tumbling over rocks, a reassuring, happy background of natural song.

Water.

Surface water attracts wildlife. Most mornings a Great Blue heron comes for a breakfast of minnows. Often we are visited by a pair of wood ducks. Once a bald eagle came and sat for an hour in a sycamore overlooking the wide part of the water. Deer, turkeys, and kingfishers make regular appearances.

A spring or stream at an elevation above the house site offers the opportunity for a gravity-fed water system, using no electricity. If a stream is below the house but has adequate fall, a small dam may provide adequate head to operate a ram pump, another no-electricity water supply system.

The quality of any surface water is directly caused by the nature of its watershed. A stream receiving runoff from an agricultural area may have bacteria from animal wastes and chemical residues from fertilizers and pesticides. A creek below a clear-cut hillside will be full of silt. After full vegetation returns the same stream may run clear.

The advantages of property adjoining or crossed by a waterway are many—the downside, less obvious, is that water is a magnet to others. Depending on the size of your waterway you may be bothered by boaters, fishermen, and floaters, the traffic that water brings.

Check the history of flooding with neighbors. Also determine laws regarding usage, damming, and diversion. And check with local officials for new laws being considered.

Coliform bacteria and giardia lamblia are two of the most common disease-causing organisms. Coliform is the standard indicator of harmful organisms in water. All surface water should be considered to have a high coliform bacteria count, which is caused by the animals that live in, on, and around it. If surface water is to be used for household purposes it should be filtered and treated.

Small streams are preferable to rivers because they are closer to the source, are generally clearer and less polluted, and attract fewer tourists.

If there is no well or surface water

If you consider buying property with no existing well and there is no available surface water, you must ensure that a successful well can be installed. Check with neighbors to find how deep their wells are, if they ever run dry, and if they know who drilled them. Your best information source will be well drillers with substantial local experience. They can tell you the odds and the cost of creating a good well.

Heart disease, cancer, and water

We once thought that hard water decreased heart disease. Some now believe that it is magnesium, not calcium in our water which reduces heart disease. Above-average magnesium content in water occurs in North and South Dakota, Oklahoma, Nebraska, Kansas, most of New Mexico, eastern Montana, eastern Colorado, western Arkansas, western Missouri, all of Texas but the southeast corner, and northwest Utah. Many of these same areas also have had the longest-lived persons in the U.S.

Rapid City, South Dakota, drinking water contains a high concentration of selenium, a mineral believed to help prevent cancer and heart disease. The rate of cancer in Rapid City is far below the national average. Of course, moving to a city to get selenium would be rather extreme since selenium is available as a supplement. It is one of a group called antioxidants.

From bad water to good

Physical contamination can result from surface runoff during periods of heavy rainfall, carrying various substances into the water source. Physical contamination includes oils, salts, dirt, and bad taste and smell from the growth of algae.

Chemical contamination occurs from mine drainage, landfill leakage, storage tank leaks, spills, fertilizer and pesticide runoff.

Biological contamination comes from municipal, industrial, agricultural, and household wastewater systems. It occurs naturally in surface water, the result of animal life. Bacteria and viruses come from animals: wild, domestic, and human. Septic tank leaks can contaminate wells.

Any water can be made safe to drink. Polluted water can safely be used if it is appropriately filtered and treated at point-of-use. If a property has all other characteristics you want in outstanding proportion, then the expense of water treatment *may* make sense. Make a thorough investigation to determine the source and extent of pollution and to determine if it will improve or if it is likely to worsen. Other considerations include cost of equipment, cost of operation, maintenance, and degree of safety. Get the advice of experts.

Water quality guidelines

- The ideal home place is far from pollution sources.
- Rural areas generally have cleaner water than cities.
- Deep wells are usually safer than shallow wells.
- Springs, creeks, and rivers are typically cleaner near their source and more polluted further downstream.
- All water sources should be considered unsafe until tested. Check with county officials and well drillers for a testing source.
- Rivers all should be considered polluted.
- Major polluters include agricultural, industrial, municipal, and military facilities.
- Avoid buying property downwind or downwater from farms that may use chemical fertilizers, herbicides, and pesticides.
- Heavily developed lakeside areas often have pollution from excessive numbers of septic tanks.
- Upstream logging operations create high amounts of sediment.
- Oceanside waterways and wells may be affected by saltwater intrusion at high tide.

On your criteria worksheet circle the water features your ideal place will have and show your preferences on water and waste systems.

Sources and recommended reading

Acid rain is discussed in chapter 27 *Places and conditions to avoid*

- Ford, Norman. The 50 Healthiest Places to Live and Retire in the United States. Bedford, MA: Mills & Sanderson, 1991.

- Goldman, Benjamin A. *The Truth About Where You Live: An atlas for action on toxins and mortality.* New York: Times Books/Random House, 1991. Eye-opening text and maps are the result of use of the freedom of information laws.

- Graves, William, editor. National Geographic Special Edition: *Water: The Power, Promise, and Turmoil of North America's Fresh Water.* Washington, DC: The National Geographic Society, 1993.

- Robbins, Jim. *Last Refuge: The environmental showdown in Yellowstone and the American West.* New York: Morrow, 1993.

- Setterberg, Fred and Lonny Shavelson. *Toxic Nation: The Fight to Save Our Communities from Chemical Contamination.* New York: John Wiley & Sons, 1993.

Water information

A free booklet, *Ground Water and the Rural Homeowner* is available from:
U.S. Geological Survey
Branch of Distribution
P.O. Box 25286
Denver, CO 80225
The USGS also has a brochure simply titled *Ground Water* which has a good map showing major ground-water areas in the United States.

U.S. Environmental Protection Agency: 800-426-4791 (Safe drinking water hotline)

U.S. Department of Agriculture Soil Conservation Service: 800-THE-SOIL

American Ground Water Trust: 800-423-7748

Organizations

National Water Well Association
6375 Riverside Drive
Dublin, OH 43017
614-761-1711

National Rural Water Association
2915 South Thirteenth Street
P.O. Box 1428
Duncan, OK 73534
405-252-0629

America's Clean Water Foundation
750 First Street N.E., Suite 911
Washington, DC 20002-4241
• Develops and distributes educational materials.

Freshwater Foundation
725 County Road 6
Wayzata, MN 55391-9611
• Provides educational programs and freshwater research.

Ground Water and Drinking Water Resource Center
401 M Street, SW, WH-550A
Washington, DC 20460
• Distributes water and drinking water documents and drinking water publications and maintains a bibliographic database.

Izaak Walton League of America
1401 Wilson Boulevard, Level B
Arlington, VA 22209-2318
• Operates Save Our Streams program and provides publications.

National Water Information Clearinghouse
U.S. Geological Survey
423 National Center
Reston, VA 22092-0001
• Supplies federal water data.

Water Environment Federation
601 Wythe Street
Alexandria, VA 22314-1994
• Presents materials on water-quality issues.

Water tests

County and state health departments may help in selecting tests and locating testing laboratories. If you can't find someone local, you can have water tested by Watercheck-National Testing Laboratories. Call them at 800-458-3330.

Water tests, purification devices, and composting toilets

Alternative Energy Sourcebook is a combination catalog and compilation of useful articles. Sort of a *Whole Earth Catalog* of energy-efficiency and alternative energy systems. Offerings include water testing and treatment systems. Includes a selection of water filtering and purification devices and composting toilets.
Real Goods Trading Corporation
966 Mazzoni Street
Ukiah, CA 95482-3471
800-762-7325

By the next century water will be more expensive than oil.
FROM THE GERMAN MAGAZINE *DER SPIEGEL*, MAY 25, 1992
AS REPORTED IN "THE DRYING GAME,"
UTNE READER, MAY/JUNE 1993

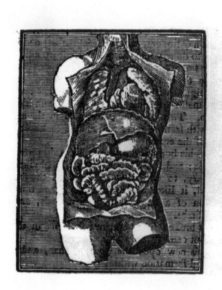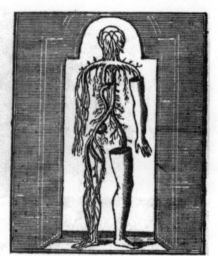

16
Health 101

Like any other activity, the practice of health involves one or more choices.
We choose to live quietly and simply, to exercise in the open air, to keep sensible
hours and not overdo physically. We choose to exercise our bodies not in
gymnasiums or on golf courses or tennis courts but doing useful outdoor physical
work. We choose to live in the country rather than the city, with its polluted air,
noise and stress. We prefer clean fresh air, sunshine, clear running water.
We choose to cut our own fuel in our own woods rather than pay
the oil barons. We design and construct our own buildings.
We grow and prepare our own food,
rather than shop in the supermarkets.

HELEN & SCOTT NEARING
CONTINUING THE GOOD LIFE

(Scott Nearing was 100 when he decided to die.
He split firewood until he was 98.
Helen is in her tenth decade and more active
than most women half her age.)

Health and place

ne of the best things we can do for our body is to put it in a clean,
healthful place. Most rural environments are more healthful places
to live than most city environments. For starters, there is more
space per person and the tree-to-automobile ratio is a lot better. There
are fewer industries per square mile spewing death into the air and
water. The conversations of city-to-rural migrants change from how
thick the smog is to how pretty the sky is. Country folks seem to walk
more slowly but take longer strides—they're less stressed but get where
they're going just as fast.

While nutritious food is the best medicine, it is clear that the place we live affects our physical and psychological health. In fact, the premise behind this book is that living in your ideal place will add tremendously to your happiness and enlightenment. This chapter provides health information for you to consider as you develop criteria for your ideal place. It will help you to find a place that is conducive to your best health. It will help you to avoid places that are bad for your health. These are different things.

Living in a large city shortens life expectancy.

NORMAN SHEALY, M.D., PhD.,
DIRECTOR OF SHEALY INSTITUTE FOR COMPREHENSIVE CARE AND PAIN MANAGEMENT, SPRINGFIELD, MISSOURI

Environmental factors contributing to good physical health are clean air, pure water, and healthy soil. Factors contributing to poor health are the reverse. They include water and air poisoned by industrial emissions, pesticides, and other agricultural residue. Less widespread but potentially worse are the retired and current toxic waste dumps which somehow manage to poison nearby residents. Chemical industry people deny the connection.

If you have a medical condition that requires treatment, then your criteria for an ideal country home will include being near medical staff and facilities; if you are presently healthy and determined to stay that way, then you should locate in an area that contributes to good health. There is evidence to suggest that the most healthful places are where there are the fewest doctors.

Better health equals fewer doctors

Most analysts and writers equate rural health quality with the ratio of doctors per capita. This does not seem to be an accurate guideline, as "counties with the

best mortality rates from all diseases have *half* as many doctors per capita as the national average, and those with the worst mortality have 8 percent *more* doctors per capita than the country as a whole." (Benjamin A. Goldman, The *Truth About Where You Live.*) One must conclude that, rather than diminishing the incidence of disease, doctors locate their practices where demand for treatment exists. It's just good business—in the biggest business.

Health-care services

The greatest reductions in mortality during the past two centuries are not from better medical treatment. The leading killers at the beginning of this century were infectious diseases. These were largely eradicated with environmental improvements: sewage systems, purified public water supplies, and better nutrition—long before the discovery of antibiotics and other medical cures.

In certain diseases, medical technology is simply inadequate. In spite of spending billions of dollars and two decades on research, cancer is still the second-leading cause of death. AIDS is a health disaster in search of a solution. For all disease, prevention seems to me easier, less expensive, and more logical than cure.

Some feel that a health care crisis exists in rural America. According to the American Hospital Association, 280 rural hospitals closed between 1980 and 1990. An estimate was prepared by the National Rural Health Association in 1988 for Congress—1,280 rural counties were federally designated "health-professional-shortage areas," with fewer than one doctor for every 3,500 residents. The problem is most acute in the South and in sparsely populated western states, but every state has at least two areas so designated.

There are notable exceptions to the above. Many small towns actively recruit ("seduce" comes to mind) doctors. Many medical schools encourage young

physicians to do at least part of their training in rural areas. The government has raised Medicare rates and by 1995 will pay rural hospitals equally with city hospitals. 'Bout time.

Some doctors are joining the city-to-country movement. In *The New Heartland* John Herbers notes that the ninety-seven-bed Baxter Hospital in Mountain Home, Arkansas, has a number of specialists who followed retirees to the area, often taking cuts in pay because they like the lifestyle of the region.

The latest in rural health care is tele-medicine. Doctors use inter-active video to "see" patients in multiple distant clinics. Doctors feel that diagnosis is just as accurate and patient monitoring is better than in person, because both doctor and patient can see each other more often.

If easily accessed health care is one of your criteria, you should make a special investigative effort to satisfy yourself. After you choose an area of interest, when you write to chambers of commerce for general area information, request a report on health care availability.

On the subject of seducing doctors, an enjoyable movie was *Doc Hollywood*. Michael J. Fox as Dr. Ben Stone is a newly-minted MD whose cruise toward the medical fast lane takes a small-southern-town detour when he swerves his Porsche to miss cows in the road and wipes out the judge's new picket fence— while the judge is still painting it. The town woos him with copious home cooking, a guaranteed salary, and the mayor's lusting daughter (well, that was her idea, and she mostly just wanted a ride to Hollywood). I give it two thumbs up for entertainment and a chuckle for reality.

Essential country skill #1: working off stress. Instructions: Find a shade tree. Sit down and lean against the tree. Chew on a blade of grass. Briefly contemplate city life. Observe wildlife, count trees, and watch grass grow. Dozing is optional.

Stress and place

Stress kills people, enjoyment of life, and relationships. It promotes heavy drinking and cigarette smoking and causes irritability. It is a prime factor in ulcers, high-blood pressure, and heart disease. It leads to alcoholism, drug dependency, divorce, and dog kicking. Get rid of it—the stress, not the dog.

The geography of healthfulness seems to be connected to a lack of stress. *Psychology Today* magazine's study on low-stress cities found them all to be small towns. An area of Polish farms in Nebraska is perhaps the most healthful place to live in America. The active stress-free lifestyle is considered the primary reason that residents there, for many decades, have lived longer than people in any other place in America. The area has freezing winters and hot, humid summers. So much for the health benefits of a gentle climate.

Being in the wrong place combined with job pressures can create a lethal amount of stress. When I was a city real estate broker I became close friends with my chiropractor. It was inevitable—I saw him several times a week because of my almost-constant tension headaches. During the years I have both lived in the country and avoided the real estate business I have not once needed a chiropractor.

Mental health

Those who study cause and effect of social problems suggest that mental illness is higher among those who change their home places often. Such a pattern, it is implied, creates a condition of being in limbo, a feeling of not belonging to a place, a loss of community, unsettledness.

Or is it that those who are unhappy are more prone to move, hoping the new place will magically cure the underlying problem—but do so impulsively and carelessly? The premise of this book is that a move can be a highly positive action—but only when it is conducted with a thorough examination of self and potential places.

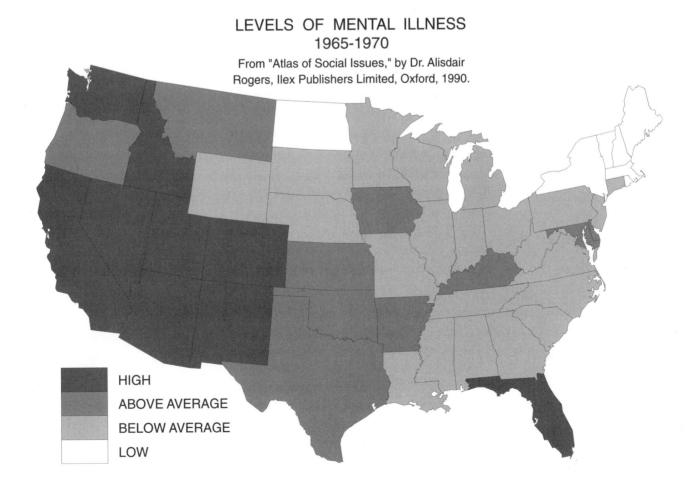

LEVELS OF MENTAL ILLNESS
1965-1970

From "Atlas of Social Issues," by Dr. Alisdair
Rogers, Ilex Publishers Limited, Oxford, 1990.

HIGH
ABOVE AVERAGE
BELOW AVERAGE
LOW

Where death and disease are caused by environmental factors

Benjamin Goldman performed a great public service by compiling *The Truth About Where You Live: An atlas for action on toxins and mortality,* a book representing the culmination of five years of work at Public Data Access, Inc. in New York. PDA exploited the Freedom of Information Act and used computer processing techniques to evaluate government information to appraise environmental and health conditions. Goldman writes:

> Across the United States, an average of four industrial accidents a day spill toxic chemicals into the environment. Factory mishaps release 370 thousand tons of toxins into the air each year. Industrial plants routinely discharge another 7 million tons of toxic chemicals into the air and water, and dump another 500 million tons of hazardous wastes into the ground—in full compliance with existing government regulations. To complete the picture, add another 4 billion tons of wastes that farms and cities discharge annually into the nation's air, waterways, and land.

The Truth About Where You Live uses many maps to provide a comprehensive picture of counties that are suffering from disproportionate shares of environmental contamination and death. Deaths from cancer and other diseases follow the nation's rivers. Runoff from pesticides and other agricultural chemicals, and industrial wastes have turned rivers into gutters of chemical soup. The counties bordering the Mississippi have some of the worst mortality rates in the country. Below the Ohio River, eighty percent of the counties bordering the Mississippi have shamefully high levels of excess death.

Death rates are generally highest in the eastern part of the country. High mortality rates exist in the coastal plain states of the Southeast, including Georgia, South Carolina, and North Carolina, in the Appalachian regions of Kentucky, Virginia, and West Virginia, and in western Pennsylvania. As measured in 1983-1985, for white males aged 45-64, the nine worst states for heart disease are: West Virginia, Kentucky, North Carolina, Mississippi, South Carolina, Georgia, Arkansas, Tennessee, and Louisiana. A factor that experts agree on is that blood pressure is significantly higher in the South. They disagree on the *why.*

In general, avoid areas where corporate farming is conducted—big companies tend to be sensitive to profits and insensitive to human needs. They use large amounts of herbicides, pesticides, and chemical fertilizers, many of which become airborne and all of which find their way into groundwater. Search for a home place in areas where soil or topography make large-scale farming impossible.

Avoid petrochemical industrial areas like the plague that they are. Stay far upwind and upriver from nuclear reactors, active and closed military bases, old dumps, landfills, waste incinerators, mining and oil sites (including exploration sites), and industrial facilities.

Goldman's book, published in 1991, derives primarily from federal data collected in the 1980s. Since then, various acts and laws have been adopted, and some Superfund sites have been declared safe for habitation. Be skeptical. Only you can be the final judge of what is a healthful place for you to live. I suggest you use the information from *The Truth About Where You Live* as a caution and a starting point, then carefully make your own current investigation.

Healthful places

Are there any healthful areas left to live? Yes. They are usually far from industrial and corporate farming areas. For your health and your family's health, take the time to identify them. Make a thorough investigation of present, past, and planned land uses around your potential home site before you commit to living there.

According to the Northwest National Life Insurance Company, the states with the healthiest people are Utah, North Dakota, Idaho, Vermont, Nebraska, Colorado, Wyoming, and Montana. Utah may be rated so high because the predominately Mormon population eschews smoking and riotous living.

In praise of home-grown food

It is one of the miracles of science and hygiene that the germs that used to be in our food have been replaced by poisons.

WENDELL BERRY
THE UNSETTLING OF AMERICA

The quality of our lives is directly correlated to the quality of our food. A huge advantage of country living is the space to grow a lot of our food. One cannot overestimate the health benefits of food grown from living, organically rich soil, unpoisoned by chemicals, the produce untouched by pesticides. And the nutritional value of produce minutes-fresh from the garden surpasses anything commercially available to even the wealthiest shopper.

Supermarket tomatoes are picked green—home-grown tomatoes are picked at their height of sun-ripened goodness. Commercial produce varieties are chosen for fast growth, uniform ripening, transportability, presentation, and profit. They are grown using chemical fertilizers, herbicides, and pesticides on soil often deficient in trace minerals essential for good health. Picked green, sprayed with wax, handled and bruised by machines and individuals working for profit alone, typical supermarket produce is deficient in vitamins, minerals, taste, and satisfaction.

Homegrown varieties may be chosen for vigor, suitability to local conditions, and flavor. Grown in clean, living, organic soil, they provide maximum nutrients and flavor. During their season they can be consumed within minutes of harvest, essentially still alive.

The quality of our health derives from the quality of the soil in which our food is grown. High-quality soil is a living thing—alive with millions of earthworms and microorganisms converting organic matter into plant food. By contrast, most commercially produced food is grown in dead or barely alive soil devoid of essential minerals. One example of the result of agribusiness soil mining is the incidence of obesity in Americans. Chromium, essential for converting fat to energy by the mitochondria of our cells, has been mined out of soil by decades of grain monoculture. The result: nine out of ten Americans are deficient in chromium.

Chemical fertilizers, herbicides, and pesticides are killers of earthworms, microorganisms, and humans. The growth of chemical agriculture has been paralleled by the growth of so-called health care (what is practiced should be called disease care)—which in 1994 became the biggest business in the country. Purposefully applying poisons to our soil and our food crops is the result of ignorance, greed, and criminal indifference to consumer health.

We can beat the grim legacy of agribusiness by growing much of our own food and by buying the rest from conscientious growers. Buy property with poison-free soil. Ideal garden soil has not been commercially farmed for decades. If you are unsure of soil quality, ask one of the many organic growers' associations that certify organic produce where soil may be tested for poisonous residue. If it is free from poisons, you can build a good garden. The key to growing healthful food is building healthful soil.

Living healthy and living long

If Dr. Roy Walford is correct with the title of his book, *The 120-Year Diet*, we're giving up on living at least 40 years too soon. The cover story of *Life*, October 1992, "Can We Stop Aging?" quoted scientists using the 120-year figure as if it were an accepted fact.

Heart disease and cancer kill 75% of us. Information widely available today, accessed and acted upon, could virtually eliminate these two killers. If we live in a healthful place, engage in healthful work, eat healthful foods, and follow a few common-sense precepts, we can live far longer than insurance companies currently predict.

Health is one of my most rewarding hobbies and about it I am biased. My bias is that most of us can achieve and maintain excellent health without help from doctors. Don't get me wrong about doctors; I think they are essential assets. I just hate to see them driving better vehicles than teachers, farmers, and writers. Seriously, each of us should be in charge of our health—which means being responsible for our health. The benefits far outweigh the effort required.

As a no-extra-cost bonus in a book that you thought would limit itself to helping you to find the perfect place to park your heart, I offer my personal list for staying healthy and living long.

BEWARE: I AM NOT A DOCTOR. THEREFORE YOU MUST TREAT ME AS IF I AM IGNORANT ABOUT HEALTH. IF YOU HAVE A MEDICAL CONDITION, CONSULT A DOCTOR BEFORE DOING ANYTHING YOU READ HERE.

Don't you just hate these stupid disclaimers made necessary because of lawsuits? Reminds me of a story: There was a terrible accident at a building site, and a construction worker rushed over to where a well-dressed woman was pinned beneath an iron girder. "Hang in there, lady," he said helpfully, "the ambulance will be here soon. Are you badly hurt?" "How should I know?" she snapped. "I'm a doctor, not a lawyer."

NONDOCTOR GERUE'S HOPEFULLY HELPFUL HEALTH HINTS:

- Move to a rural place that has healthful air, water, and soil.
- Eat a low-fat (20 percent or less) diet with minimal amounts of meat and dairy products but lots of fruit, vegetables, and grains. Grow food or buy organic. Only eat foods that are delicious.

 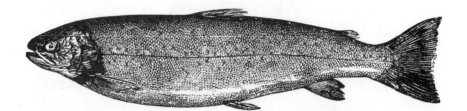

- Use antioxidants—vitamins A (beta carotene), C, and E, and selenium. Antioxidants are the best health news in decades—read all about them.
- Use best-quality vitamin and mineral supplements. Very few diets provide optimal nutrient levels. Educate yourself.

- Exercise (brisk walking qualifies) at least three times a week for a minimum of 30 minutes each time. Country living automatically takes care of this. "The sovereign invigorator of the body is exercise, and of all the exercises walking is best" (Thomas Jefferson). When you visit the city, laugh at elevators and those who ride them. Have a little fun—ask elevator waiters for directions to the stairs. Don't be surprised if they don't know where the stairs are. Indulge in activities you enjoy. "A satisfying sex life is the single most effective protection against heart attacks" (Dr. Eugene Scheimann). Erma Bombeck relates to that: "The only reason I would take up jogging is so that I could hear heavy breathing again."
- Don't smoke. Don't breathe others' smoke. "Now that I'm gone, I tell you: don't smoke, whatever you do, don't smoke" (Yul Brynner, cancer victim, in a posthumous anti-smoking commercial).
- Avoid stress. When people are rude, smile—it'll totally confuse them. Live below your means. Maintain perspective. "One way to get high blood pressure is to go mountain climbing over molehills" (Earl Wilson).
- Work hard at something you feel good about.
- Get adequate rest. Ignore rules dictating how many hours adequate is—trust your body's messages. "The amount of sleep required by the average person is about five minutes more" (Max Kauffmann).

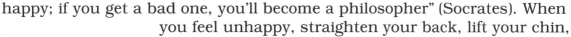

- Avoid unprotected sun exposure. Use sunscreen. Get a broad-brimmed hat that reminds you of one of your heroes. (According to NASA, in 1992 the ozone layer hole was three times the area of the 48 contiguous states.)
- Touch. Give and receive hugs and massage.
- Be happy—live where you prefer, do the work that impassions you, be with one you love. Married people seem to be happiest. "By all means marry; if you get a good wife, you'll become happy; if you get a bad one, you'll become a philosopher" (Socrates). When you feel unhappy, straighten your back, lift your chin, show your teeth, and act happy. Soon you will be.

- Stay mentally active—forever. Garden. Read. Think. Debate. Write, paint, sculpt, craft. Mow your lawn creatively. Study nature.
- Laugh a lot—especially at those who disagree with you, and at all politicians. "Laughter is inner jogging" (Norman Cousins). "He who laughs, lasts" (Dr. Robert Anthony).
- Give of yourself to others. "When you cease to make a contribution, you begin to die" (Eleanor Roosevelt). "If you want to lift yourself up, lift up someone else" (Booker T. Washington). "You cannot do a kindness too soon, for you never know how soon it will be too late" (Emerson). "Long-range studies imply that doing something with other people, especially something for them, is the most powerful of all stimuli to longevity and health" (Jon Poppy).

- Install a full-length mirror in your bathroom. Make a list of all of your positive accomplishments. Tape the list to the mirror. If the naked truth in the mirror causes suicidal depression, read the list. Then follow the suggestions in this list.
- As Peter McWilliams observed: Understand that life is not a struggle— it's a wiggle.
- *Expect* to live well past 100 years. Remember Eubie Blake's words: "If I had known I was going to live this long, I'd have taken better care of myself."

Sources and recommended reading

- Ford, Norman. *The 50 Healthiest Places to Live and Retire in the United States.* Bedford, MA: Mills & Sanderson, 1991.

- Goldman, Benjamin A. *The Truth About Where You Live: An atlas for action on toxins and mortality.* New York: Times Books/Random House, 1991.

- Herbers, John. *The New Heartland: America's Flight Beyond the Suburbs and How It Is Changing Our Future.* New York: Time Books, 1986.

- Setterberg, Fred and Lonny Shavelson. *Toxic Nation: The Fight to Save Our Communities from Chemical Contamination.* New York, John Wiley & Sons, 1993.

EPA Right-To-Know Hotline: 800-535-0202. An information specialist will direct you to a state agency that can give you information about toxic conditions in specific locations.

To lengthen thy Life, lessen thy Meals.

BENJAMIN FRANKLIN

Happiness is good health and a bad memory.

INGRID BERGMAN

Never deny a diagnosis, but do deny the negative verdict that may go with it.

NORMAN COUSINS

17
Community
lost and found

There can be no vulnerability without risk;
there can be no community without vulnerability;
there can be no peace, and ultimately no life, without community.

M. SCOTT PECK

Grappling with definition

e are inclined to think of community as a group of people who live near each other, have common interests, socialize, and perhaps solve mutual challenges together. In truth, most think of community as simply a neighborhood of friends.

Community is much more. Community always includes the natural features of its place, for those features shape all the people who live there as the people shape the features. The features are the landform, the trees and the shrubs and the grasses, and the animals domestic and wild, large and small, feathered and finned and furred. Features include the land and the things within the land, the soil and the minerals. Community includes all the parts of the place that comprise its economy, and in this all features of the place contribute. Without all these parts, community is incomplete and cannot thrive.

Natural community is similar to bioregion, but bioregions exist independent and above political boundaries, while community must sometimes consider those boundaries in matters of law and taxes and representation. Community is even more similar to an ecosystem, an interrelated system of parts that coexist in harmony.

When it exists freely, honestly, and fully, community occupies that essential place between the individual and the public sector of society. There are certain important human social conditions that effectively can only be dealt with by the community. A fundamental reason why most cities don't work is that community functions have been usurped by public entities. A public entity can never understand and be sensitive to an individual the way a community can. The public entity's actions are often destructive of community.

In speaking of community, then, we are speaking of a complex connection not only among human beings or between humans and their homeland but also between the human economy and nature, between forest or prairie and field or orchard, and between troublesome creatures and pleasant ones. All neighbors are included.

WENDELL BERRY
"CONSERVATION AND LOCAL ECONOMY," IN *SEX, ECONOMY, FREEDOM & COMMUNITY*

It seems to me that the healthiest communities function as extended families. The young are taught by the examples of the adults. Social disturbances are handled locally, without the need for public institutions.

My sense of community derives from having lived in many places, both urban and rural. I believe that the qualities of the natural environment, a sense of place, common interests and values, and shared experiences create the condition we call community. A community is composed of people who belong to one another and to their place. It exists to receive membership and to give service. The commonality of the features and conditions of a place causes membership. The health of the individual—mental, physical, and economical, is inextricably tied to the health of the community. A community is most healthy when it is self-sustaining.

Community provides a sense of belonging. There is good reason to believe that much modern unhappiness—even mental illness—is the result of moving too often and with too little thought. A change in venue can improve our mental condition if it is well thought out—indeed, that is one of the premises of this book—but the modern nomad moves carelessly, with insufficient thought or commitment.

Community life is by definition a life of cooperation and responsibility.
Private life and public life, without the disciplines of community interest,
necessarily gravitate toward competition and exploitation.
As private life casts off all community restraints in the interest of
economic exploitation or ambition or self-realization or whatever,
the communal supports of public life also and by the same stroke
are undercut, and public life becomes simply
the arena of unrestrained private ambition and greed.

WENDELL BERRY
ESSAY: "SEX, ECONOMY, FREEDOM & COMMUNITY"

While most urban places have lost community because public entities have taken over its function, most rural areas have well-established communities, both in small towns and out in the country. Community is more viable in low-density population areas because people depend on each other more.

Even those of us who cherish privacy, enjoy self-sufficiency, and have a high level of independence need to be responsible to other people and know that we have others' support. Ever since our ancient ancestors huddled in caves with others community has been one of the strongest of human bonds. Lives have been lost defending it.

The longing for community is one of the oldest themes
in our nation's young history.

OSHA GRAY DAVIDSON

Nothing defines and exposes community so clearly as a perceived common threat. Rural Missourians rallied together to fight a misnamed, so-called Natural Streams Act which threatened to create unbearable police state conditions for those of us with flowing water on our land or living on a watershed—essentially everyone. Many of these people were residents of my county whom I had never before met. The threat to our freedom brought us together—it exposed and identified our larger community.

The current strong interest in renewing connection to community is the result of wide-spread recognition that largely we have lost it, especially in urban areas. That recognition provides an important part of the answer to the question of why so many are moving away from cities.

Examples of community

Indications that a strong sense of community exists in places you investigate will include viable volunteer fire departments, well-attended PTA meetings, strong voter turnout, low crime rates, thriving local economies. It is also evident by the attitude of people you meet on the street and in local stores. Common courtesies. Smiles and greetings to strangers. Genuine expressions.

Economic cooperation is evident where communities are healthy. In some places food growers are interfacing with consumers to create local food systems. Organic growers' organizations and buyers' cooperatives have resulted, to the benefit of all.

The old and the new

In some areas community appears to be divided between old-timers and newcomers. Newcomers commonly focus on the common challenge of learning how to live in the new place. They would do well to remember that old-timers have lived and lasted in the place under all of man's and nature's conditions. It is wise to observe how they do things. With time, some from each group will integrate the other.

Your strongest initial connection will be with those who have similar backgrounds, who share your values, and who came to the place by somewhat the same path.

Finding, building, and preserving community is a vital part of our human condition but we have lost the practice. Consider carefully your motivations to become absorbed into a strong existing community.

How to use community as a criterion

Find out where like-minded people are going. Read the following chapter on demographics and chapter 22 on states (political, not mental). If strong community is a very high priority for you, you may wish to consider an intentional community (see chapter 26).

Once you have targeted a specific county, make contact with people there. Ideally you will visit. Purposely get lost. Go into a likely looking homestead and explain your situation. Keep doing this until you find someone who will take the time to talk to you and show you their place. A few hours spent this way will tell you much about local conditions and attitudes. And you may begin a friendship that will continue after your move.

You might place a small ad in the local newspaper asking for contacts by people who have recently moved there. Phone calls to the newspaper editor, banker, insurance agent, county clerk, school superintendent, and chamber of commerce are additional ways to gain feelings and information about the community.

Fitting in

Every community demands conformity to its laws,
expects the acceptance of its customs and folkways,
and prefers to have none but native sons at its firesides.

HELEN & SCOTT NEARING
LIVING THE GOOD LIFE

Helen and Scott tried to persuade people in their adopted Vermont community to make some adjustments in their conduct. It didn't work out very well and it frustrated the estimable Nearings, who took community very seriously in those demanding, early homesteading days. The lesson is well made: existing communities are resistant to change.

Most rural communities are gracious and welcoming to new residents. It is wise to accept early social invitations even though you may be busy getting settled. If you wait until you "have time" you may find that the invitations have stopped. There likely will be ample opportunities for service work. Volunteer fire departments, PTAs, 4H clubs, recycling groups, food buyers' co-ops, and service clubs are always looking for additional help. This is an excellent way to show the community who you are and for you to understand it. Just don't push your personal agenda and you'll do fine. In *Little Town Blues*, Raye C. Ringholz writes of the different priorities of outsiders from locals in a small Utah town.

> Not of the predominant Mormon faith, environmentalists and vegetarians as well, they still live comfortably and are accepted in the tight-knit community of ranchers because they don't attempt to force their ways on long-time residents.

Country folks are often poor but proud. Poor, that is, by urban definition. It will not do to push them or talk down to them. Restrain yourself from telling them how "we did it back in Metropolis." They get all they want of Metropolis on television. And you did *leave* Metropolis for good reasons. If you are very lucky, one of the natives will take a liking to you. Most old-timers are proud of what they know and will share hard-won knowledge with someone who really listens. Listen carefully and you may avoid painful and costly mistakes. Give them respect and you will be respected.

As for advancing your well-researched, well-thought-out, perfectly logical, totally irrefutable solutions for saving the natural world from destruction by ignorant and greedy people, keep it to yourself—or write a book. Show what you believe by how you conduct yourself. If it makes sense to the natives, why, in 20 or 30 years some of them may begin to follow your example. You *will be there* in 30 years, won't you? They will.

Recommended reading

Berry, Wendell. *Sex, Economy, Freedom & Community.* New York: Pantheon Books, 1993.

—————. *Fidelity: Five Stories.* New York: Pantheon Books, 1992.

A community identifies itself
by an understood mutuality of interests.
But it lives and acts by the common virtues of trust,
goodwill, forbearance, self-restraint, compassion, and forgiveness.
If it hopes to continue long as a community, it will wish to and will have to—
encourage respect for all its members, human and natural.
It will encourage respect for all stations and occupations.
Such a community has the power—not invariably but as a rule—
to enforce decency without litigation.
It has the power, that is, to influence behavior.
And it exercises this power not by coercion or violence
but by teaching the young and by preserving stories and songs
that tell (among other things)
what works and what does not work in a given place.

WENDELL BERRY

*A strong sense of identification with a particular place
means making a bond with the other people who live there
—whether you always agree with them or not.
Common ground in the geographic sense
creates common ground in the social sense.*

DANIEL KEMMIS
MAYOR OF MISSOULA, MONTANA

*Now we are all poor folks down here,
we live on fresh air and mountain scenery,
and we have so many ways
you've just got to like some of them.*

JOHN CONKLIN "UNCLE JOHNNY" HARLIN

Crime-ridden city

18
Demographics
and
social conditions

It is easy to travel the United States and be impressed
both with the commonalities of existence
that all its residents share
and with the diversity that is still imposed
by vastness, the wide range of climate and physiography,
the residue of history, differences in resources and agriculture,
and variations in ethnicity and culture.

CALVIN BEALE

Go west, young man.
No, north! No, south! No, go back east!

he history of Americans has been to move. We moved west because of minerals, free homesteading land, weather, prosperity, and Horace Greeley's bombast. Since the West was fully settled we have moved to wherever economic conditions flourished. Movement is much more prevalent than stability—the average American moves five times during his lifetime. How many people do you know who live in the same city or county in which they were born?

For most of this century more people left rural areas than moved there. By the late 1960s, social and economic conditions began to slow this migration; in the 1970s there were more people moving to rural areas than away from them. That trend continues today. Of the 2,288 counties classified as nonmetropolitan in 1992, more than 67 percent gained population between 1990 and 1991.

For our purposes, what is happening on a national scale is of less importance than what is happening in specific regions and counties. Some rural counties are in fact losing population, especially in the Great Plains states, the western corn belt, and the Mississippi delta region. Areas where gains are most prevalent include the Rocky Mountain states, the Northwest, the upper Great Lakes area, the Ozarks, various areas of the South, and rural areas of the Northeast.

Counties that are destinations for retirees continue to be the fastest growing, and recreational counties are the second-fastest growing. Slower but continued growth is occurring in counties with an economic base in manufacturing or government. Farming and mining counties continue to lose population, except those mining counties that are now considered recreation areas, notably in the Rockies. In all cases, population gains are greatest in rural counties adjacent to metropolitan counties. Apparently we want our country homes and our shopping malls, too—or city jobs are still supporting new country dwellers.

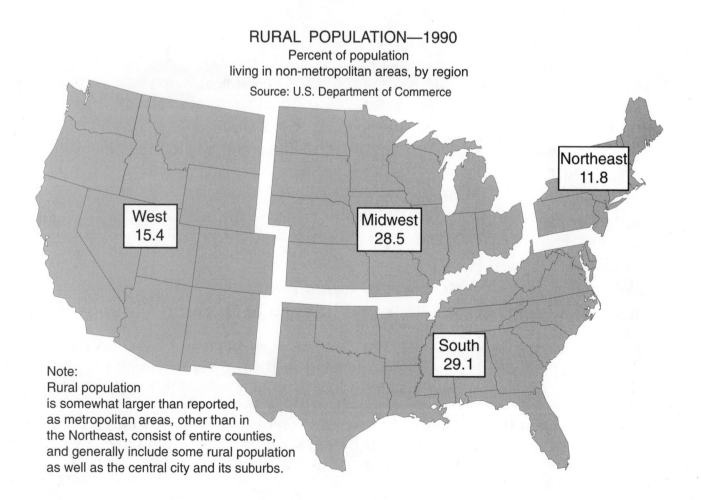

RURAL POPULATION—1990
Percent of population
living in non-metropolitan areas, by region
Source: U.S. Department of Commerce

Northeast
11.8

West
15.4

Midwest
28.5

South
29.1

Note:
Rural population
is somewhat larger than reported,
as metropolitan areas, other than in
the Northeast, consist of entire counties,
and generally include some rural population
as well as the central city and its suburbs.

I suspect that most people would live in a rural area if economic circumstances permitted. This is supported by the conclusions of the Gallup polls cited earlier. The fact that retirees are moving in such great numbers to rural areas is further evidence. Modern industry has both followed the people to the country and it has relocated and the workers have followed (see chapter 12—*Making a living*). The information age combined with computer technology has freed many workers to work in the country for city clients or bosses. I like to think of all this as The Great Migration to the Boondocks.

Immigration and ethnicity

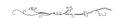

*The United States is spending huge amounts trying to
create a cultural presence in Latin America.
But we are doing it an easier way.
Little by little, with 30 million Latin Americans
already here, we are taking over this country.*

NOBEL PRIZE-WINNING NOVELIST GABRIEL GARCIA MARQUEZ

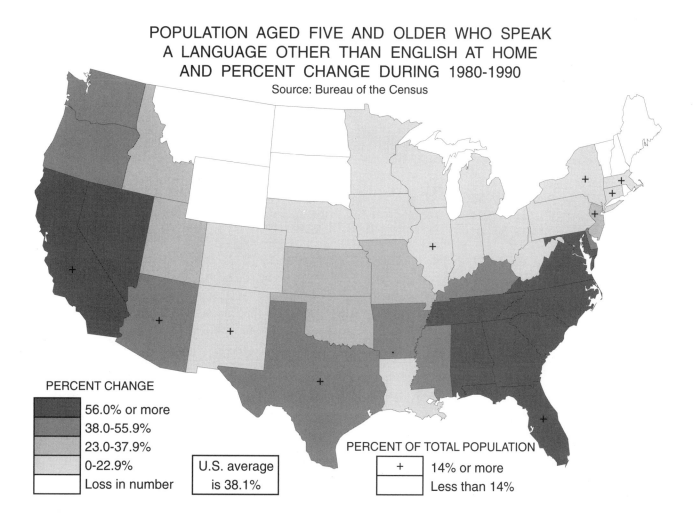

POPULATION AGED FIVE AND OLDER WHO SPEAK
A LANGUAGE OTHER THAN ENGLISH AT HOME
AND PERCENT CHANGE DURING 1980-1990
Source: Bureau of the Census

PERCENT CHANGE

	56.0% or more
	38.0-55.9%
	23.0-37.9%
	0-22.9%
	Loss in number

U.S. average is 38.1%

PERCENT OF TOTAL POPULATION

+	14% or more
	Less than 14%

The ethnic mixing of America is speeding up—33 percent of 1980-1990 U.S. population growth was from immigration. The Immigration Act of 1990 now allows 675,000 legal immigrants per year. In addition to this flow, large numbers of illegal immigrants move into coastal and land border areas each year. Most immigrants settle in cities but, increasingly, many are going straight to the suburbs. Immigrants and minorities have higher birthrates than the majority population—the sum of immigration plus birthrate accounts for the fact that the ethnic minority population is growing faster than the majority population.

The strongest influx of immigrants is in the Southeast and the Southwest. There is very strong Mexican immigration in California, Arizona, and Texas. It is predicted that the Hispanic vote will predominate in California by 2040. The media tells us that the dominant culture of Miami has become that of Cubans, who are also moving in large numbers to New York City and northeast New Jersey.

Asian populations are fast expanding in Seattle, San Francisco, Los Angeles, and San Diego and are settling as well on the east coast. *American Demographics* (10-93) reported that Atlanta's Asian Americans are more visible than its Hispanics. Business signs written with Oriental characters have become common in Atlanta suburbs.

Even interior areas have experienced strong immigration—during the 1980s, 15,000 Hmongs, a tribal group from Laos, settled in Minnesota. Sizable Hmong populations are also established in Wisconsin and in Georgia.

The *Los Angeles Times* reported the most common last names of 1992 homebuyers in L.A. The top ten, by ranking number of homes bought, were: Lee, Smith, Garcia, Kim, Lopez, Hernandez, Nguyen, Rodriguez, Johnson, and Gonzalez. Of the top 50, 17 were Latino, and 11 were Asian.

University of Michigan demographer William H. Frey is concerned that a "Balkanizing" trend is occurring, with minority-dominated immigration and "white flight" leading to "sharply divergent racial and socioeconomic structure areas in broad regions and states." Several states with strong foreign immigration also have strong out-migration to other states. These states include Texas, Illinois, New York, and New Jersey.

This is not an unknown American condition. Within each region of the United States there are places of vibrant ethnicity and pervasive local attitudes, not just from those who have come here from another country. Place creates character. The attitude of a New England farmer is strange to a Creole shrimp fisherman. Wyoming cattle ranchers have little understanding of Alabama cotton growers.

Beyond native American differences, newly arrived Americans bring with them characteristics and traditions that sometimes clash with local customs and laws. Language and clothing styles are the most obvious differences but others are more dramatic. Cultures that commonly eat dogs, for instance, do not blend well in areas where valued pets run loose. In Asian nations fishing is done not for sport but for food and requires no license.

If you would have a problem living in an all-white (possibly bigoted) area, if you want your children to be exposed to a racial mix, or if your Norwegian parents insist that their grandchildren retain that cultural conditioning, you will need to do extra research. During consideration of any area, write or talk to local people to see who they are, who they favor, and what their biases are. Again, the local newspaper is revealing of local characteristics.

Prejudice and bias linger longer in the country, where tradition is strong and attitudes are less buffeted by the media. TV is not always a barrier breaker—I know people who would not allow their children to watch the Cosby show even though it was the #1-rated family sitcom.

Beyond obeying laws, most of us treat our fellow humans with respect, as we wish to be treated. By no stretch does it follow that we should live in an ethnic atmosphere with which we are uncomfortable.

Where is everybody going?

More than five million Americans move from one state to another each year. The strongest migration is to retirement counties, which constitute one-fifth of all nonmetropolitan counties. States of greatest retiree influx include California, Florida, Arizona, and Washington. Those with the heaviest percentage losses are West Virginia, Oklahoma, Louisiana, Iowa, and North Dakota.

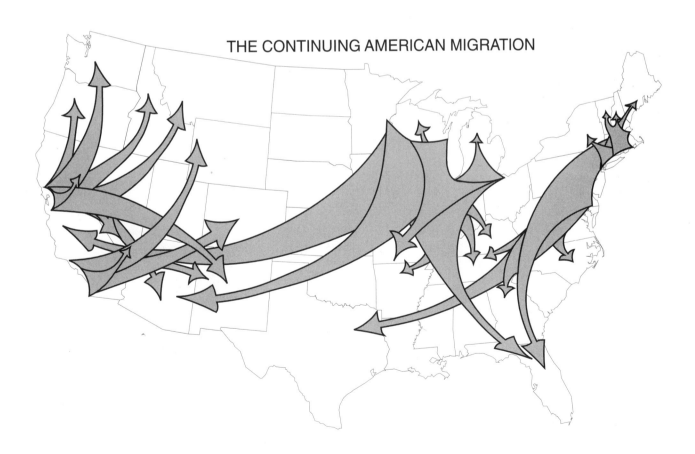

THE CONTINUING AMERICAN MIGRATION

Urban refugees are largely shunning the Sun Belt and are instead moving to areas of clean air, beauty, recreation, and perceived safety. The strongest migration to rural counties is occurring in the following regions.

Rocky Mountain states

After life in the smog, former west coasters find Rocky Mountain air exhilarating, the open spaces intoxicating, and the skiing superb. But, beyond real estate agents and merchants, not all rural residents are happy about the invasion. As in Seattle and parts of Oregon, there is anger against California "equity refugees" who sell expensive Golden State homes and build or buy big homes in the mountains, driving up demand and prices.

And then there's the water shortage.

Time (9-6-93) featured an article with a paragraph title: "Sky's The Limit, The Rocky Mountain home of cowboys and lumberjacks has become a magnet for lone-eagle telecommuters and Range Rover-driving yuppies. So far, it's been a booming good time."

> For all its steam, the Rockies boom has its pitfalls and built-in limitations. For one thing, it cannot go on forever in the continued absence of a general economic recovery. . . . The region's scarcity of water poses as much of a challenge as it always has. The northern tier of Montana, Idaho, and Wyoming, with plentiful

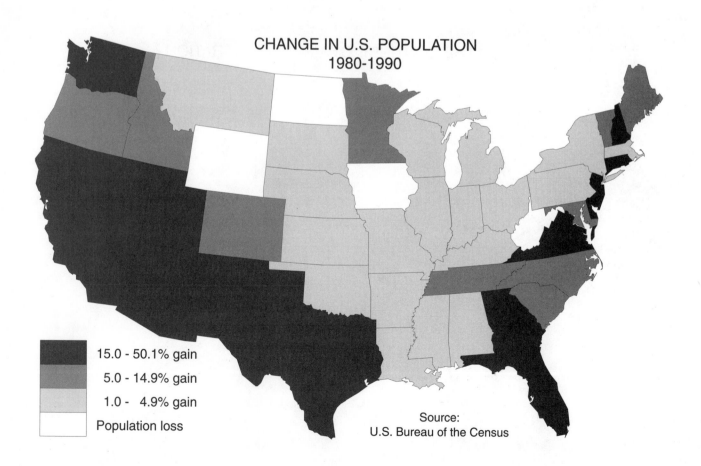

CHANGE IN U.S. POPULATION
1980-1990

15.0 - 50.1% gain
5.0 - 14.9% gain
1.0 - 4.9% gain
Population loss

Source:
U.S. Bureau of the Census

rivers and low population density, expects no problem satisfying its pockets of growth. The semi-arid southern tier of Utah, Colorado, and New Mexico, however, has to give water high priority. *Denver is now judged to have only about 20 years' worth of identifiable water sources left.* (My emphasis)

William Kettredge is a short-story writer living in Missoula, Montana. In "The Last Safe Place," a follow-up in the same issue of *Time,* he says:

> You hate seeing your paradise overrun by latecomers from some seaport. Many are coming to the Rockies to retire. Their children are long out of school. They're on fixed incomes and resist supporting education. But these good folks don't seem to give a damn about the welfare of our next generation. They want to buy into our functioning culture on the cheap. What's drawing these crowds? It's not so much, I think, the beauties of nature, or cheap land, as it is safety. Sanctuary. As we know, our old America fantasy—a New World and social justice all around—has gone seriously defunct. Millions of citizens in our cities quite justifiably count themselves disfranchised. Some are angry, armed, and dangerous.

From a different perspective, Steamboat Springs, Colorado, is actively recruiting "lone eagles" as part of its economic development strategy. The term describes professionals who work at home—perceived as "clean industry" that brings prosperity to the community without any downside.

Midwestern states

Since 1940, the United States has added at least 13,000 square miles of inland waters (exclusive of Alaska), largely in the form of reservoirs created by dams. Whatever the primary purpose of the dams, they have usually attracted people for both recreation and permanent living. The effect has been particularly great in those inland states that lacked natural lakes. For example, in Oklahoma, Missouri, Arkansas, Kentucky, and Tennessee, there was a 133 percent increase in inland water area from 1940 to 1970, compared with less than 25 percent in the rest of the United States. The great majority of counties with major dam reservoirs in these states have had rapid population growth.

CALVIN BEALE

With beautiful scenery, four distinct seasons but moderate winters, numerous large, clear reservoirs, and low prices, the Ozarks area has been attracting retirees and back-to-the-landers since the 1960s. Even after all the growth it is still pretty much just a sprinkling of retirement enclaves and small towns in huge areas of farms and wooded hills and hollows. Not all midwesterners opt for gentler climes— many are attracted to the beauty and recreational aspects of Wisconsin and northern Michigan, still close to major cultural and commercial centers.

Southern states

From Tennessee to the coast and southward through the Appalachians, urban refugees from east coast cities and Midwest industrial areas are following industry and staking claims to the rural dream. Georgia and North Carolina are growing at above-average rates. Florida continues to attract huge numbers of people in spite of rising prices and growing congestion.

Northeastern states

Maine, Vermont, New Hampshire, and upstate New York are filling with second homes and permanent residences for refugees from the big cities who choose to stay in the region.

Social habits

Traditional rural social habits follow patterns established by work and religion. In most rural American areas today natives' social habits revolve around home, work, community, schools, and church. The tendency is to socialize with those individuals that one meets locally and whose values are shared.

City migrants bring their social habits with them, subject to place conditions. A common newcomer lament is how far one has to travel to socialize. In the country everybody is further apart and the space condition definitely causes less socializing. In our area residents typically cherish visitors but are loathe to leave home. The common end to conversations is "Come visit us—we'll be home."

After the fast pace and congestion of city living some rural immigrants feel lonely and isolated. I know of more than one person who left our area because they never did adjust to living beyond the sidewalks. If socializing is a prime requisite for you, you may wish to locate close to a town of some size. Put that on your criteria worksheet.

Culture

It is incorrect to assume that culture is lacking in country. Naisbitt and Aburdene have a section in *Megatrends 2000* entitled "From Broadway to the Boondocks."

> One reason behind record-breaking audiences for opera, theater, and symphony is that people in small and medium-size cities and in rural areas can attend hometown productions in some very impressive places. . . . In remote Orono, Maine, private contributions built the stunning $7.5 million Maine Center for the Arts on the University of Maine campus. In 1986 the 1,628-seat concert hall opened with a gala bash featuring musicians Isaac Stern and Yo-Yo Ma. During intermission audiences can walk through the museum of pre-Columbian sculpture that encircles the hall. Best of all, locals can attend world-class performances in their own backyard instead of driving five hours to Boston.

City residents are acting out their country desires by square dancing, line dancing, wearing cowboy hats and driving four-wheel-drive vehicles. Country

music stars pack city amphitheaters. Even the stars are changing their habits. Nashville has long been the country music capital of the world, but with over thirty big-name performers now based in town, Branson seems destined to inherit the title. Even there, the cross-over continues—the stars range from Andy Williams to Johnny Cash.

Most rural places do offer far less "high culture" than metro areas. Your lifestyle criteria should reflect whether you need to find a country home within reasonable driving distance to cultural centers.

Crime

Anybody can be good in the country; there are no temptations there.

OSCAR WILDE

Graffiti artist, 1811

Federal and state prison populations in 1970 were 196,000, in 1980 330,000, in 1990 773,000. By the end of 1992, 884,000 Americans were in prison (Bureau of Justice). The U.S. has the highest incarceration rate for any industrialized nation in the world. Shame on us.

North Carolina is often held up as the new ideal form to which our society is evolving. An excellent education system, high rates of employment, a good highway system, a great diversity of homesite choices, including nearly every type of rural setting. Yet on National Public Radio (11-5-93) I heard a piece on a serious North Carolina crime problem. It seems that there is insufficient jail space to incarcerate new criminals, so inmate sentences are being shortened or curtailed. "Build more jails," the injured and fearful citizens implore. But there are inadequate state funds to build new prisons.

Another innocent bystander shot in New York yesterday.
You just stand around this town long enough and be innocent
and somebody is going to shoot you. One day they shot four.
That's the best shooting ever done in this town.
Any time you can find four innocent people in New York in one day
you are doing well even if you don't shoot 'em.

WILL ROGERS

U.S. Attorney General Janet Reno
worries that tough, mandatory minimum sentences have filled limited jail space with two-bit crooks, enabling more dangerous criminals to get out early because of prison overcrowding.

(Nina J. Easton and Ronald J. Ostrow, "Ms. Reno Objects," *Los Angeles Times Magazine*, 10-31-93.) Back in North Carolina, the governor's office reports that 60% of felony parolees are back in jail within three years, convicted of new felonies.

The police, the courts, and the jails will never stop crime—only people can do that. My view is that the causes of crime are family breakdown and community breakdown. These conditions occur in rural areas but with less frequency than in cities. Family discipline, school discipline, and community disapproval of hoodlumism is typically stronger in rural areas. Moreover, criminal activity is not as profitable in sparsely populated areas.

Parents beware: milk theft is a common initiation requirement among turf gangs.

Every year when it's Chinese New Year here in New York,
there are fireworks going off at all hours.
New York mothers calm their frightened children by telling them it's just gunfire.

DAVID LETTERMAN

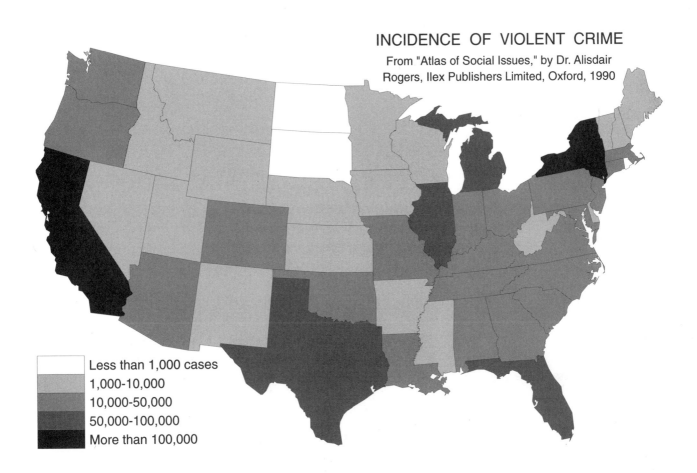

INCIDENCE OF VIOLENT CRIME

From "Atlas of Social Issues," by Dr. Alisdair
Rogers, Ilex Publishers Limited, Oxford, 1990

Less than 1,000 cases
1,000-10,000
10,000-50,000
50,000-100,000
More than 100,000

Potential community conflicts

Some old-timers resent newcomers who arrive with loose money, fancy cars, and city attitudes. Others are simply amused. It's amazing how place creates values—after a few years in their chosen home, *old* newcomers often share the same attitudes toward *new* newcomers as natives. You may, too.

Private property rights are often ignored in the country where large private holdings contribute to a public land image. And established patterns often conflict with changing needs. Our farm was owned for 15 years by city people who used it only for summer vacations and occasional long weekends. The natives used the stream road, which passes about 150 feet in front of the house, to travel through the hollow and hunt the property during deer and turkey season. For years one neighboring property owner took city hunters through the property to a part of his land remote from his house. The first year we were there I allowed the activities to continue because we wanted to be *good* new neighbors. But the hunters' trucks driving through before daylight woke us up and the shooting destroyed our peace and quiet and caused us safety concerns so the next year I stopped it. The deep resentment from that neighbor continues even now, ten years later.

Determining the complete nature of communities is sometimes difficult without spending substantial time there. We have friends who bought a place on a North Carolina mountain, worked hard for a year building their homestead, and then, when they had time to socialize, discovered that the clan in their immediate area were not at all friendly—in fact, they were downright hostile to newcomers who showed intentions of staying. After enduring various insults and even threats of violence, they went looking elsewhere. After they identified their next area they ran the following ad in the local paper:

> ## SITUATION WANTED
> Mature, responsible couple experienced in rural living seeks small farm or country home to caretake for absentee owner. Maintenance and protection of your property in exchange for living quarters and garden space.

They received several offers, chose one, moved there, and lived rent-free for a year while they assured themselves that this time they had indeed found their

Fences should be built strong, so you and your neighbors can lean on them while determining what's hot and what's not

ideal place. They and I recommend a lease agreement signed by all parties, stipulating the terms of the caretaking agreement. This ensures that there will be no surprises, like being told to move out on short notice. Offering references should favorably impress the owner that you are good people, and may eliminate the requirement of a security deposit.

During the seven years between finding my place and moving there I had two caretakers. They received free rent in return for minimal maintenance and improvements. The first was a family that had purchased an acreage nearby that lacked a house. After living at my place for three years they decided to sell their land and move closer to a city. The second caretaker, a single woman, later bought land nearby. In both cases, they and I profited by the experience.

Living in an area for a year, either caretaking or renting, provides time to experience the climate and the community, develop income, and to look at property and become aware of values. If you have the time, it is an excellent way to verify that you have indeed found your ideal place.

Country people have a different focus than city people. They are more attuned to nature and natural rhythms. A neighborhood of long-established subsistence farmers is not where you will likely be able to engage in conversation about the latest best-seller list. If one of your treasures is a lifetime subscription to the *New Yorker* or if you find discussions about the weather incredibly boring you may be disenchanted with life in the slow lane. Your criteria worksheet should reflect this.

That is not to say that country folk are less intelligent or even less well-read. Personally, I think the fact that they were living and surviving in the country *first* says a lot for their smarts. It's just that city living tends to be faster, more tense, and more focused on what's hot and what's not. Country living smooths one out. Rural folks tend not to get very excited about fads. I suspect there were few sales of pet rocks in the Ozarks. On the other hand, if you know anyone who would like to buy some rocks *real cheap*, why, send them on by. For no extra charge we'll even give each rock a proper name.

If an area has been losing population or gaining very slowly, then the cultural makeup of the citizenry is likely to be that of the natives. But if the area has been growing rapidly you can expect to find a large number of people just like you who have moved there from the cities. Certain areas are so popular with urban refugees that the newcomers outnumber the old-timers. The resulting community culture often is that of city people learning how to live in the country.

Country culture, attitudes, and habits are the result of people from various backgrounds finding out what works. Land creates the human character—the harder to extract a living, the tougher and more independent the residents.

Independence

Country folk had to be independent to survive—a commonality between peoples of sparsely populated areas. Independence sometimes evolves into isolationism. Ozark natives have a deserved reputation of low regard for "revenooers," partly a result of moonshine and tax collectors not mixing well. A government agent was killed near our place in the 1950s because he got too close to the still in a cave up one of our side hollows. The farmers around Mechanicsville, Iowa, have exhibited similar qualities. In *Broken Heartland,* Osha Gray Davidson reveals:

> In 1931, when the government began testing all dairy cows in Iowa for tuberculosis, scores of armed area farmers vowed to shoot the first son-of-a-bitch to touch a Cedar County cow.

The farmers thought the testing was a good idea—they just didn't like being told that they *had* to do it.

Politics

Rural citizens are usually conservative, especially regarding finances. When cash money comes hard the tendency is not to part with it easily. With the city-to-country movement now in its third decade, some rural areas are showing the effects of increased numbers of liberal voters. In some counties the newcomers have become the majority. I find it sad that natives in these places are losing control.

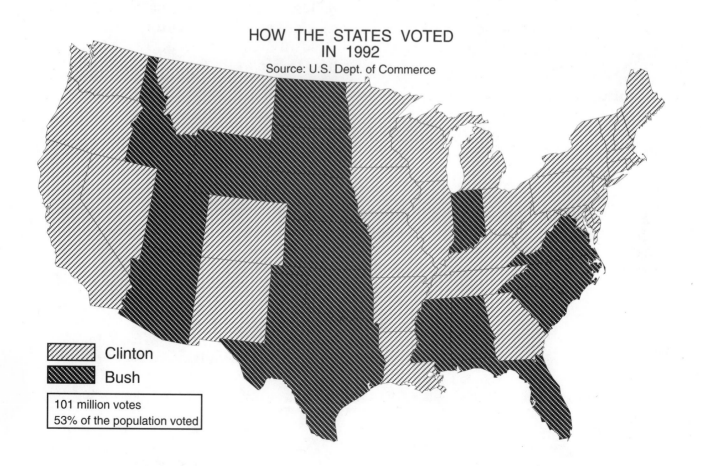

HOW THE STATES VOTED
IN 1992
Source: U.S. Dept. of Commerce

Clinton
Bush

101 million votes
53% of the population voted

City visitors are surprised to learn that the old-timers in our county, many living below the so-called poverty level, overwhelmingly vote Republican. They are astonished to learn of the poor couple who refused to sign up for an assistance program urged on them by university researchers. The scholars were disconcerted by the response: "Why, that would be like taking *charity*, wouldn't it?" Entitlement was not the issue. Values was.

Political leanings can quickly be uncovered by reading the local newspaper and talking to local people. Feed store operators, restaurant workers, the person repairing your flat tire—one or two carefully worded questions may give you more information than you expected. Voting history may be found with the county clerk.

Religion

There is only one religion, though there are a hundred versions of it.
GEORGE BERNARD SHAW

Rural churches in the Ozarks are often small and numerous, spaced according to horse-and-buggy times when trips were necessarily of short distance. Judging from the number of cars out front, congregations may be as few as four or five families. Denominations reflect those found in nearby towns and cities, which typically have larger facilities.

If finding a church of a particular denomination is of high priority for you, write it on your criteria list, next to demographics. You can learn of the churches in any area through the local newspaper or the chamber of commerce.

He charged nothing for his preaching, and it was worth it, too.
MARK TWAIN

Alcohol

Years of decadent California living conditioned me to shopping habits that don't work in the Bible Belt. Shortly after moving to the Ozarks I inquired of a clerk in the local grocery store where I might find the beer. I may never forget the sight of the young man drawing himself to his full height (about five-five) and proudly declaring: "Sir, it is the policy of Town & Country Supermarket to not sell alcoholic beverages!" Upon my pressing, his good manners prevailed and he did tell me where the town's only "package store" was located.

Some counties south of us in Arkansas are "dry" and most ban the sale of alcoholic beverages on Sunday. Some counties actually have laws prohibiting the transportation of more than a modest amount of beverage through their counties even though legally purchased in more liberal counties. Do not take such laws lightly—if stopped for a traffic violation your car may be searched. Rural law enforcement personnel tend to be very serious about their authority. It is not inconceivable that they will strike you as humorless.

Sex

Country adults take their role model responsibilities seriously. Traditional rural values include matter-of-fact but not "modern" attitudes toward sex. Children who regularly see animals breeding lack the curiosity of city kids. But attitudes toward talking about sex are conservative. If you are coming from one of the more liberal cities be aware that in many rural areas modern, open sexual conversations are considered totally unacceptable, especially within hearing distance of women or children.

There are sexual distinctions that may seem archaic. In our county it is a custom for drivers to acknowledge approaching cars with a wave. (I find it not only neighborly but nostalgic—reminds me of my early sports car-driving days, when MGs, TRs, and Healeys were uncommon enough that we elite waved—only—at each other.) I quickly adopted the practice. But I noticed that female drivers rarely returned my wave. I finally deduced that it is inappropriate behavior—such provocative communication from a man to a woman one does not know and who is away from her spouse.

Homophobia is prevalent in the Bible Belt and what fairly are called redneck areas, both of which tend to be conservative and traditional. Homophobia exists so strongly in our county that two prominent business people finally left the area after continued, serious telephone threats.

Some rural areas have an imbalance of the sexes. Herman, Minnesota, population 485, has an excess of 68 bachelors aged 20 to 50 over eligible women in the same age group. The town is especially interested in attracting a plumber, a lawyer, and an accountant. Check it out, ladies.

Enclaves

Even today, in areas isolated by topography and poor roads, there are groups of people who are far out of the mainstream, are culturally unique, who live in the shadows of civilization. They may exhibit simplistic attitudes and behavior, may have intermarried, may be clans distrustful of others, as evidenced by the earlier story about our friends' experience in North Carolina.

While remoteness increases this likelihood, there is no way to know for certain whether such a condition exists without visiting the area and talking to shopkeepers, the sheriff, the residents and, ideally, the local census takers, whose duties have taken them into the most remote areas.

Radical groups

Militants, clans, cults, and other secretive groups like to headquarter in the remote country, where their unique ways will not attract attention. The local sheriff will be aware of such groups and their location.

On your criteria worksheet . . .

Of all criteria, social conditions are the ones most likely to be overlooked and the ones that could most easily destroy your happiness in an otherwise ideal place. Consider well your needs and preferences and next to demographics write them down.

Don't be fooled by what you see today.
The present trickle will accumulate into a river, then a flood.
Try to imagine the eventual transformation.
In the next century, most middle-class
Americans will be living in the penturbs. . . .
Penturbs—the fifth region of opportunity—is the new frontier.
JACK LESSINGER

A. Largesse Hogg, headed for the pork barrel

19
Services and taxes

It seems correct to say that we did not foresee the extent
to which the growing number of older people
would include many people with
(1) retirement incomes large enough to make them mobile,
(2) the option of retiring at a comparatively early age, and
(3) a desire to choose a rural or small-town setting
for their retirement despite the poorer quality of
medical and community services
that many such areas have.

CALVIN BEALE

t is a fact that many rural counties and communities provide minimal services. The reason is both cultural and economic. Country people are independent and loathe to pay someone else to do things they can do for themselves. Many rural communities predictably reject ballot measures that would raise taxes to provide services perceived as not critical. "Critical" often is limited to law enforcement, schools, and roads.

Transportation and roads

Thanks to the interstate highway system, it is now possible to
travel from coast to coast without seeing anything.

CHARLES KURALT

The interstate highway system is finished and the U.S. Department of Transportation, state transportation departments, and road engineers are now working on the National Highway System, which will connect the interstates and principal arteries. The new roads will be designed to serve commuter and commercial traffic, and will connect cities, ports, airports, border crossings, public transportation facilities, and major travel destinations.

By city standards country roads range from adequate to deplorable. County roads are usually dirt or gravel while state roads traversing counties are usually paved. If you expect to commute to work you will want land near a good highway. If you will work at home and clients will not need to visit, you may wish to buy property far from highways, which will lower land costs, lessen traffic noise—which travels far in country quiet—and raise the level of privacy.

Some states help finance rural transportation systems for those who don't drive, typically older folks. Most do not. School buses serve nearly all areas sending children to public schools. Taxis are usually only found in cities—so if you take one to the country, don't lose it.

Schools

A child's education should begin
at least one hundred years before he is born.
OLIVER WENDELL HOLMES

Schools were discussed in "Concerned parents," in chapter 4. Rural schools parallel city schools in that they are a reflection of the values of the residents. Community interest and support for student activities is often every bit as valuable as tax dollars. Don't expect as many frills as big-city or affluent suburban schools offer—Olympic pools and multiple tennis courts are unlikely. There are notable exceptions—visit schools to assure yourself of facts.

Law enforcement

Small towns often have a modest police force and a small jail. County areas are usually serviced by a sheriff and a minimal number of deputies. In low-population areas one local dispatcher may coordinate calls for the sheriff, police, fire departments, and the ambulance service.

Our county of 9,500 has a sheriff and two minimally-trained deputies who provide their own cars and guns. We provide the sheriff's car and we buy everybody's bullets. Bullets are not a big budget item. The sheriff is not quite as good looking as Andy Griffith was in Mayberry RFD, but he smiles just as big, especially with the approach of election time. Our deputies are several notches

above Barney Fife and we give them a whole box of bullets. Like the judge, the sheriff is elected by county voters. I can best explain the condition of our county jail by reporting that repeat offenders are only those with really bad memories. The dispatcher, the jail, and the sheriff's office are in the courthouse building in our county seat, which is also the main town in the county—its population is several less than a thousand and holding steady.

Fire protection

Unless you live in town, you would do well to learn to depend on yourself. Rural areas may or may not have fire departments. If they do they are probably staffed by volunteers. In our county there are twelve member-supported volunteer fire stations spaced to provide minimum response time. Even so, most house fires result in loss of the structure, with the firefighters' work confined mostly to preventing the fire from spreading. Some only respond to members' fires, which helps to keep annual dues paid on time. In many rural areas, the state conservation department maintains a firefighting capability primarily to protect forested areas but available for non-structural emergency private use.

Utilities

Rural electric service is provided by a variety of business entities. Ours is a co-operative, owned and operated by members. Electric rates are affected by the ownership entity, the type of fuels used for generation, and whether the owners invested in nuclear generation— expect the shut-down and cleanup costs of nuclear facilities to be substantial. The property you buy will either have existing electricity to the house, it will be available to be brought in at a price, or it will be too far away to be affordable. There are the alternatives of home generation by photovoltaics, water, and wind, in addition to back-up generators powered by gas, diesel, or propane.

Where there are electric power poles and lines there will usually be telephone lines. If you plan to use a modem, be aware that some old rural phone lines may have line noise that will affect fax-modem transmissions.

Radio and TV reception is weaker in the country and worst of all down in a hollow or valley. If TV is important to you a satellite dish receiver may be in your future. New models are small and give excellent service.

Waste disposal

Even small towns usually offer trash pickup service. Most areas have some sort of recycling operation, either administered by a town or by a local group—in our county some of the all-volunteer fire departments.

In most rural areas there is no trash pickup. This is an opportunity. In truth, there is very little that needs to be sent to a landfill. We sort for recycling, compost all food trimmings and leftovers, and burn paper products that we can't recycle. We buy in bulk to minimize containers. It's amazing how quickly you can find ways to cut down on so-called waste material. It's a good feeling to evolve from being an Earth trasher to being an Earth saver.

Sewage disposal

Rural sewage disposal systems are usually private. They may be as simple as an outhouse, as modern as an indoor composting toilet, as elegant as a greenhouse/ water hyacinth system, or as common as a septic tank and leach field. Whichever system you encounter or build, you will be responsible for maintenance.

Outhouses and composting toilets need periodic emptying, hyacinths are cut and added to the compost pile, and septic tanks need to have sludge pumped out every couple of years or so. A leaking septic tank can pollute a well.

Health care

This subject is covered in chapter 16—*Health 101*.

Libraries

No place affords a more striking conviction of the vanity of human hopes, than a public library.

SAMUEL JOHNSON

Did that get your attention? At first this cynical quote perplexed me. Samuel Johnson (1709-1784) was an eminent English lexicographer and writer. He wrote a dictionary and is widely considered to be the greatest man of letters in English literature, so it is safe to assume that he used words correctly. One would also expect him to have greatly valued books and the places where they are kept. A dilemma.

Aha! Research reveals another Samuel Johnson (1696-1772)—this one a philosopher and clergyman—one of the founders of King's College, present-day Columbia University. His view was that the sensible world is made up of ideas man receives directly from God. That explains the concept that books are examples of man's vain hopes. Methinks we have found the source of the quote.

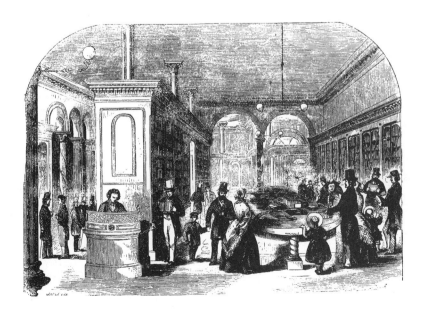

Funding for rural libraries is often inadequate or entirely absent. My only serious country living regret is the distance to a large library. Our very modest county library is funded by donations and fundraisers and is maintained and staffed by volunteers.

Notable exceptions to these stark conditions are found in those small towns that contain colleges and universities.

Taxes versus services

The income tax has made more liars
out of the American people than golf has.
Even when you make [a tax form] out on the level,
you don't know when it's through
if you are a crook or a martyr.

WILL ROGERS

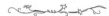

Most of us complain about taxes. If you are one of us, here's where you get to walk your talk—here's where convictions meet the pocketbook. Here's where you get to *choose* your taxes. *And your services.* Because, bureaucratic waste aside (now there's an oxymoron), the two go hand in hand, or hand in pocket. Although we can do nothing—legal—about the onerous federal income tax and social security tax, by carefully choosing the state and county that we will move to, we can *choose* the state income tax, state sales tax, county property tax, use taxes, and fees that we will pay.

Low taxes support minimal services but maximum freedom. Ideally, we buy only as much service as we really need. As one of my criteria, I listed low taxes. I got them. With the exception of the state conservation department, all fire protection in our county comes from volunteer departments that are funded by membership fees and fundraisers such as recycled materials sales and auxiliary activity. State roads are blacktop; county roads are gravel. There is no trash pickup. There is no planning commission and no zoning commission. If we choose to build a pyramid or a bowling alley in our front yard, we are limited only by imagination, energy, and finances. Common sense seems to do the job just as well as if we had zoning laws. There is also no building inspector. You would not believe how low our taxes are.

The historical record shows that voters in our county almost always vote against new tax proposals. Our county commissioners understand from the get-go that they have a steep uphill battle making any "improvements." Schools, roads, a small sheriff's department, a jail no sane criminal ever wants to return to, and the bare minimum number of county employees necessary to meet state requirements. That's it. I bought our land in 1976—the property taxes are lower today than they were back then.

Some rural areas, especially those close to cities, provide and charge for almost as many services as the cities. Just remember: if you get more services, you pay for them. And in the case of planning, zoning, and building officials, loss of freedom. Your choice.

Property taxes vary substantially from county to county. Unlike income and sales taxes, the lion's share of which goes to state governments, revenues from property taxes are split 96 percent to local governments and only 4 percent to the state. Fees and miscellaneous revenues are more evenly split, with 57 percent going to local governments and the remaining 47 percent to the state (USDA, AR-31, June 1993).

State sales taxes range from zero to nine percent. Counties and municipalities often add to this. Local officials can give you the rates.

States that do not charge state income taxes have to make up that loss by charging more someplace else. New Hampshire is an example of a state that does not tax income or (most) retail sales. Sound good? In *Country Careers* Jerry Germer states that it is not uncommon to have a New Hampshire property tax bill of $3,600 or more on a $100,000 home.

Mark your criteria list according to your specific needs and desires for services—and taxes. Remember: the best tax is the one not due. This is also the time to write your needs and preferences for electricity, telephone, and radio and TV reception. Review chapter 11—*Cost of living* if necessary.

The art of taxation consists in so plucking the goose
as to obtain the largest amount of feathers with the least amount of hissing.

JEAN BAPTISTE COLBERT

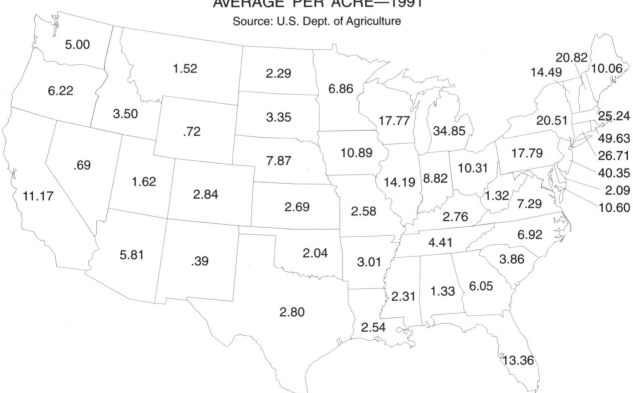

AGRICULTURAL REAL ESTATE TAXES
AVERAGE PER ACRE—1991
Source: U.S. Dept. of Agriculture

Downtown Oklahoma City, 1889, just after the opening of the Cherokee Strip to homesteaders

20
To build
or not to build

Buying unimproved property
versus buying improved property

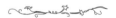

*At a certain season of our life
we are accustomed to consider every spot
as the possible site of a house.*

HENRY DAVID THOREAU

Unimproved land

f your dream includes building a house, then buying bare land may
be on your mind. An alternative which gives more property
choices is to buy land with an old house on it that you can live in
while you build. If the place is really old it probably will not add
appreciably to the land cost, especially on a larger parcel. A caveat—
the existing house may be sitting on the choicest building site on the
entire acreage. That was our dilemma—take it down, move it, or rebuild it?

Another option is to buy a mobile home for temporary living during
construction. Once your home is built you may be able to sell the mobile unit for
nearly as much as you paid for it. If you choose this route you will have to provide
temporary electric, telephone, water, and waste lines.

Buying undeveloped land will require additional research and inspections. You must ensure the availability of water, electricity, and telephone service. This will mean talking to local well drillers about the cost of a well and pressure system and the odds on finding good water within a reasonable depth. You will want to verify this information by talking to adjacent landowners. If you are not yet comfortable with the concept of a composting toilet, local backhoe operators can tell you the cost and probable effectiveness of a septic system. Some soils have inadequate drainage characteristics; you may need a percolation test. You need to ensure that you will have legal ingress and egress rights. There may be building permit costs and requirements. You will need to check for zoning restrictions to make sure you can do with the land what you wish and to determine the cost and time required for doing it.

Part of the foregoing may not apply if you buy a lot in an existing subdivision or town. But you must check zoning laws for uses permitted, building codes, and whether there is an architectural review board that must approve your plans. In some subdivisions you must build within certain size and style guidelines and you even may only be allowed to paint your castle an authorized color. Of course, to my mind, if any of these conditions exist you are not in real country.

In addition to getting the design you want, one of the big advantages of building a new home is that you can use modern materials and technology. Home energy conservation technology has made great progress in the last few years and can greatly enhance your comfort and lower the cost of maintaining a comfortable climate inside your home.

Building materials will cost as much and maybe more than in the city because of trucking costs. The wages of rural craftspeople are less than their city kin and often less than they are worth. In our county, you can hire a good plumber or electrician for $10 per hour. Carpenters get between $5 and $10, depending on experience and skill level. If you are not ready to wear the hat of general contractor you will need to pay someone to fill this role.

If you decide to build, do so within the time frame required by the Infernal Revenooer Service to avoid paying godawful capital gains taxes on the sale of your present home. Their rules tend to change irregularly, so read a book, call your accountant, or—ugh—contact the I.R.S. for current regulations.

Improved property considerations

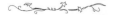

No house should ever be on a hill or on anything.
It should be of the hill. Belonging to it.
Hill and house should live together
each the happier for the other.
FRANK LLOYD WRIGHT

Rural residences range from ultra-modern dwellings to old farmhouses unburdened with plumbing or wiring. Electricity did not make it to some rural counties until the 1950s. Inadequate and improper wiring is a serious fire threat and should be upgraded before use.

Buying property with a well-designed modern home is most costly but will give you quality and convenience. The two primary reasons for buying land with old houses are low price and atmosphere. Old farmhouses are typically given little value by the local tax assessor, real estate appraisers, and sellers and buyers. In many cases that is appropriate, as the cost of bringing them up to modern standards can be substantial. Most of these old places are uninsulated, have inadequate electrical wiring, inadequate or nonexistent plumbing, may have a colony of bats living in the attic, and will probably leak in the lightest rain. Most important, the foundation may be deficient.

They also have architectural character. Heart. The atmosphere of an old place can be steadying, reassuring, quieting, can be a powerful influence on how you feel about living in that place.

An existing house means that certain necessities are already in place. An existing road saves the cost of paying a bulldozer or grader operator to put one in. A good existing water supply system takes away the possibility of drilling a dry hole and the cost of drilling, pump, pressure tank, and plumbing. Electricity already to the house means a substantial savings over having to contract with the local utility to bring it in or buying and installing a home generating system. It also means the poles are in place, so telephone lines may be installed if they are not there.

Where there is an existing house, there also are likely to be outbuildings. An old barn, garage, root cellar, or workshop can add a lot to the utility of any property. And then there are the smaller evidences of human habitation. Existing or old garden spots. Flower beds. Fruit and nut trees. All these and more may be present on an existing homestead.

As with much in life, making the decision of buying improved or unimproved land is something of a weighing act. Quality versus character. Convenience versus cost. The cost factor will change if you have construction skills and want to use them. Most important are your feelings. You probably already have a preference for building or buying an existing house. My purpose here is to alert you to the appropriate considerations so that your choice will be informed.

So now, on your criteria worksheet, write your needs and preferences for buildings—existing or to be built.

The Puritan. SEVEN ROOMS AND BATH

$2,504 MONTHLY PAYMENTS $40

The Conway. FIVE ROOMS AND BATH

$1,614 MONTHLY PAYMENTS $30

21
Prices

To know tomorrow,
first consider yesterday

he characteristics of value are demand, scarcity, transferability, and utility. Land and home prices are affected by more—they are influenced by interest rates, greed, fear, and inflation.

Real estate price movement used to be pretty predictable—always upward. There was a time in the 1970s when we didn't worry about paying top price for any property because within a few months the market value was up by ten percent. It was hard to go wrong. No longer. In the last few years, in both cities and rural areas, prices have been behaving like bad acrobats—leaping and crashing.

The breathtaking urban and suburban price jumps of the 1970s and 1980s were initiated by the demand of 76 million baby boomers born between the mid-1940s and the mid-1960s. Schools overflowed and the biggest school building boom of all time commenced. More high schools were built in America in 1967 than in any year before or since.

After finishing school the boomers got married and started rearing families. They wanted homes of their own just like Mom and Dad. Rural landscapes disappeared as pastures became sprawling subdivisions. During the 1970s the baby boomers created a huge demand—the subdividers provided the supply. Soon speculators—which many of us became—bought anything they could get for a low down payment and rented it out, putting up with plugged-toilet-in-the-middle-of-the-night calls because they knew they were going to become wealthy if they hung on long enough. In the early 1980s we suffered a recession. Then in the middle and late 1980s the market went crazy as the last of the boomers and the speculators made a final run.

The conditions of the 1970s created a new home-ownership paradigm. A home was no longer a treasured place that would stay in the family for generations. A home was now an investment. Traditional home ownership values were replaced by portfolio enhancement considerations.

The population bulge that is the baby boom market force has moved to the right side of the graphs. In the mid-1990s boomers are aged roughly 30 to 50 and most have already bought their first home. Today's women are waiting longer to have children and are having fewer of them. The demand for first homes, the foundation that holds up the house of real estate, has weakened and waned.

That's why part of the house is falling down. That's part of the reason for record foreclosures and the S&L wipeout—that and greed and changing market conditions influenced by world forces.

The world changed quickly in the late 1980s. All within a few years, the Berlin Wall thundered down, the world decided to take a well-deserved depression break,

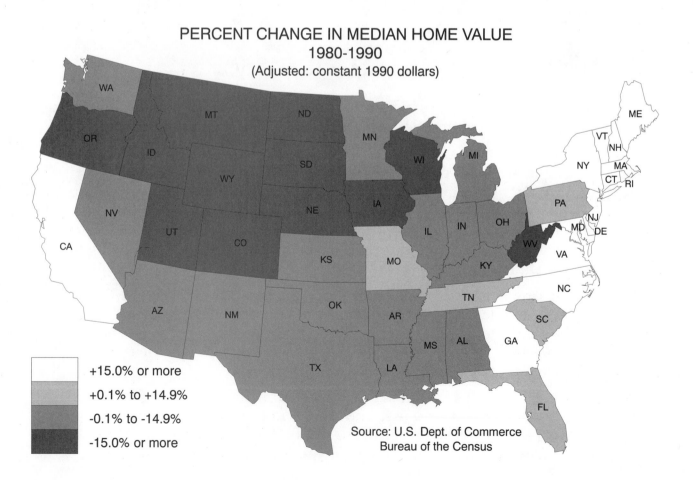

PERCENT CHANGE IN MEDIAN HOME VALUE
1980-1990
(Adjusted: constant 1990 dollars)

+15.0% or more
+0.1% to +14.9%
-0.1% to -14.9%
-15.0% or more

Source: U.S. Dept. of Commerce
Bureau of the Census

and the Cold War melted and evaporated.

All but the fiercest hawks conceded that Star Wars was history. All but the blind noticed the national debt, the S&L depositor rape, a prolonged national recession, and the absence of an identifiable evil enemy. Desert Storm proved that the U.S. is more than adequately armed to deal with second-rate military forces. And so the feds closed military bases and canceled contracts for planes, missiles, and military R&D. California, the seventh most productive political unit in the world, paid the price. The financial earthquake continues to rumble. Inflated home equities—

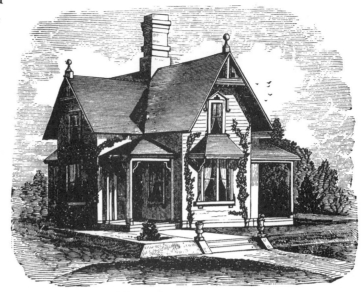

Proposed design for a cottage to cost $1,800.

paper fortunes—are disappearing like designer ice cubes in cappuccino.

Prices are not reacting equally throughout the land. Not all areas were dependent on defense. Certain hot spots like Washington, D.C., and Houston caught fire. Houston laid claim to becoming the capital of the world or something.

So where are we? Is nothing about the real estate market dependable anymore? Are all the old rules out the window? No. Everything still acts and reacts as it did before. It's all predictable. Not an easy task, but possible. It's still a matter of supply and demand, interest rates, inflation, and greed. But market factors change much more quickly than ever before, and the predicting business has become a guessing game.

So what's a hopeful buyer to do? Well, it depends on why, where, and how you are buying. You can either buy according to your time desires or according to your financial criteria. Hard to believe but true, there are many areas where slow, steady growth is

Proposed design for a small frame cottage to cost $2,000.

still the norm. Those are good places to live if you still have to work. And prices are still within reason.

Rural property prices today

Prices for farmland, which includes forest land, peaked in 1981. Since then they have plummeted. The average value of U.S. farmland in 1992 was $685 per acre.

Rural home sites and small acreages for homesteads may be more or less expensive per acre than land suited for full-scale farming, depending on location, demand, and seller motivation. A scan of United National Real Estate's winter 1994 catalog *United Country* revealed the following:

- Arkansas: 3 B/R, 1.5 bath home, storage buildings, pond, three acres—$58,750.
- Colorado: 46 acre valley, well, no house, 20 minutes to metropolis—$66,000.
- Georgia: 2 B/R, 1.5 bath home on five acres, $45,000.
- Idaho: 80 acres, good soil, creek, one hour to Jackson Hole—$75,000.
- Kentucky: 109 acres, hilly, wooded, spring, fronts creek, 10 minutes to county seat—$29,000.
- Minnesota: 3 B/R home on 8 acres, 5 miles to town—$39,000.
- Missouri: Completely remodeled 3 B/R 2-story on 13 acres, barn, pond—$59,900.
- New Hampshire: 3 B/R 2-story on 43 acres—20 open, rest wooded, stone walls, brook—$139,500.
- New York: Renovated 100-year-old Greek revival 4 B/R home on 110 acres of tillable [land], pasture, woods, ponds—$68,000.
- Ohio: Old 4 B/R home on 300 acres, open and wooded, 1/2 mile creek frontage, 8-acre lake, springs—$129,000.
- South Carolina: 2 B/R cabin on 24 acres overlooks 12-acre fishing lake, two miles to town—$120,000.
- Tennessee: Trout and catfish farm on 33 acres, 3,000 gpm springs, 8 ponds, concrete raceways, buildings—$125,000.
- Virginia: Cabin beside big spring-fed stocked pond, wooded 40 acres, nine miles to town—$50,000.

Splashing cold water on your face may restore you to the moment. If that doesn't work, consider that all these properties have probably sold by now.

Future prices

Guessing the speed of urban and suburban real estate price movement is a high-stakes game intensely played by investors, bankers, and developers. My personal bet is that there will be a ten-to-twenty year period of undulating adjustment while inflated urban prices meet the effect of rural migration, immigration, and the reality of global economic forces. Until NAFTA, GATT, the EEC, and other alliances have shown their influence, predicting city prices is a crapshoot.

What's the future for rural real estate prices? Part of the answer can be found by studying the census reports of the last 30 years. The 1980 census showed that the 40-year movement from country to city has reversed. Now in the last part of the 20th century, Americans find that cities are unhealthy, unsafe, and expensive. It is reasonable to predict that the movement to rural America will accelerate.

The picture of population migration from city to country is coming into focus. The movement is incremental. Central city dwellers move out to the suburbs. Suburbanites move out to small towns or to real country. Like the circular wave created by a disturbance in calm water, the movement is outward, ever outward.

University of Washington real estate professor Jack Lessinger studies these things. He predicts:

> Prices will rise in penturbia. They must, to reflect growing populations. . . . In newly developing counties, land values will rise, in metropolitan counties they will fall. Gradually, the two will become more equal in value.

Anticipating the demand for rural property, many people are now buying second homes as a hedge against higher prices and as a way of more easily making the transition from city to country.

Baby boomers are turning their backs on faded corporate dreams and are converting big-city equities into small-town cottages and rural businesses. Legions of ex-Californians have already moved to Washington, Oregon, Arizona, Colorado and Nevada. East coasters are filling Maine, Vermont, the Carolinas, Georgia, and Florida. Midwesterners are migrating to Wisconsin, Michigan, Missouri, Tennessee, Kentucky, and Arkansas. So—are country prices going up? Does a goose go barefoot?

Decision time

For most of us, price is an important criterion, but not the most important. My advice is to identify the area to which you are most drawn, check it out with both paper research and personal visits, and then buy as much land as you can afford.

If what you want is more than you can presently afford, a good compromise is to buy your country property now but then stay in the city at a high-paying job until the property is paid for. Every city refugee I have ever talked to agrees that having one's property paid for before moving to the country is a wise choice—often the one factor that determines the difference between a successful rural rooting and a retreat back to suburbia. Having 40 acres and independence in a few years is better than instant gratification but the pain of making property payments from lower country wages.

Another answer to affordability is to buy further "out." Prices decline as miles to the nearest city increase. And really inexpensive property can be had where the utility lines have not yet appeared. Utility line extensions are expensive but new photovoltaic technology makes generating one's own power a reasonable alternative. Cellular telephone service may soon make telephone lines unnecessary.

A common dilemma is choosing between more property later and less property sooner. The question of buying more land but then spending more time in the city to pay for it is a conundrum, one of those life decisions that makes one feel lonely. Talk it over with your family and be true to your strongest needs. There is no right or wrong answer. Take your time. You will note that price is down at the bottom of the criteria worksheet. That's because all the preceding factors are best decided without a dollar consideration. To buy your ideal property may mean having to wait before moving to it. I've lived through it and I think the goal is worth the price.

On your criteria worksheet, write what you now believe should be the maximum price you will pay for your property. Divide this price by the minimum acreage you desire and you will have the per-acre price that you can pay.

Sources

United National Real Estate
4700 Belleview
Kansas City, MO 64112
800-999-1020

Farmland price information is available from:
U.S. Department of Agriculture
National Agricultural Library
10301 Baltimore Boulevard
Beltsville, MD 20705

Suburban cottage designed to cost $2,500.

But what luck it is
to have one place in the world
where you know, whatever overtakes you,
if only you can make it there once more,
you have it all.

C.W. GUSEWELLE
FAR FROM ANY COAST

Part III
Finding
your ideal
country home

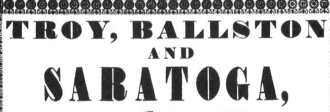

TROY, BALLSTON
AND
SARATOGA,

DAILY LINE OF
COACHES.

This line will commence running on the first day of July, leaving each place at half past 8 A. M. every day. Passengers wishing to travel from Saratoga to Lebanon Springs, will find this line not only the most expeditious but cheapest.

Passengers for Pittsfield, Northampton and Hartford by taking this line will dine at Troy, lodge at Pittsfield, and arrive at Hartford early the next day. The road is now put in the best order, and all that is now wanting is that liberality which the establishment merits.

☞ *Seats taken at G. W. Wilcox's, York House, Saratoga,* and at all the Principal Houses in Troy.

L. V. & J. B. REED, Proprietors.

J. S. KEELER, *Agent,* Troy.
S. DEXTER, *Agent,* Saratoga.

TROY, JUNE 25, 1834.

N. B. On the arrival of the ERIE or CHAMPLAIN, Parties can be accommodated with coaches to Saratoga or Ballston the same evening.

22
Regions, bioregions, and states

❦

In the United States there is more space
where nobody is than where anybody is.
That is what makes America what it is.

GERTRUDE STEIN

❦

Economic-cultural regions

alvin Beale, senior demographer at the U.S. Department of Agriculture, is said to have traveled in well over half of the nation's approximately 2,400 nonmetropolitan counties (Peter A. Morrison, *A Taste of the Country*). Perhaps because of his habit of getting into the field as much as possible he was the first to notice, in the late 1960s, that some metropolitan areas were losing population to the countryside. This was the beginning of a return to the trend of the first 200 years of our history—minus the 1940s, 1950s, and most of the 1960s, when machinery reduced the need for farm hands, and country people moved to industrial jobs in cities. Beale developed the following map and designations of twenty-six economic-cultural subregions.

26 Economic-Cultural Subregions
Developed by Calvin Beale,
Senior Demographer, U.S. Dept. of Agriculture

1. Northern New England • St. Lawrence
2. Northeastern Metropolitan Belt
3. Mohawk Valley and New York • Pennsylvania Border
4. Northern Appalachian Coal Fields
5. Lower Great Lakes Industrial
6. Upper Great Lakes
7. Dairy Belt
8. Central Corn Belt
9. Southern Corn Belt
10. Southern Interior Uplands
11. Southern Appalachian Coal Fields
12. Blue Ridge, Great Smokies, and Great Valley
13. Southern Piedmont
14. Coastal Plain Tobacco and Peanut Belt
15. Old Coastal Plain Cotton Belt
16. Mississippi Delta
17. Gulf of Mexico and South Atlantic Coast
18. Florida Peninsula
19. East Texas and Adjoining Coastal Plain
20. Ozark • Ouachita Uplands
21. Rio Grande
22. Southern Great Plains
23. Northern Great Plains
24. Rocky Mountains, Mormon Valleys, and Columbia Basin
25. North Pacific Coast
26. The Southwest

Northern New England-St. Lawrence

Density and prices are rising due to the influx of young professionals, environmentalists, and homesteaders, largely from the Boston-to-New York area. The region receives a lot of media attention and has developed a self-conscious rural/small-town culture. The main economic base is manufacturing, but many urban professionals have begun small businesses, and tourism is strong.

Northeastern Metropolitan Belt

The most densely populated nonmetropolitan area in the country stretches from southern Maine to northern Virginia, averaging about 140 persons per square mile. Most areas are within commuting distances to job centers. Many second-home and vacation homes in this region.

Mohawk Valley and New York, Pennsylvania Border

Similar conditions to the above. Very little real country—dominated by major cities of Buffalo, Rochester, Syracuse, Albany. High-tech industrial plants. Finger Lakes region.

Northern Appalachian Coal Fields

Long history of polluting industrial and mining operations combined with uncertain economy creates a negative condition.

Lower Great Lakes Industrial

Between and beyond the cities of Milwaukee, Chicago, Indianapolis, Detroit, and Cleveland are many small cities and towns. Heavy industrialization near the lakes. Rural areas are primarily concentrated agricultural operations—farm sizes are increasing.

Upper Great Lakes

Negligible agriculture, continued resource-based economy. Strong water-based recreational activity by tourists, second-homers, retirees, previous residents. Northern half of lower Michigan is growing rapidly, creating typical growth problems.

Dairy Belt

. Stable, predominately rural area of farms, influenced strongly in the western portion by the Minneapolis-St. Paul metro area.

Central and Southern Corn Belt

Over 85 percent of land is in farms. Many small towns. Moderate manufacturing. Population declining as farms are consolidated into agribusiness operations. Population decreasing.

Southern Interior Uplands

Thousands of small tobacco farms. The region has lately been characterized by a reduction in agriculture and an increase in manufacturing. Recreational activities have been increased by development of the Tennessee and Cumberland rivers. Large areas of rural conditions.

Southern Appalachian Coal Fields

Narrow, winding hollows and rugged hills, very little level land. Very rural, many small towns, poor. Beale notes that the deeply dissected Cumberland Plateau country of southern West Virginia, eastern Kentucky, and smaller parts of Virginia and Tennessee has been the classic area of white poverty in the United States. As coal prices go, so goes the economy. Heavily mined, the area has suffered severe environmental degradation. Stay far from water that may be contaminated by mining operations. The other caution is: bring money with you—this is a very poor place to make a living.

Blue Ridge, Great Smokies, and Great Valley

Eminent countryman Wendell Berry said that if he were free to move, he'd look in the mountains of western Virginia. (Donald McCaig, *American Homeplace*) That's a high recommendation. An area of magnificent scenery.

Southern Piedmont

Nearly half of all rural residents work in manufacturing. Economic emphasis is on textiles, furniture, new products. Agricultural activity is low and decreasing. Rural densities fairly high. Atlanta is the dominant economic influence.

Coastal Plain Tobacco and Peanut Belt

Rapidly changing area. Emphasis has shifted from agriculture (tobacco, peanuts, soybeans) to industry with substantial influx of companies seeking low labor costs. Wide distribution of business and residences. Nonmetropolitan population outnumbers the metropolitan population. North Carolina sometimes held up as the example of where we are headed demographically as a nation.

Old Coastal Plain Cotton Belt

Predominately agricultural. Substantial rural land with low population density.

Mississippi Delta

Rich soil, high pollution, and high poverty rates with distinct racial aspects.

Gulf of Mexico and South Atlantic Coast

Tobacco, peanuts, soybeans. Area has lost much population to industrial areas. High percentage of the widely-distributed rural population is black and poor.

Florida Peninsula

More than one-fourth of rural residents are 60 years old or older. Most of the area is dominated by retirement, recreation, and attendant service industries. Fast population growth since 1960s has substantially raised rural land prices and living costs. No letup in sight to continuing huge immigration rates by Americans, Cubans, Haitians, and others. Rural land is disappearing.

Ozark-Ouachita Uplands

The Ozarks area is the result of a great uplift from an ancient sea area. What we see today are not mountains, but hollows, carved by water over 250 million years—that which eroded more slowly we call hills. Hills and hollows are mostly covered with mixed hardwood forest plus pine and cedar. Generally poor, rocky soil, but garden sites are available in all but rocky hilltops and glades. Except for bottomland fields, farmland is predominately pastures. Old subsistence farm sites make ideal homesteads. Winters range from harsh in the north to mild in the south. Weather changes are common, depending on wind direction. "If ya don't like the weather, jist wait a few minutes." Rainfall averages 39-45 inches. Lots of springs, streams, ponds, lakes. Historic atmosphere. "Even the landscape fosters the feeling that you can simply glance over your shoulder into the past," wrote Phyllis Rossiter in *A Living History of the Ozarks*. Popular retirement destination, especially around man-made lakes. Low land and housing costs, both in small towns and boondocks. Ideal for those who love nature, a nourishing environment. Negatives include low wages, insects, occasional ice storms and tornadoes. Spotty population growth.

Rio Grande

A mixture of semi-arid to arid plateaus and mountains. About two-fifths of the population are Mexican-Americans; one-tenth Native Americans. Very low density. Water determines where agriculture is possible. Scattered mining activities. Southern New Mexico is attracting retirees. Economies are often supported by transfer payments. Santa Fe has social friction between poor natives and rich immigrants.

Southern and Northern Great Plains

Sparse and declining population. Small towns struggle to survive. Declining groundwater supplies for irrigation may dictate bleak future economic picture.

Rocky Mountains, Mormon Valleys, and Columbia Basin

Dominant Mormon influence in Utah and surrounding edges of other states is being diluted by continued immigration. Economy is basically agricultural—ranching, dairying, irrigated crops, and dry farming—plus coal, oil, gas, and uranium mining. Strong recreational economy around Lake Powell and national parks in southern Utah. Much of the region is very dry.

North Pacific Coast

Heavy rainfall, mild climate, timber, lush ocean coast, valleys, mountains. Timber industry future is uncertain as lumbermen and environmentalists struggle for control. Agriculture flourishes in Willamette River Valley. "Cloud Belt" image shows that Sunbelt is an imperfect synonym for population growth. Strong immigration has caused resentment among Washington and Oregon residents who now discourage immigrants, especially those from California.

The Southwest

Las Vegas growth continues at very high rate. Phoenix growth is strong. Arizona, southern California, and southern Nevada continue to attract retirees. California is suffering from defense industry cutbacks. Strong Asian and Mexican immigration. Substantial native-born American outmigration to Rocky Mountain area. Agribusiness operations in San Joaquin and Sacramento valleys continue to poison groundwater. North-versus-south water battles continue.

Bioregions

*The valley in which we lived was designed by nature
as an isolated, self-contained economic and social unit . . . .*

HELEN & SCOTT NEARING
LIVING THE GOOD LIFE

In *Dwellers in the Land: The Bioregional Vision,* Kirkpatrick Sale says the word bioregion was

> first propagated by writer Peter Berg and ecologist Raymond Dasmann . . . working through an organization called Planet Drum [see Resources below] and a newspaper irreverently called *Raise the Stakes,* who brought the concept to a wider audience.

On the matter of definition, Sale offers:

> The natural region is the bioregion, defined by the qualities Gaea has established there, the *givens* of nature. It is any part of the earth's surface whose rough boundaries are determined by natural characteristics rather than human dictates, distinguishable from other areas by particular attributes of flora, fauna, water, climate, soils, and landforms, and by the human settlements and cultures those attributes have given rise to. The borders between such areas are usually not rigid—nature works of course with flexibility and fluidity—but the general contours of the regions themselves are not hard to identify by using a little ecological knowledge.

Sale wrote in 1985 that about forty bioregions had been identified across the North American continent. Examples of bioregions are the Ozarks Plateau, the Sonoran Desert, and the Central Valley of California. Within bioregions are distinct ecosystems, each contributing to and overlapping other systems. Jim Robbins explains their process in *Last Refuge:*

> As charismatic as the grizzly bear is, however, there is a movement among conservationists and scientists to swing the spotlight away from animals with popular appeal, like the wolf, or bear or mountain lion, to recognize instead the myriad and intricately related life-forms—from microbes to fungus to insects to mammals—that make up an ecosystem. Research in the past few decades has shown just how dependent an ecosystem is on each part. Tiny microbial soil dwellers, like bacteria and fungi, decompose logs, grass and other organics into minerals that growing plants can use. . . . And so the goal of a sustainable ecosystem is not just to protect the grizzly bear habitat or wolf habitat, but to keep as much of the ecosystem intact as possible, to preserve biodiversity.

States and counties have artificial boundaries—bioregions have natural boundaries. This is readily apparent from an airplane—children (and perhaps a few adults) are confused to find no state boundaries on the ground. For our purposes here, we can use bioregions to identify our ideal area, but we use states and counties to gather information, as that is how we humans presently organize data.

The value of thinking on a bioregional level is that we consider natural conditions and natural laws. To fulfill our present mission—finding our ideal home place—we consider human conditions such as taxes, roads, utilities, and services, but our greatest consideration should be for the natural conditions of climate, landform, soil, vegetation, and water. Thinking in these terms will allow us to think beyond political boundaries during our search. This is a big change for most people, so I include the following information classified by states.

States

Come and visit us again. . . .
But for heaven's sake, don't come here to live.

TOM McCALL
WHEN HE WAS GOVERNOR OF OREGON

Every state has something special to recommend it but certain states are attracting most city-to-country migrants. Fast growth drives up prices and creates resentment by natives. Oregon and Washington residents most notably have lashed back at Californians invading their states. It is to be expected that natives or long-time residents of other states will have similar negative feelings against those whom they perceive are negatively affecting the quality of their places.

Since the 1960s, homesteaders and back-to-the-landers have been moving to rural parts of Missouri, Tennessee, Arkansas, North Carolina, Kentucky, Oregon, Washington, Wisconsin, Michigan, Oklahoma, Maine, Vermont, New York, West Virginia, Virginia, South Carolina, Minnesota, and Georgia. The Sun Belt—California, Arizona, Nevada, New Mexico, Texas, and Florida—has been attracting retirees for years. The Texas economy rollercoasts with oil prices but the hill country still attracts urban refugees. Florida has become expensive and crowded, and is humid in summer—still the sun lovers flock there. Colorado is the favorite destination of Californians looking for a Rocky Mountain high. Many of those who like big open spaces are choosing Idaho, Montana, and Wyoming. Most other states have pockets with outstanding geographic features. Water concerns are growing in the West—with the exception of western Oregon and Washington, most western states have inadequate water except along rivers, and even there water rights may preclude use by new settlers.

Retirement destinations are no longer limited to the popular stereotypes of Florida and the Southwest. Widespread in-migration has occurred in the Ozarks, the New England coast, the southern Blue Ridge, the Texas Hill Country, the Puget Sound area, the Upper Great Lakes, the Sierra Nevada foothills, western Oregon, east Texas, and the Tidewater areas of Maryland and Virginia. All of these locations involve dispersed settlement, and not merely aggregations of people in towns.

CALVIN BEALE

California is a special state. Blessed with multiple climates, landforms, and features, it seems an ideal place. It was. California is perhaps our clearest example of what happens to a place when too many people move there—over 30 million humans have changed Eden into an overcrowded, overpriced nightmare. Businesses and individuals are leaving the central and southern parts of the state for the same reasons—high prices, high taxes, pollution, too much government, and dangerous social conditions. Northern California has some very nice low-density country but residents there pay high fees and taxes needed to keep the floundering giant financially afloat.

Use the previous map to indicate your initial regional preferences—those states that fit your topographic and climate criteria. You may find you are attracted to several. Mark them all.

Resources

Chambers of commerce

You can find chamber of commerce listings in the annual *World Wide Chamber of Commerce Directory,* available in most libraries. You can also find chambers through the U.S. Chamber of Commerce, 1615 H Street NW, Washington, DC 20062, or phone them at 301-468-5128. Most chambers will send you packets of info including maps and real estate company listings.

State chambers of commerce and tourism departments

State chambers and tourism departments are usually located in each state capital. A good source of maps, tourist guides, demographics, climate information, industry, taxes, etc. Tell them what you want. The volume of material you receive will show the priority placed on attracting tourists and residents.

Real estate company

United National Real Estate
P.O. Box 11400, 4700 Belleview
Kansas City, MO 64112
800-999-1020
United National catalogs contain a huge number of available country properties. Their motto is: "No one knows the country like we do," and it seems appropriate. I found my property through a United affiliate in 1976. Area catalogs showcase rural properties listed by their affiliates in 41 states. The national catalog *United Country* is available for $4.95 by mail. Allow three to four weeks for delivery or send $7.95 for first-class delivery, which they say will get it to you in seven to ten days. They accept credit card orders by phone. Or you can receive the catalog free of charge at any of their affiliated offices. After you have decided on an area, call them and they will send a free regional catalog which will list their various affiliated offices in many towns. They also publish *American Treasures*, a catalog of historical properties, many of which are listed on the National Register. *American Treasures* costs $3.95, whether you pick it up or have it delivered by pony express.

Bioregional organization

Planet Drum
Box 31251
San Francisco
Shasta Bioregion, CA 94131
Source for information on the bioregional movement.

Books

- The *National Atlas of the United States of America* contains 765 maps and charts. It is out of print but can be found in many public libraries.

- Encyclopedias are a source of, well, encyclopedic information. Each of the major sets has substantial entries on each state.

- Downing, Joan, editor. *America The Beautiful*. Chicago: Childrens Press, 1990. This is a set of books, one for each state. Although classified as juvenile literature I found them in the adult book section of my library, and the ones I have used appear to be well researched, written, and designed, totally suitable for adults. Of course I'm just a large, semi-old child. Subjects include geography, history, government, economy, industry, culture, and population density, distribution, and growth.

- Sale, Kirkpatrick. *Dwellers in the Land: The Bioregional Vision*. San Francisco: Sierra Club Books, 1985.

- Shattuck, Alfred. *The Greener Pastures Relocation Guide: Finding the Best State in the United States for You*. Englewood Cliffs, New Jersey: Prentice-Hall, 1984.

Essential country equipment #7—the turkey

This is the original model much favored by Ben Franklin as the finest example of American qualities: keen eyesight, superb hearing, and so smart it could tutor Harvard Law School students. (The currently favored chesty model was developed by breast-fetish bio-engineers.) Specimens of this classic design may be found in wooded areas around homesteads except from mid-November to early January—during this period they vacation in Puerto Vallarta.

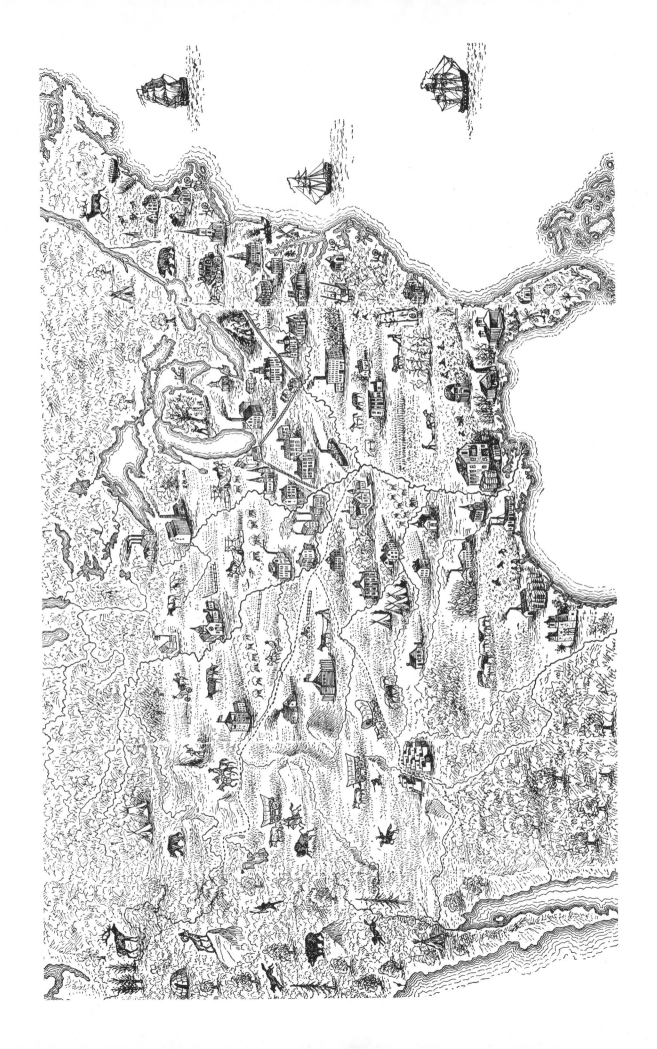

23
Real country, boondocks, and old subsistence farms

I am speaking to city people.
This leads me to say that there are
two kinds of country and of country life,
—the country of the city man and the country of the countryman.
These prospects are wholly unlike, for the country is seen
from opposite points of view, and with different preconceived ideas.
The city man looks outward to the country:
it is his respite and release.
The countryman is part of the country:
it is his realm and his support.

LIBERTY HYDE BAILEY
THE OUTLOOK TO NATURE

Real country—a condition of the mind

eal country—for some, it is the land just past the last city bus stop, the
last suburb beyond the previous last suburb. The single field of
grazing cattle between two towns that have not yet grown together.
For others it is further out—the area variously called exurbs,
rhuburbs, slurbs, fringe areas, or the edge. For still others, it means
outback, bush, or boondocks.

Your concept of real country is unique to you and probably dictates not only distance from city but certain conditions and features. Population density, size of property holdings, and types of human activities are all factors that contribute to the sense of real country.

Jack Lessinger coined the word penturbia to describe the fifth area of American development, "small cities and towns, and subdivisions, homesteads, industrial and commercial districts interspersed with farms, forests, lakes and rivers." In some places the interspersion has become very thin. The so-called farm country in Massachusetts has a density of between 100 and 250 people per square mile, only 2.5 to 6.4 acres per person. Bostonians may consider that to be real country.

Most of us would agree that real country means an area of sparse population. Then we would argue about the definition of sparse. For my wife and me, it is being surrounded by hundreds of acres of forested hills and hollows, the nearest small town 14 miles and 30 minutes away and the nearest modest shopping center a one-hour drive. (In addition to our large garden we have a large pantry, a large freezer, and a root cellar.) There is nearly half a mile of thick woods between us and our nearest neighbor.

The state maps in appendix B show the rural areas in each state. Areas indicated by shading have a population density of less than 50 people per square mile (or even less in some cases), which equates to at least 12.8 acres per person. For some of us, this is too crowded. For others, after living in a concrete jungle it may feel like the wild frontier.

Why did I set the limit at 50 people per square mile? Well, that's how I found the data, in *America The Beautiful*. How the people who produced that wonderful set of books acquired that data is a mystery to me—census takers could never create those non-county lines. I visualize a wide line of trustworthy Boy Scouts dependably marching through each county, honestly counting people. "Good morning, ma'am, you're 87." "What! How impertinent!" (Courtesy is in the mind of the oath taker.)

As urban centers have grown outward, country has become closer to more people. Real country today may be less than an hour's drive from towns with major schools, hospitals, shopping centers, and cultural facilities. Some of the best of these towns are small state capitals and college towns.

Boondocks

Boondocks—what a wonderful word. In Tagalog, the primary Indonesian language of the Philippines, *bundok* means mountain. Etymologists persuade that bundok was combined with sticks (as in "out in the sticks") to get boondocks, which now means a remote rural area. And you thought you were only going to learn geography here.

Boondocks is a challenging word to work with. Is it: boondocks *are* serious country, or boondocks *is* serious country? It's at moments like this that I wish the

girl in front of me in high school English had not been so devastating. Well, they/it are/is. In the boondocks, four-wheel-drive vehicles are appropriate, as are supplies adequate for extended periods. Water is an issue. Considerations include lack of electricity and telephone. Other than wood, energy for heating and cooking is often imported. Photovoltaic charging systems currently available can make living in the boondocks much more comfortable. Lights, tools, radios, and even computers may now be powered by batteries recharged by the sun.

Boondocks land prices are usually very low. If you are proudly independent with a high level of country skills, and your idea of adequate space is similar to that expressed by Daniel Boone: "If I can see the smoke from my neighbor's fire, it is time to move," then the boondocks may be the place of your ideal home.

Unless you have lived in a primitive manner before, you might try camping in a remote area for a few weeks, better a few months, best a full year. Expect procuring water to be a substantial challenge. Without a well and electric pump, water sources may be limited to springs, streams, and lakes. Plan to purify. Take a lot of books. Take a close friend.

Abandoned small farms

According to the U.S. Department of Agriculture, the number of farms has dropped every year since 1950, from 5.6 million then to 2.1 million in 1992. Regrettably, none have dropped onto politicians' heads. In prime soil areas farm consolidation has occurred, and around cities many former farms are now shopping centers and subdivisions. Still, there are thousands of old subsistence farms in real country just waiting to be discovered. The former owners were generally too poor to use chemical fertilizers, herbicides, and pesticides, so the land is probably clean, although the family dumpsite will typically be found in some low spot.

These abandoned farms are often ideal country home places. Many may be found in Michigan, northern Wisconsin, southern Missouri, northern

Arkansas, Kentucky, Tennessee, and other southeastern states, particularly in hilly areas. They are often owned by city people who only occasionally visit "grandmother's farm."

I especially like old subsistence farms for many reasons:
- They have land too poor and/or too hilly for agribusiness operations.
- They have established water sources.
- They are in communities of small farms.
- They are often reasonably priced.
- They have a set of buildings which, even if ramshackle, can be used for temporary shelter and storage.
- They have old garden sites, maybe fruit or nut trees.
- They have history.
- They have nostalgic surprises: remnants of stone walls or split-rail fences; family cemeteries; old-fashioned rose bushes; daffodils that in spring appear in a row where a long-ago fence protected a farmwife's flower garden from chickens, cows, horses, hogs, and dogs.

If all of the above is too wild for you, the next chapter on small towns and villages may include *your* definition of country.

*The new heartland can be seen
on the outer fringes of metropolitan areas;
around small towns far removed from the large cities;
along rivers, coastlines, and reservoirs;
near recreation and retirement areas;
on marginal farmland; along country roads;
and on remote land that is barren
except for its physical beauty.*

JOHN HERBERS
THE NEW HEARTLAND: AMERICA'S FLIGHT BEYOND THE SUBURBS
AND HOW IT IS CHANGING OUR FUTURE

Sugarhill Farm, Woodstock, Vermont, 1885.

24
Small towns and villages

Where all the women are strong,
all the men are good-looking,
and all the children are above average.

GARRISON KEILLOR

f your ideal place is a small town or village, then this chapter is for
you. The quality and the character of small towns, the likelihood
of change, and the nature of small-town communities are all
factors that bear consideration.

Small-town change

It is tempting to romanticize small towns and life therein—easy to be
influenced by nickel-ice-cream nostalgia. Some of us grew up in a small town;
most of us are only a generation or two away from one. Memories persist of clean,
uncrowded, crime-free communities, of warm evenings on front porches, of kissing
giggling girls (or boys) behind lilac bushes. Those who are a generation away
undoubtedly have heard family stories about small-town life, aka "the good old
days."

Sadly, I find that I cannot generalize about small towns. I'd like to say that they
reflect our heritage, our roots, whence cometh the values that are the foundation
of our national soul. I'd like to say that they exude a sense of community. I'd like
to point out that small town inhabitants can be counted on to smile and wish us a

good morning or good afternoon—and mean it. I'd like to say that small towns are like good parents and grandparents, a dependable source of trust, support, and encouragement. In my fantasy wish-list, small towns change their human faces with births and deaths, but their hearts keep the same predictable beat.

Well, some do, some can, some are, and some will. But many small towns are no longer trustworthy. Too often today, in the time a person gets to know one well, it changes into something else. Osha Gray Davidson reviewed two books relating to current dilemmas of small towns *(Mixed Media, Utne Reader* May/June 1993). In the first we are presented with part of the picture:

> Some rural communities are being destroyed by economic decline, others by infusions of prosperity.

(Raye Ringholz, *Those little town blues: Voices from the Changing West).* In the second:

> Once-stable villages in New Hampshire, Connecticut, Vermont, and upstate New York are being "pureed by progress"—blended into an increasingly diffuse, culturally ambiguous, and urban-influenced mass.

(Ron Powers, *Far From Home: Life and Loss in Two American Towns).*

The price of a good community is eternal vigilance.
You get the master plan and you think it's done. But it isn't done.
It's a living document. The community is changing every day
and somebody has to be paying attention all the time.

Terrell J. Minger
Robert Redford Institute for Resource Management

The destruction of small-town qualities has become a common lament. The condition is widespread but it is far from universal. Change is always inevitable, but destruction of community is not. The lifeblood of a small town, of a community, is the people. As with marriage and friendship, good conditions prevail when the participants are motivated by love and respect to protect, preserve, and enhance. Small towns preserve their heart and their health when residents make it happen. Many communities have adopted slow-growth or no-growth laws, but that's only part of the solution. Any community is composed of all its factors and features and unless attention is paid to them all something inevitably will go awry.

Bona-fide small-town atmosphere is the result of generations of people who have lived by the demanding natural rules of a place. The elements of small-town quality are natural beauty, stable economy, strong community, low population density—and time. Only in low-density beautiful, natural places is the human spirit preserved and nourished. Compacting people causes certain social disease. Again, never forget—*all cities once were villages.*

The one small-town quality that does not change

*So live that you wouldn't be ashamed to sell
the family parrot to the town gossip.*

WILL ROGERS

There is one thing that is constant in all small towns. It was true in Ben Franklin's time and it will be true when our great-great-grandchildren are trimming their lawns with programmed-solar-powered-beam-guided grass zappers. HOLD THE PRESSES! As the news anchorpersons say: "This just in"—my just-received Late Spring 1994 *Real Goods* catalog (see Real Goods Trading Corporation under *Alternative technology* in *Resources* at the end of the chapters) includes "The First Solar Robotic Lawnmower." I kid you not.

> The Solar Turtle IS reality, a solar-powered robotic lawn mower . . . utilizes an
> electronic brain programmed by fuzzy logic . . . .

Un-bloody-believable. You set the thing out in the lawn and forget about it. When the sun charges its batteries it goes to work at up to 20 inches per second. Automatic height adjustment. Grass too wet? Not to worry. The turtle takes a nap until conditions become optimally dry.

Well I guess that proves the saying: "What the mind can conceive we can achieve." I wrote what I thought was a far-out example of future technology a few months ago and here some Belgium engineers have made me as outdated as the concepts of "waste not—want not" and waiting for sex until the second date.

So where were we? Oh yeah: the one thing that is constant in all small towns, and will last longer than anything of which *I* can conceive, is this: small-town life is not very private. Someone once noted that in a small town a car with the wrong directional signal blinking endangers no one because everybody knows where the driver is really going.

*A small town is a place where everyone knows
whose check is good and whose husband is not.*

SID ASCHER

When everyone you meet smiles and greets you, when the bank employees all address you by your name, when your neighbors put out your trash cans because you forgot, it is not because these are members of a superior species living on a higher plane than mere city dwellers. It is at least partly because everyone knows that the least slight, the most minimal of neighborly indiscretions will become instantly known by everybody in town and remembered for at least three generations. "Why yes, my dear, don't you know—he's the grandson of Robert Booboo—you remember—he's the one who didn't even *notice* poor, old Mr. Wretched struggling with his stuck gate that bad winter of ought-seven, and poor, old Mr. Wretched like to have had a heart attack. Mmm, yes, that was his *grandfather*."

Ayup, that there's the gate old Mr. Wretched like to done hisself in on and Robert Booboo just passed right on by without a howdy-do.

In some ways our county (about 9,500 population) functions rather like a small town. A friend of ours who lives two ridges to the north once appeared on a television show featuring his wood carvings. A few weeks later he received a letter from a viewer in Arizona addressed to "The wood carver" at the wrong post office—but in our county. That was enough to do the job.

We live 14 miles from our nearest town. We do our banking there and buy as many things as we can, considering selection and prices. We get to that town on average about twice each month. We know few people there. Yet I have been stopped on the sidewalk and addressed by name by total strangers. The ensuing conversations left no doubt that the strangers knew much more about me than my name.

I can't say that I mind living in a place with these conditions. Now if I lived right in town, I might. Think about it. If you cherish anonymity for your virtues or your vices, you may not be comfortable in a small town.

Suburbs in disguise—"towns" to avoid

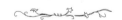

*Everybody when they come to the suburbs
they want the trees and bunnies and birds, okay?
And that's why we put two swans out there and
feed the damn ducks so all the frigging geese
and ducks come around and people say,
"Gee, I work out in a place where they have
paths and running tracks, ponds, birds.
Do you have a running track where you work?"*

DEVELOPER TO AUTHOR JOEL GARREAU
IN *EDGE CITY: LIFE ON THE NEW FRONTIER*

Caution: New Towns are designed to seduce you. The design is elegant but flawed. The concept is ancient—the dream of creating a perfect human environment in a natural setting has persisted throughout history. The most famous recent attempts began with Reston, Virginia in 1962, continued with Columbia, Maryland in 1967, and include Jonathan, Minnesota and Irvine, California—a town fast becoming a city. The idea of planned cities goes back at least to Miletus, Greece, which was planned during the fourth century B.C. During the Middle Ages, over 400 new towns were built in England, Wales, and Gascony, as well as about a dozen in Switzerland and Germany. But I digress— again.

The current craze in urban planning is the effort to villagize the suburbs. San Francisco architect Peter Calthorpe is impressing his Transit-Oriented Development design on Laguna West, an Apple-computer facility near Sacramento. Calthorpe advocates dense communities where cars are passé. He envisions linking workers to their jobs with light rail transportation. A noble plan. But the number of riders a light-rail system needs per day to be cost effective is seven thousand and the probable number of car commuters who will change to rail has been determined to be 12 percent. So, to make light rail cost effective requires fourteen and a half million square feet of office space—more than downtown St. Louis or Cincinnati.

Miami architects Andres Duany and Elizabeth Plater-Zyberk, of Seaside, Florida fame, promote their Traditional Neighborhood Development, codes that any jurisdiction might adopt. TND mandates mixed-use developments designed as small towns. On paper the effort is laudable: de-emphasize the auto; build paths

Excuse me, aren't you Robert Booboo's grandson?

so people can walk to work and shopping; create small parks where inhabitants can talk and play chess. To ensure atmosphere, the codes require white picket fences and ornamented front porches. The imagery is seductive, a developer's dream. Nostalgia sells, and big investment money is betting that the concept will reap profits.

These are designer towns, suburbs with psychology, homes with chutzpah, nouveau nostalgia, yuppie high camp. The purported goal is to de-emphasize the automobile and encourage a village atmosphere. The result is artificial villages— the product of a "you can have a brand new 'grandma's town' and we're prepared to give it to you for a price" marketing strategy. As always, the purpose is to generate profits, which the high density almost guarantees.

The homes are expensive. And there part of the absurdity is found. These counterfeit communities are being built for those who yearn so strongly for the qualities of small towns that they are willing to enslave themselves to large monthly mortgage payments to fake it in a suburb. To parody an old song—I owe,

Suburban house, about 1850. Daguerrotypist unknown.

I owe, so off to work I go. How can there be high-quality life with employment slavery? There cannot be. The "quality" is a veneer.

Developers and bureaucrats say New Towns are noble attempts to create a quality environment. However clever the words, the primary goal is profit. The analogy with agribusiness is compelling: give consumers what they have been conditioned to want: a colorful, blemish-free product—and to hell with nutrition.

In *New Towns: another way to live* Carlos C. Campbell states:
> Planning commissions and zoning boards are nothing more than smoke screens for the real decision makers—bankers, politicians, and bureaucrats.

New Towns tend to be heavy on control. They often embody numerous associations, councils, and institutions to control social conditions. In the view of city planners, the ideal town has ideal control of its less-than-ideal citizens.

Main Street is another consumer hot button—witness the success of Main Street at Disneyland. Husband-and-wife team Duany and Plater-Zyberk have transformed Mashpee Commons, a Cape Cod shopping mall, into an old-fashioned Main Street. In Kentland, Maryland, they redesigned a regional shopping center to emulate the nature of a traditional town square.

The allure of small town realness is irresistible. Millions of tourists travel to small towns each year to taste that realness. Quick quiz question: how many artificial villages will become tourist destinations? Joel Garreau suggests some guiding questions:
> Will we ever be proud of this place . . . will we ever feel—for this generation and the ones that follow—that it's a good place to be young? To be old? To fall in love? To have a Fourth of July parade? Will it ever be the place we want to call home?

New Towns and Edge Cities, like suburbs of any name, exacerbate the serious issues of water scarcity, sewage treatment, and social tension. They are the yuppie hot spots of today, the slums of tomorrow—good ideas come too late. Inner-city sickness spreads outward in expanding concentric shock waves. Suburban sprawl is the leading edge of city cancer—artificial villages are simply compacted suburbs more prettily packaged.

With regard to suburban development, Jack Lessinger is clear:
> In our vast inventory of land, suburban real estate is the one type least suited to the emerging consensus. . . . *Suburbia will go down with the ship*—along with the entire system of the Little King's consumption economy. . . . we will see miles of 2,500-square-foot behemoths, their wide windows broken and patched, their many rooms divided and subdivided into nondescript apartments, and, betraying the indignities of poverty, the former proud front lawns will be littered by junk automobiles and broken furniture.

One last example of the efforts to build a perfect town: Visionary architect Paolo Soleri has designed and, with the labor of students is building a self-contained community in the desert north of Phoenix. An apse-shaped work area, housing, restaurant, gift shop, swimming pool, gardens. A "town" in a sprawling concrete monolith. I have visited Arcosanti three times over the last twenty years. It doesn't seem to be happening very fast. The main source of funds appears to be tour admissions and the beautiful bronze wind chimes the students cast. It takes a lot of chimes to build future-town.

Avoid fast change

Change is irresistible and small towns are susceptible. If you desire an old-fashioned small-town atmosphere that will persevere, research population trends and growth plans before committing to any place. Ask the mayor, county clerk, newspaper editor, and bank president if they know of any companies considering a move to your chosen hamlet. If large companies move in they will cause rapid change. It is a matter of percentages. If your target town has a present population of two or three thousand and a big company builds a factory or headquarters there that will employ several hundred, the odds are great that the essence of that place will quickly change. Talking to key people in town will gauge local inclination toward fast growth, especially company headquarters, factories, and shopping malls—developments that can change and dominate the atmosphere of a small place.

Prosperity begets change. L.L. Bean has brought excessive success to Freeport, Maine. The mail-order giant's 90,000-square-foot store first only attracted shoppers and tourists. But the crowds attracted what locals call "Bean sprouts," over 100 new stores hawking everything from perfume to furniture. Today, more than 2.5 million shoppers per year produce traffic jams, thick exhaust, and escalating real estate prices.

Where to look for a small town

The North Central region has more small towns than any other U.S. area. Glenn Fuguitt of the University of Wisconsin has compiled data on nearly 5,600 incorporated towns of fewer than 2,500 population located in nonmetropolitan counties in this region. That is 30 percent of all incorporated places of all sizes nationwide.

Away from megalopoli, the Northeast is composed of hundreds of small towns, each separated from the next by woods and farms. The South and the Midwest have numerous towns that once served as commercial hubs for farms in their area. In many cases their role has changed but those that have survived often have great character. In the mountainous West many old mining towns have survived the depletion of the minerals that created them.

There are still many small towns with traditional values, strong community spirit, and a warm atmosphere created by the character of good people. The best choices are insulated from fast growth by distance, inferior roads, or topography— for instance, by being in a small valley with hills impossible to develop, or backed up to a river or lake with steep hills on the other side. Those that have limited space for growth are most likely to retain their present qualities.

College towns

Change is less likely in towns where the economic base is one of long-term commitment. Some of the nicest small towns are college towns. They have stable economies based on the college, allied "intellectual" enterprises, and service businesses. The country immediately surrounding these towns is also an excellent place to live. The population ebbs and flows with the scholastic year. The intellectual climate of the college generally sets the tone for community. It's a great place to raise children.

State capital towns, county seats

Small state capital towns tend to be conservative and stable. An employment base exists from the multiple state departments and with the various service industries that support them. To a lesser degree, the same is true of county seats.

Looking

A super way to discover small towns and villages is to spend time driving the back roads of your preferred area. Take your time. Get lost. Once you find a town that appears ideal talk to everyone you see. Have lunch. Use your criteria list and rate the town on how well it meets your needs. Subscribe to the local paper. Drive the surrounding area. Keep talking to people—beyond the natural beauty and architecture, the essence of a place is found in its people. If there is a library, read back issues of the newspaper—nothing will more quickly give you a picture of the social character of a place.

If you are unable to go to an area but would like to begin your search, write to the state chamber of commerce or board of tourism and tell them you may be interested in moving to their state. They will send you an information packet which will include a map. You can also contact real estate people in your areas of interest. United National Real Estate agents will send you brochures on available properties. If you would like to know more about a specific town, order a newspaper subscription. It will probably be a weekly. The local news, letters to the editor, social calendar, and political campaigns will give you instant insight into the values of that place.

Now make notes on your criteria worksheet.

*For any American who had the great and priceless privilege of being raised
in a small town there always remains with him nostalgic memories
of those days. And the older he grows the more he senses
what he owed to the simple honesty and neighborliness,
the integrity that he saw all around him in those days.*

DWIGHT D. EISENHOWER

Sources, resources, and recommended reading

Chambers of commerce

You can find local chambers through the U.S. Chamber of Commerce, 1615 H Street NW, Washington, DC 20062, or phone them at 301-468-5128. Most chambers will send you packets of information including maps and real estate company listings. Some rural chambers are so small they can't afford to mail information packages—perhaps an indication of a superior place to live. In that case you will have to rely on the state chamber.

Newspapers

Subscribe to the local newspaper and you will quickly check the pulse of the area. The best source for subscription information about each of the U.S.'s 1,651 daily newspapers is Editor & Publisher's *International Yearbook*. For information on the nearly 7,000 weekly papers, check out the *IMS Directory of Publications* or *Gale's Directory of Publications*.

Placing an ad in the Personals section of the classifieds requesting contact with others who have moved there from the city is a way to get information and maybe make friends—possibly a place to stay when you visit. Expect to hear from every real estate agent in the area.

Books

- Campbell, Carlos C. *New Towns: another way to live.* Reston, Virginia: Reston Publishing Company, 1976.

- Crampton, Norman. *The 100 Best Small Towns in America.* New York: Prentice-Hall, 1993.

- Fuguitt, Glenn V. and David L. Brown and Calvin L. Beale. *Rural and Small Town America.* New York: The Russell Sage Foundation, 1989.

- Garreau, Joel. *Edge City: Life on the New Frontier.* New York: Doubleday, 1991.

- Lessinger, Jack, Ph.D. *Regions Of Opportunity: A Bold New Strategy For Real Estate Investment With Forecasts To The Year 2010.* New York: Time Books, 1986.

- Ringholz, Raye C. *Little Town Blues: Voices From the Changing West.* Layton, UT, Gibbs Smith, 1992.

Everyone has deep in their heart
the old town or community where
they first went barefooted,
got their first licking, traded the first pocket knife,
grew up and finally went away
thinking they were too big for that Burg.
But that's where your heart is.

WILL ROGERS

In the country town we gain in contact with our neighbors.
We know people by the score, by the hundred. . . . Our affairs
become common with one another, our joys mutual, and even our
sorrows are shared. . . . It all makes life pleasantly livable.

WILLIAM ALLEN WHITE

GREAT LAND ENTERPRISE AT LUNAVILLE!

ROUSING OPPORTUNITY!

Five Hundred Acres on the Sunny Side of the Moon
to each Subscriber.

WITH LOTS OF ROCK FOR BUILDING PURPOSES!

When one half the stock is taken, an Atmospheric Engine will be erected in the crater of Popocatapetl to furnish refined air to the settlers, and a Steam Squirt will be placed on Goat Island to play water on the Moon, so that the inhabitants will have always enough—never too much, and never too little; thus avoiding the drouths and drenchings to which the earth's people are liable. Balloons also will be provided to start daily from different available points on the earth.

NOW IS THE TIME TO SUBSCRIBE!

25
Subdivisions

Land subdivisions, developments, projects,
retirement communities, planned unit
developments, destination resorts,
etc., etc., etc.

A few miles off the road is the site of a
planned community dating from the nineteen-sixties.
It was to have wide streets and a fountained square,
but construction was delayed and then indefinitely postponed.
Ghostless ghost town, it had been named Neptune City.

JOHN MCPHEE
BASIN AND RANGE

Land subdivisions

ural land subdivisions are typically very large acreages purchased by corporations and then subdivided into parcels, usually from one-half acre to ten acres in size. During the 1960s and 1970s, thousands of subdivisions were created on mountain, desert, or swamp land in Florida, California, Nevada, and other states. Most companies used slick advertising and powerful sales methods to sell the parcels to naive city people longing for a piece of country. The lots were priced at only a few thousand dollars. They were worth much less—with few exceptions they were essentially useless.

The Rockefeller Brothers Fund released a report in 1973 on *The Use of the Land*. It revealed:

> In 1971 an estimated 625,000 recreational lots were sold by over 10,000 subdividers. . . . For the nation as a whole, at least six recreational lots were sold in 1971 for each second home constructed. . . . In California, between 50,000 and 100,000 acres of rural land were subdivided annually in the late 1960s and early 1970s by recreational lot sellers. By 1971, however, houses had been built on only 3 percent of the lots sold in the previous decade.

The pitch was: "You're getting in on the ground floor—this area is going to boom—in a few years you'll make a killing!" Promised roads, utilities, services, and escalating values almost always failed to materialize. The lots, sold with enticingly low down payments and modest monthly payments (Those of us in legitimate real estate at the time used to joke: "Fifty dollars a month—forever!"), often were abandoned and sat vacant, available to anyone who paid the back taxes. As soon as the development company had taken the easy money, and before spending any of it on improvements, it either declared bankruptcy or simply disappeared. Today some of these rip-off developments can be seen from interstate highways in the western desert—they're the ones with big faded signs, barely discernible dirt roads, sometimes one or two small houses far out in the sagebrush.

Well, the feds received complaints—whew, did they ever!—and it is now more difficult for unscrupulous developers to make a dishonest buck. That is not to say that some aren't trying to relive their lucrative wayward youth. If you are tempted to buy land in an undeveloped subdivision, do twice the amount of checking as for any other property. Beware of slick promotional material with "artist's rendition" of clubhouses, lakes, marinas, and golf courses. And just don't believe sales claims that values are going to rise substantially and soon.

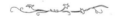

I just got wonderful news from my real estate agent in Florida.
They found land on my property.

MILTON BERLE

Consumer protection

The Department of Housing and Urban Development (HUD) enacted legislation to protect subdivision property buyers from misrepresentation, fraud, and deceit. Many states have similar statutes. The federal law requires that purchasers of certain properties must receive a property report disclosing such items as availability of utilities, soil problems, distance to schools, restrictive covenants, oil and mineral rights, special assessments for roads or other improvements, and payment terms. Properties that are usually exempt from this law include lots with buildings, subdivisions with fewer than 100 lots, and lots of 20 acres or larger.

Please note that the property report is *not* an indication of government approval of the project—it simply reveals pertinent facts. If you are interested in this kind of property be certain to carefully read the report. The law requires that a purchaser sign a statement that he has received the report and gives a seven-day cooling-off period during which the buyer may cancel the purchase agreement (in writing) and receive his deposit back.

There is a solid reason for the right-to-cancel-law. Real estate salespeople in subdivisions know they will probably only get one shot at buyers, so they are trained and conditioned to be very aggressive—to make the sale *today*. Do not be persuaded by the glib "You have a seven-day right to cancel; make your decision today while it's convenient; you can always change your mind later." Other pressing matters may interfere, and *later* often comes too late.

Housing subdivisions, retirement, and recreational developments

*Many people think of retirement communities
as large compounds of the elderly
living among themselves with little contact or interest
in the native population around them,
the kind of places found in Arizona or Florida.
In the Ozarks and other regions where elderly people go to live,
the retirees are likely to be segregated by neighborhoods,
but so pervasive are the natural surroundings and the native culture
that their influence cannot be escaped in the low-density settings
which have sprung up in recent years.*

JOHN HERBERS
THE NEW HEARTLAND

There are many housing subdivisions that may be attractive to country home seekers. Retirement communities are sometimes found in small subdivisions of homes on large lots or small acreages surrounded by forests and hills. Ski resorts, fishing lakes, and man-made facilities center many new communities that can only exist because of transfer payments such as retirement checks. These areas are often far removed from urban centers, so they offer year-round service employment for younger people.

With any subdivision, which may also be called a development, project, retirement community, planned unit development, or destination resort (new names appear yearly), be sure to receive and carefully read a copy of the Covenants, Conditions, and Restrictions (CC&Rs). This is not the same document as the property report. CC&Rs frequently are spelled out in a thick packet of pages with small print. It's tough reading—great stuff for insomniacs—but you do not want to miss details such as, for instance, that resales must be made through the development company, that you must build a house of at least a certain square footage, or that you must paint your house every two years—the exact color that the architectural review board dictates. You also need to find out what fees owners must pay for common area maintenance, insurance, accounting, etc.

Some subdivisions, especially condominiums and planned unit developments, are specifically aimed at retirees and second home buyers. Many of these places end up with a substantial number of renters—who will not share owners' attitudes. While it is impossible to predict how new developments will go, local property management people or real estate agents will be able to tell you what the score is with a project more than a year old.

Shadow governments

When considering any planned community beware of the power of shadow governments. Usually spelled out in the CC&Rs, homeowners associations may control most aspects of life within their jurisdiction, down to the color of the curtains in the windows fronting a street. These shadow governments have the power to levy taxes (assessments), legislate (create rules and regulations), and enforce (police power to force homeowners to obey their edicts). And the officers are often elected by votes having a dollar basis, rather than the democratic one-person-equals-one-vote concept.

Shadow governments regulate the nature of landscaping. They decide how many pets are allowed and what size. They decide the age of inhabitants—many forbid anyone younger than 45. If your adult child dies, you may be prohibited from taking in your grandchild. In some places shadow governments have become virtual dictatorships. Owners who sue them usually find that courts uphold their actions.

If you purchase property in a planned-unit or condominium development, about the only way you can have any real effect on how things are run is to become active in homeowner association affairs. If you like politics and meetings, you'll fit right in.

Tax sales

If after all this you still feel that this is the type of property you want, visit the county courthouse and ask to see the delinquent tax list. You will find that subdivision lots are listed most frequently. If you feel that these lots are a good investment you can often buy them for the back taxes. But be aware that, even after a tax sale, within a specified time period the previous owners can come forward, pay the back taxes, interest, and expenses, and regain title. Ask the tax collector what the laws are in that county.

Resources

If a subdivision is large enough and is promoted in interstate commerce, it must be registered with the following agency. Ask for the free booklet *Before Buying Land . . . Get the Facts*. And request a list of other materials it currently has available regarding country land.
U.S. Department of Housing and Urban Development
Interstate Lands Sales Registration Division
451 Seventh Street, S.W.
Washington, DC 20410

A booklet: *Buying Lots from Developers*, stock number 0-23-000-00295-7, is available for fifty cents from:
U.S. Superintendent of Documents
Government Printing Office
Washington, D.C. 20402

State real estate commissioners have information on subdivisions within their jurisdictions. Planning commissions, building departments, and real estate boards will have the address and phone number, or call the appropriate state government information center listed in *Resources*.

Daniel Webster's birthplace, Salisbury, New Hampshire, c. 1893

Downtown Minneapolis, 1854. Daguerrotype.

26
Intentional communities and eco-villages

A country living alternative

Intentional communities are a viable option for country living by
people of all ages and backgrounds. As most residents of
intentional communities are experienced in country ways, they
might provide a helpful transition from city life to living alone or
with family on your own land. Community members tend to be
supportive and nurturing. If you choose to join them, the same will
be expected of you.

The editorial staff of the *Directory of Intentional Communities* (see
Resources at end of chapter) grappled with the issue of definition and initially

decided to include any group of two or more people who wished to be in the book. Later, they chose to narrow their inclusions to those who "aligned themselves with a philosophy of non-violence and freedom for members to leave the group at any time." After the Waco, Texas, nightmare that is a choice we all can relate to.

History

Many intentional communities have evolved from the counterculture communes of the 1950s, 60s, and 70s. The community of today, while still at odds with business-as-usual politics and business, is generally much more conservative in its approach to right living. In a *Directory* article entitled "Communities for the Mainstream" Julie Mazo points out that

Even the *Wall Street Journal* found it relevant to report on the evolution of the people and places once called hippies and communes, as gray hair grows more plentiful among the Woodstock generation.

Marilyn and Tom Ross, in *Country Bound!* note that the communes of this decade are not the turf of freewheeling hippies intent on doing drugs and having sex. Those I have visited are populated by people with the same motivations described in this book's chapter 4—*Who are you?* Community residents are like the rest of us who choose to live in the country—they simply prefer to live with others in a group environment.

Sizes, sites, and philosophies

Intentional communities range in size from two or three people to 300. Their physical sites range from city houses to 5,000 acres of country land. The average is perhaps 20 people on 80 acres. Some were founded to promote a particular philosophy or religion, although the majority appear to be open to diverse personal beliefs. Most are located on rural land and are ecologically oriented. All ages are represented. Many provide schooling and communal nurturing for all resident children.

Three examples

Perhaps the best-known intentional community is The Farm, founded in 1971. Approximately 250 residents and about 40 businesses flourish on its 1,750 acres in southern middle Tennessee. Businesses and enterprises include the Soy Dairy, Solar Electronics, the Book Publishing Company, and the Dye Works. A school offers basic skills plus foreign languages, fine arts, and apprenticeship training. The Farm is home to the Midwife School—babies are delivered regularly. Their Kids to the Country program maintains a nature enrichment program for urban children.

Founded in 1937, Celo Community is the oldest land trust community in America, and one of the most successful. It comprises some 30 family units living on 1,200 acres of North Carolina land owned by the community. Members purchase "holdings" which are confined to the realistic needs and uses of each family. Celo community members are diverse in background, occupation, and in religion, and make their livings independently (membership includes craftsmen, farmers, teachers, and doctors). A number of successful projects, services, and schools have been developed, some with a national clientele. Celo has a two-year waiting list of potential new members.

Situated on 1,000 acres of south-central Washington, Ponderosa Village is typical of newer communities. Begun in 1980, there are now 52 residents of all ages and many backgrounds. Their stated organizing concepts are self-reliance, freedom, voluntary cooperation, personal growth, and a place of security in case of serious problems. Land, houses, and gardens are individually owned. Visitors are welcome and camping is available, but call or write before visiting. (Update: A Ponderosa Village classified ad in the June 1994 issue of *Real Goods News* states that they now offer "free one-day self-reliance seminars.")

A philosophy of balance

Intentional communities typically live more peaceably than the rest of the world. Many communities make decisions by consensus, and state that they are continually working to improve skills in non-competitive conflict resolution. Group needs are balanced with individual members' needs.

In a *Directory* article, "Individuality and Community," Griscom Morgan reported:
> A philosophy of balance lies behind the intentional community endeavors that arose from the work of Arthur Morgan and Community Service, Inc. A sociologist studying Celo Land Trust in North Carolina perceived that Celo's longevity since 1939 [sic] is based on a wide horizon of diversity rather than disciplined conformity to an ideology. The researcher found this to be anachronistic in that the opposite condition is widely accepted as necessary for the survival of intentional communities. . . . are all outgoing in their involvement with the wider society. None of these communities conform to communal stereotypes. Rather, they strive to be open-ended, living organisms. Their group lives are designed around the changing needs of diverse individual members who are continually evolving in the ever-changing order of the universe.

Eco-villages—attempts to redesign human habitat

As reported by Jay Walljasper in "At home in an eco-village" (*Utne Reader* May/June 1992), Europeans and some Americans are working with a concept called eco-village. Eco-villages are cooperative communities embodying current technology that aim to live in harmony with nature by growing their own food, generating their own energy, and handling their own wastes. They use computers, fax-modems, and modern mail services to communicate with their customers or bosses. Housing consists of duplex and triplex units clustered in small groups, all oriented toward common buildings, open areas, parking, and office facilities. The eco-village concept allows inhabitants to buy individual living units, have access to common land and facilities, and have wide latitude in how collective or private they choose to be. From my ex-real estate broker perspective, they are small, energy-efficient, ecologically-oriented, planned-unit developments. Very modern— oriented toward social and environmental sensitivity. Sane living for those who want to be close to others.

EcoVillage at Ithaca, New York, will ultimately have about 500 residents. About one-third of its 176 acres will be used for housing, the rest for gardens, ponds, orchards, and nature preserve. A common parking lot is planned with paths leading to homes. Residents will share such items as lawnmowers, snowblowers, and washing machines. Private, semi-private, and public areas will attempt to recreate strong social networks—community.

Researcher Per G. Berg, at Sweden's Institute for Future Studies, is helping to build Marielund, a 40-household eco-village near Uppsala, Sweden. He says the aim is: "A home, but a home from which you can explore the rest of the world. It's the best of village life. The best of modern life."

The New Alchemy Institute and many intentional communities have been striving toward these same goals for decades.

Resources

Celo Community, Route 5, Box 79, Burnsville, NC 28714. 704-675-5525

The Farm, Summertown, TN 38483. 615-964-3574

Ponderosa Village, 203 Golden Pine, Goldendale, WA 98620. 509-773-3902

Those interested in learning more about intentional communities are referred to the *Directory of Intentional Communities*. If it is not in your library, it is available from the Communities Publications Cooperative, Route 1, Box 155, Rutledge, MO 63563. The Directory lists 355 North American and 56 international communities and presents nearly 40 articles on the overall intentional community scene, including "Guidelines for Contacting & Visiting Communities."

A special issue of *In Context* on eco-villages was published by the Context Institute, Box 11470, Bainbridge Island, WA 98110.

A book I have not read is *Builders of the Dawn: Community Lifestyles in a Changing World*, Sirius Publishing, Baker Road, Shutesbury MA 01072.

The contact for EcoVillage at Ithaca is: Anabel Taylor Hall, Cornell University, Ithaca, NY 14853.

Per G. Berg is at Institute for Future Studies, Box 6799, 113 85, Stockholm, Sweden.

The New Alchemy Institute, 237 Hatchville Road, East Falmouth, MA 02536. Started in 1969 by John Todd and Bill McLarney, New Alchemy performs wonders on its 12 acres. It serves students, teachers, households, and small-scale farmers with research and education projects on food, energy, water, and waste treatment systems. A mail-order catalog is available upon request. My just-received information is that the organization is undergoing restructuring.

27
Places and
conditions to avoid

Everyone has gone back to a place
that they remember from childhood
and seen an apartment complex or a K-mart.
When I was growing up,
we were on the edge of the Everglades.
Now we're in the middle of mall hell.

CARL HIAASEN

Places that boom—and bust

alvin Beale reported that many mining, resort-retirement, or exurban fringe counties grew by 40 to 50 percent or more in population from 1970 to 1980, especially in the West and Florida. He observed that growth at these rates is next to impossible for a small community to handle. Water and sewer facilities, schools, medical and social agencies, crime rates, roads, and other issues and services are impacted hard, and local agencies are unable to cope. He noted that it is important to determine what part of the growth cycle a place is in.

In *Country Careers* Jerry Germer wrote
In the last century, mining towns like Virginia City, Nevada, or Park City, Utah, became ghost towns practically overnight when their single economic base was exhausted.

The boom and bust syndrome common to mountain towns that are dependent on mining employment first causes fast demand for services and then later closes stores and empties schools. Areas heavily into agriculture also have an uncertain future. The trend is for fewer people using larger machines to farm more acres. These areas are likely to continue to decrease in population.

Any place where one or two companies or military bases dominate the employment scene is a disaster waiting for a layoff. The exception is when the companies are very stable, for instance Hershey Chocolate Company, in Hershey, Pennsylvania, population 7,407. Given the human penchant for anything sweet, Hershey will be selling kisses for a very long time.

Not just small places boom and bomb. Joel Garreau relates how during the 1980s New England was electrified by an economic boom so strong that in one decade it lifted New England from the poorest region in America to the richest. The extraordinary business growth used up prime space so fast that growth stopped, then nose-dived. In the early 1990s the Massachusetts Miracle became the Massachusetts Massacre. Wyoming's population soared 41 percent in the 1970s, based on coal and oil demand. In the 1980s worldwide oil prices dropped and thousands of Wyomingites lost their jobs and left the state.

City fringe areas

Part of the difficulty of measuring city-to-rural migration patterns is that cities have annexed suburban areas and even rural areas, and continue to try to increase their official metropolitan area. In *Where To Make Money: A Rating Guide To Opportunities in America's Metro Areas*, G. Scott Thomas reports:

> The federal government has given the metropolitan designation to some areas that are decidedly unmetropolitan, places like Grand Forks, ND, Casper, WY, Enid, OK.

The purpose is power—salaries and profits fed by votes, taxes, and government largesse. These expansion areas will be used to prop up the cities as they continue to decline. The fringes of these areas may appear rural, but they are often affected by city regulations and city taxes. Buy land far from these city fringes disguised as country.

Unsafe at almost any speed—growth and development

Economic growth is not only unnecessary, but ruinous.
ALEXANDER I. SOLZHENITSYN

During my search in the 1970s I consciously avoided areas close to major highways or railroads, two criteria for major manufacturers. If you treasure open space, peace, and quiet you will avoid small towns and their surrounding areas that have locations and features attractive to large corporations in their quest for lower wages and taxes and fewer regulations.

When developers and preservationists clash, the latter often lose. In *Edge City* Joel Garreau says developer John Tilghman Hazel, Jr., has so rapidly transformed entire Northern Virginia landscapes that his vanquished opponents have been "reduced to describing him in satanic terms—no less than the Prince of Darkness and the Father of Lies."

I can imagine the outcry: "This guy is anti-capitalism!" Nope, just anti-growth for growth's sake and especially for ideal country places. Yeah, I know our economy is based on the growth theory. And the next dictum is that the government must keep growth happening. That's part of why economists' predictions are worthless—too much meddling with natural laws. To know where the economy was going we have watched where the politicians were going. But, through overuse, they seem to have worn out the steering mechanism—money.

Politicians appear to believe that human laws are more intelligent than natural laws. I once accepted an invitation to a luncheon with our visiting congressman. The conversation was mainly on the agricultural economy and the various new government programs being considered. The congressman and the others lamented at length that "nothing seems to work anymore." The devil made me do it—with manifest naiveté, I observed: "Supply and demand used to work quite well." Instant silence and lowered eyes. Forks pushed salad around. I boldly pushed forward: "Perhaps we should consider having fewer, not more programs." Well, that was that—I was never invited again. Damned troublemaker.

It's not that simple, of course. Strict supply and demand would result in the super-rich lions and we poor lambs. Alas, until the Golden Rule becomes universally, genetically implanted, we humans will continue to need some traffic signals to keep us from tromping all over each other.

Growth does not equal progress or health. And fast growth can destroy the good qualities of any place or community. I will keep reminding you that cities once were villages and small towns, ideal places now ruined by growth.

Growth for the sake of growth is the ideology of the cancer cell.

EDWARD ABBEY

Finding a place that is growth resistant will help ensure that the qualities that attracted you will remain. There are some land characteristics that restrain or retard growth, like scarce water, or huge deserts with no valuable minerals underground. Those are not what we're looking for. The ideal country place has highly desirable features but is a place that no industrialist or developer would give a second look. A developer's or manufacturer's list of negatives includes poor transportation routes, insufficient work force, anti-growth laws, land parcels too small to be profitably developed, wild-eyed obstructionists, snail darters, and spotted owls. All of which indicate a potential ideal home place.

It is not uncommon to find country townspeople who honestly believe that growth will raise their quality of life. Calvin Beale, in a 1985 talk titled "Rural Development in Perspective," told of a billboard outside a small town in Wisconsin. The sign read:

WELCOME TO GALESVILLE
The Garden of Eden
Industry Invited

Said Beale:

> Here, in a nutshell, the basic modern dilemma of rural America is expressed. On one hand there is the ardent assertion of the idyllic, fulfilling quality that life in a small community can have, but then tempered by the necessity to invite the serpent of industry into the garden if people are to have the means to live there.

If you are considering living in or near a small town, talk to the people there who make growth happen—bankers, bureaucrats, and business people. Act like you might favor some growth and check their reaction. If you want things to stay the way they are as long as possible avoid places with growth-oriented chambers of commerce. If they persist they will get growth—but they may destroy the soul of their town.

People in wonderful small towns often just don't understand how quickly growth can destroy the qualities of their community. Following the lead of states, many low-population areas are wooing business. Typical is the following ad from the *Los Angeles Times* February 13, 1994:

OHIO COUNTY—KENTUCKY

Our community is the best-kept secret in America. An abundance of talented, friendly labor to help you reach the potential you deserve. Labor costs are favorable because of the area's low cost of living. We need small to medium size expansion or developing industries. Let us help you help us. Incentives, training, quality of lifestyle. Contact:

Judge Larry Whitaker, 502-283-3213
Judge Dudley Cooper, 502-298-4400
or Wayne Evans, 1-800-844-3553

By the way, I suspect the two judges in the ad are county judges, officials elected to administer county business affairs; in some Midwest counties they are called county commissioners, in others, judges. Some even do settle minor legal disagreements.

Unchecked economic growth can quickly become a curse. Paradise can be found and lost in short order, especially if it is within commuting distance of cities and therefore desirable to large corporations. Tyson's Corner, Virginia, went from country crossroads to sloppy suburb in a single decade. Controlled-growth programs are the typical response of town planners. Personally, I recommend a town too small to afford or need a planner.

I hammer on this theme of avoiding potential development because I know the pain it can cause. Once you find and buy your ideal country home place you will likely make substantial improvements. You will invest yourself in the place. Inevitably the place will become even more special to you.

In 1932 Helen and Scott Nearing purchased a remote Vermont maple farm and then spent nearly twenty years building gardens and stone buildings. In 1947 a paper company began denuding the mountain above them. Once the trees were gone, ski slopes were developed and advertised. By the fall of 1951, those activities plus unannounced drop-ins so destroyed their lifestyle that they moved to Maine and, at advanced ages, started over.

I have advised against buying too little land. Even moderate-size parcels may provide inadequate protection of peace and quiet. In *An American Homeplace* Donald McCaig finds farmer/writer Wendell Berry contemplating the possible need to leave his cherished 75 acres of Kentucky land because a developer had bought the acreage next door and planned to "erect and sell dozens of tacky weekend camps." When the plan faltered, Berry was able to buy the land and preserve his place.

A really large parcel next door is a gilt-edged invitation to developers. In the Afterword of *Maine Farm* Stanley Joseph writes that

> Developers have subdivided the four hundred acres bordering our land [part of Helen and Scott Nearing's place] into forty lots, and million-dollar houses are going up.

One can imagine what that will do to the peace and quiet. And the taxes. Beemers and polo ponies. There goes the neighborhood.

Development typically moves out from cities and towns in more or less concentric rings, often burgeoning at highway intersections. Sometimes it takes big jumps. Features such as rivers, lakes, and other tourist attractors are like magnets to developers. Beware of buying near large plots held by speculators waiting for the right time to build new communities or commercial developments. Staying far from main highways and railroads helps ensure low development potential but is no guarantee by itself. If a development is announced near your private Utopia, about all you can do is prepare to suffer the sights, sounds, traffic, and increased taxes, sell and move, or loudly announce your own plans—a large skunk ranch operation.

Sounds

*One good thing about living on a farm is that you can
fight with your wife without being heard.*

FRANK McKINNEY "KIN" HUBBARD

Sounds seem to travel farther in the country, where background covering din is reduced to bird songs and wind through the trees. When our winds reverse their normal pattern I sometimes hear the sounds of a gravel dredging operation many miles away.

One way to discover potential negative sounds is to camp on the property. In *Goodby City Hello Country* Julie Hayward and Ken Spooner relate the experience of a family who had fallen in love with a beautiful piece of land in northwestern Arkansas. After making a deposit and signing a contract, the family camped on the property. That night, "As they tried to sleep they heard the roar of trucks on Highway 70." The next day they walked away from their deposit and bought another property, one with appropriate country night sounds—hooting owls and yapping coyotes.

Theme centers, recreation resorts, reservations

Yes, reservations. Who would have thought that activity on Indian reservations might one day destroy surrounding settlers' rural atmosphere? Well, at least one has and others are sure to follow. It might be considered poetic justice.

Foxwoods High Stakes Casino has current revenues estimated at $600 to $700 million per year. Nevada? Nope, southeastern Connecticut, an area of tiny villages, rolling hills, and centuries-old farms. The Mashantuckett Pequot, a Native American tribe numbering about 350, found financing in Malasia and a management team in Atlantic City. Agreeing to pay the state 25 percent of slot

machine revenues or $100 million per year, whichever is more, bought state approval. In two years the casino went from an entrepreneurial dream to an enterprise that dominates the area, employing 8,050 and generating a stream of 25,000 cars per day.

The Pequot and local non-Native Americans are now engaged in a modern Indians-versus-settlers war on the issue of annexing more land to the 1,230-acre reservation. (Pequot is from Pekawatawog, "the destroyers." They were the most feared tribe in New England until the colonists massacred most of them in 1637. Two reservations were created in 1655 on Connecticut's Mystic River. Now they're getting even.)

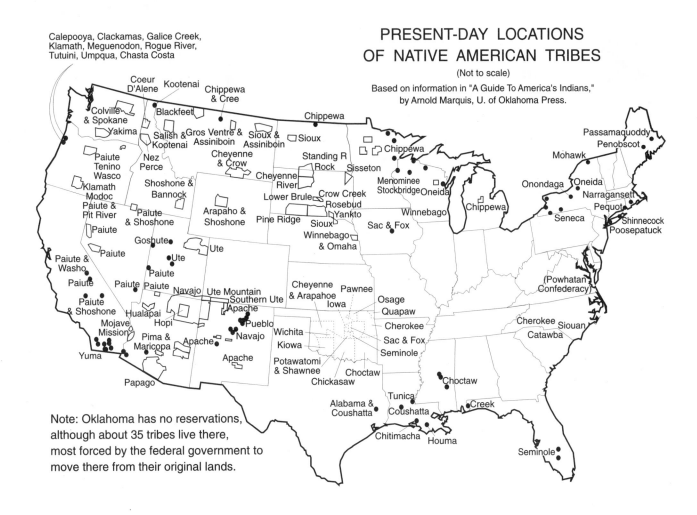

PRESENT-DAY LOCATIONS
OF NATIVE AMERICAN TRIBES
(Not to scale)

Based on information in "A Guide To America's Indians,"
by Arnold Marquis, U. of Oklahoma Press.

Calepooya, Clackamas, Galice Creek,
Klamath, Meguenodon, Rogue River,
Tutuini, Umpqua, Chasta Costa

Note: Oklahoma has no reservations,
although about 35 tribes live there,
most forced by the federal government to
move there from their original lands.

The weapons today are referendums and zoning laws. Things look bad for the white man. Future tribal plans include building two golf courses, a theme park, tennis courts, a skeet-shooting range, and a $100-million museum and research center.

Foxwoods has become a model for other reservations across the U.S., which to a certain extent are "nations within a state," hoping to cash in on the gambling bonanza. States see gambling as the least objectionable way to raise revenue since the creation of sin taxes. Donald Trump and other casino magnates are likely drooling with anticipation at this new-found opportunity.

A caution is in order regarding the preceeding map of Native American locations. Many state reservations can be located only by studying large-scale maps in an atlas—and I advise you to do so. For instance, the Pequot are mentioned in various books but their location is not mapped. About four percent of California's 200,000 Native Americans live on one of 83 reservations. Altogether, the U.S. government recognizes 545 tribes. In an April 1994 speech, President Clinton reiterated the government's commitment to self-determination and sovereignty for tribal governments.

Remote locations may preclude development—reservations most likely to be used as casino locales are those situated within easy driving distance from large population centers.

While Walt Disney World, near Orlando, is the largest U.S. theme park and attracts the most visitors, Dollywood in Pigeon Forge, Tennessee, Silver Dollar City in Branson, Missouri, Six Flags over Texas in Arlington, Texas, and the many Lion Country Safari and other theme parks attract millions of tourists each year. Theme parks initially need a large parcel of low-priced land—read rural. Once established, the parks generate other businesses, higher prices, higher taxes, and high traffic volume. Goodbye country.

Disney's latest effort is a proposed historical theme park near Manassas, Virginia, near Civil War battlefields. They bought a big plantation, quietly bought options on a total of 3,000 acres, won the governor over, and are confidently working their way past zoning challenges and outraged citizens. The "little guy" property owners in Prince William County feel pretty sure that the projected 77,000 cars per day will have a negative effect on their peace and quiet. One nearby landowner refers to the proposed development as "Disneyopolis."

Places that are just too beautiful may create the small-town-turned-resort syndrome that has become a paradigm in the West. Tourism is often seen as economic salvation for small towns losing their people to other places with more jobs. A sprinkling of tourism may leave a town intact but spectacular natural features often bring big development and big change. In *Little Town Blues: Voices from the changing West,* Raye C. Ringholz shows how heavy tourism has drastically changed Sedona, Arizona, Jackson Hole, Wyoming, Aspen, Colorado, and Moab, Utah—in all cases started by locals seeking to increase jobs.

> If there's a mountain to hike or ski, redrock backcountry to explore, a waterway to play on, or a desert oasis to green into a golf course, it's being developed by entrepreneurs with hordes of tourists and recreationers hard on their heels. Within a few short years, the immigrants follow and authentic mining camps, rustic cow towns, pioneer farming communities—historic signatures of the American West—succumb to cosmetic changes that leave them little resemblance to their original selves. Even worse, they all start to look alike.

Development of all kinds increases traffic, taxes, and prices. It inevitably increases the number of land-use laws and regulations. While casinos, theme parks, recreation resorts, and other tourist attractors may be fun to visit, they all have the potential to drastically change an area, perhaps destroying the community that drew you there. Whether such development will occur depends on local attitudes and natural features. The combination of seductive scenery and aggressive local business people almost guarantees that such development will occur.

Military installations

Military bases are often major polluters with no one to keep them in line. They should not be considered a stable employment base. And their male personnel should not be allowed near your daughters without a chaperone. (Just kidding—I was one and I was nice. Honest.) Military installations are notorious polluters, as shown by the following map.

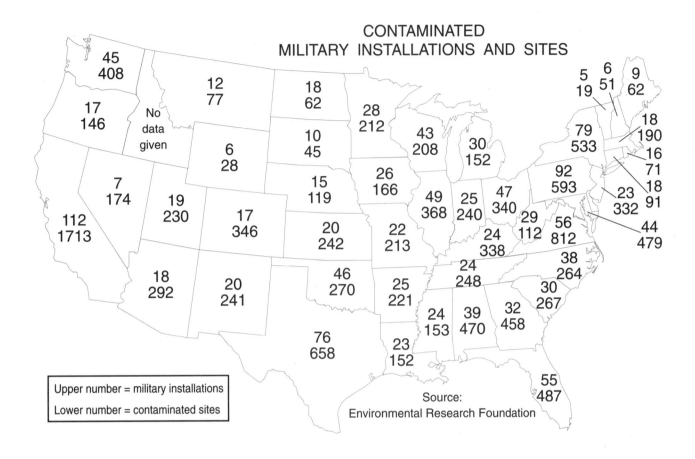

CONTAMINATED MILITARY INSTALLATIONS AND SITES

Upper number = military installations
Lower number = contaminated sites

Source: Environmental Research Foundation

Flight paths—the invasion of paradise

Modern jet airports require large amounts of space. New ones are typically built away from cities in sparsely populated areas. Living under a designated flight path is enduring a sound track from hell. As you narrow your search you will want to determine if your chosen area includes airports and their attendant flight paths. I recommend you make a very thorough investigation. From maps and conversations with locals, find out where the nearest airport is located. Find someone there who can show you on a map where the local flight paths are. Talk to your potential neighbors. Contact the Federal Aviation Administration. If you can't get the information you need, call your congressperson. Call the President. Unless you love airplanes more than life itself, call God if necessary, but do get the facts on all flight paths in your chosen area, including those used by military aircraft. It is that important. While my experience is out of the ordinary, I have visited people who live under flight paths and conversation necessarily stops when a jet goes overhead. I like airplanes. They are a safe, efficient way to travel. But over a residence and a garden they are noise pollution and air pollution.

I had lived on my place for several weeks and was working in the garden one morning when an earth-shaking roar came up the hollow. The hair on my neck stood straight out as the roar materialized into a very-low-flying bomber painted a dull gray with no identifying marks, with what appeared to be metal shutters covering the windshield. It came directly at me. I staggered, my intellect did a full stop, I braced myself to die. A cerebral neuron finally fired and I realized that I was experiencing the beginning of the end of the world. This Darth Vader-like apparition was from the evil empire, sneaking in under radar, committed to vaporize some nearby secret military target. My world would end with a blinding nuclear explosion. The monster thundered by directly overhead, its bomb doors clearly visible.

Time passed. Surprised that I still lived, I went in and used the telephone. A neighbor calmed me. Somewhat. It was one of ours. It was a training mission. A pilot was being trained to fly under Russian radar. More would come. They practiced 500 feet above the ground, inches above my airspace. They practiced using instruments only. None had crashed—yet. They came, I was told, from a Strategic Air Command base up near Kansas City. They came on an infrequent, unpredictable, but endless basis. Yes, letters had been written. There was, I was told, nothing to be done about it.

It was for more than the usual reasons that I celebrated the end of the Cold War. And I freely admit that I experienced selfish thoughts when military budget cuts were announced.

Occasionally one still comes over. Just often enough to sustain a sadness—just often enough that I never forget my puny insignificance in a world that still stays prepared to destroy itself.

The National Priorities List (Superfund sites)

EPA Administrator Carol Browner has stated that 73 million people live within four miles of the more than 1,300 toxic sites on the federal priority list for decontamination. In the last 14 years, with an expenditure of nearly $9 billion by government and billions more by private industry, the Superfund program has concluded cleanup on 220 sites.

Nuclear power plants

Radiation leaks are caused by fools like me,
but only God can build a nuclear reactor
93 million miles from the nearest elementary school.

STEWART BRAND

Following is a list of the 111 operable nuclear reactors in the United States as of December 31, 1991. Eight additional units had received construction permits by the end of 1990. Rising costs, lower electricity demand because of energy conservation, regulatory delays, and citizen opposition may preclude new construction of nuclear reactors.

Alabama=5
  Browns Ferry 1, 2, & 3, Decatur
  Joseph M. Farley 1 & 2, Dothan
Arizona=3
  Palo Verde 1, 2, & 3, Wintersburg
Arkansas=2
  Arkansas Nuclear 1 & 2, Russellville
California=5
  Diablo Canyon 1 & 2, Avila Beach
  San Onofre 1, 2, & 3, San Clemente
Connecticut=4
  Connecticut Yankee, Haddam Neck
  Millstone 1, 2, & 3, Waterford
Florida=5
  Crystal River 3, Red Level
  St. Lucie 1 & 2, Ft. Pierce
  Turkey Point 3 & 4, Florida City
Georgia=4
  Hatch 1 & 2, Baxley
  Vogtle 1 & 2, Waynesboro
Illinois=13
  Braidwood 1 & 2, Braidwood
  Bryon 1 & 2, Bryon
  Clinton 1, Clinton
  Dresden 2 & 3, Morris
  La Salle 1 & 2, Seneca
  Quad Cities 1 & 2, Cordova
  Zion 1 & 2, Zion
Iowa=1
  Duane Arnold, Palo

Kansas=1
  Wolf Creek, Burlington
Louisiana=2
  River Bend 1, St. Francisville
  Waterford 3, Taft
Maine=1
  Maine Yankee, Wiscasset
Maryland=2
  Calvert Cliffs 1 & 2, Lusby
Massachusetts=2
  Pilgrim 1, Plymouth
  Yankee Rowe 1, Rowe
Michigan=5
  Big Rock Point, Charlevoix
  Donald C. Cook 1 & 2, Bridgman
  Fermi 2, Newport
  Palisades, South Haven
Minnesota=3
  Monticello, Monticello
  Prairie Island 1 & 2, Red Wing
Mississippi=1
  Grand Gulf 1, Port Gibson
Missouri=1
  Callaway 1, Fulton
Nebraska=2
  Cooper, Brownville
  Fort Calhoun 1, Fort Calhoun
New Hampshire=1
  Seabrook 1, Seabrook

New Jersey=4
  Hope Creek 1, Salem
  Oyster Creek 1, Forked River
  Salem 1 & 2, Salem
New York=6
  Indian Point 2 & 3, Buchanan
  James A. Fitzpatrick, Scriba
  Nine Mile Point 1 & 2, Oswego
  Robert E. Ginna, Rochester
North Carolina=5
  Brunswick 1 & 2, Southport
  McGuire 1 & 2, Cowens Ford Dam
  Shearon Harris 1, New Hill
Ohio=2
  Davis-Besse 1, Oak Harbor
  Perry 1, North Perry
Oregon=1
  Trojan, Prescott
Pennsylvania=9
  Beaver Valley 1 & 2, Shippingport
  Limerick 1 & 2, Pottstown
  Peach Bottom 2 & 3, Lancaster
  Susquehanna 1 & 2, Berwick
  Three Mile Island 1, Middletown

South Carolina=7
  Catawba 1 & 2, Clover
  H.B. Robinson 2, Hartsville
  Oconee 1, 2, & 3, Seneca
  Summer 1, Jenkinsville
Tennessee=2
  Sequoyah 1 & 2, Daisy
Texas=3
  Comanche Peak 1, Glen Rose
  South Texas 1 & 2, Bay City
Vermont=1
  Vermont Yankee, Vernon
Virginia=4
  North Anna 1 & 2, Mineral
  Surrey 1 & 2, Surrey
Washington=1
  WNP 2, Richland
Wisconsin=3
  Kewaunee, Carlton
  Point Beach 1 & 2, Two Creeks

Source: U.S. Dept. of Energy, *World Nuclear Capacity and Fuel Cycle Requirements*, 1992.

Factories, power plants, and paper mills

In case you become too depressed to read the entire following chapter on toxic pollution, be advised to stay far upwind and upstream from any factory that discharges into the air or water, or dumps hazardous wastes nearby. And remember that wind directions occasionally reverse.

Power plants use enormous amounts of water for cooling and change local aquatic and marine ecosystems. Power plants burn various fuels and emit huge plumes of smoke. Even the most advanced flue scrubbers occasionally fail.

Paper mills create a smell that must be experienced to believe. White paper is bleached by a chlorine process that releases deadly dioxins into waterways.

In addition to pollution, factories generate equipment sounds which, in the quiet of country, may travel substantial distances.

Agribusiness cropland and meat production

Small family farms add much that is good to the atmosphere and quality of a community. Big operations—corporate farms—tend to use large amounts of fuel, chemical fertilizers, herbicides, and pesticides. Pesticide spraying may result in drift, air-borne toxins floating over to your property. U.S. cotton farmers use over 16 million pounds of pesticides each year. Feed lots and other intensive livestock operations generate substantial animal wastes and smells. Groundwater pollution is common near these facilities. Being downwind from feedlots discourages breathing. If you have a pet dog, be aware that most farmers and ranchers have the legal right to shoot any dog bothering livestock. And right-to-farm laws properly protect farmers from lawsuits by people who move to the country, then complain about manure smells and the noise generated by all-night machinery operations.

LULUs

Locally undesirable land uses are those enterprises and practices that our current society supports but that no one wants in their neighborhood—the NIMBY syndrome. Wastes—from household garbage to radioactive spent fuel rods from nuclear power plants—are being sent from affluent metropolitan areas to poor, low-population places. Waste management companies target vulnerable counties, then gain permission to dump their refuse by making political donations, creating a few jobs, and spreading dollars around schools and other high-profile community services.

Northeastern municipalities increasingly are paying for the privilege of dumping their garbage in inland states hundreds or even thousands of miles from their own backyards. Wendell Berry reports that eastern states are trucking garbage to his home state of Kentucky. Tiny Sierra Blanca in western Texas receives daily box-car loads of sewage sludge from New York City. It will soon become the dump site for radioactive waste from Vermont and Maine. The waste management company

expects to make a $168-million profit over the next five to eight years—a crumb of which is being spent to override local citizens' protestations that the practice is poisoning their land.

Check with the county clerk, county health office, planning department, and state waste management permit officials to determine if this is happening or being considered in your targeted areas. Frankly, in addition to pollution considerations, I would avoid buying property in any county where elected officials would consider letting such a thing happen.

A landfill's brother-gone-bad is a hazardous waste dump. These facilities are often simply ponds lined with clay into which toxic liquids are poured. Often uncovered, rains fill and overflow the ponds. Vegetation downwind from these places often dies. I know of a northern California housing subdivision that was constructed within a quarter mile downwind of one such pond. The women there experienced a high rate of pregnancy problems and babies were born with abnormalities. Landscaping vegetation routinely died.

Prisons

At the end of 1992, the federal prison system was estimated to be operating at 52 percent over capacity. Taken together, state prisons were estimated to be operating at 118 percent of their highest rated capacity.

The current trend is to build more prisons. According to *Corrections Compendium,* state prison construction budgets are up 73 percent since fiscal year 1987. Over 40 states are building new prisons or expanding existing ones. The latest political response to escalating crime is the concept of "three strikes and you're out," which will require even more prisons. Check with someone at the state level to determine sites being considered for new prisons. The governor's office can direct you to someone who knows.

Laws, codes, and regulations

We have lost many of our original freedoms guaranteed by the Constitution. This has occurred gradually over a long period of time and we don't think about it much anymore. We just accept the condition as one of the many features of modern life that we must submit to.

Freedom is one of the basic tenets of high-quality life. One of the most pleasurable conditions I found in my adopted county was the almost total lack of laws, codes, and regulations for building. There is no zoning commission to say what must go where; there is no building inspector to demand fees or sets of plans and to make surprise inspections. The only "enforcement" I have experienced came from the local electric co-op, whose lineman inspected the rewiring work I had performed in our house. It was more of a free service to be sure the wiring was safe. I welcomed the inspection; had a recommendation been made I would gladly have made the appropriate correction.

The downside to lack of codes and enforcement is that buildings may be built using unsafe methods and designs.

Again, the farther you locate away from cities the more likely you are to find such conditions as in my county. Beware of "rural" counties that lie within metropolitan areas where city codes and regulations are enforced. Such enforcement is not only degrading of personal freedom, it requires taxes to pay for it. Paying salaries and overhead for people to enforce city rules and regulations is not a part of high-quality country living.

Eminent domain

Eminent domain law allows the state to condemn and take your property for the public good, as for a park or a new highway. Most of the many dams built by the Corps of Engineers created lakes on land once owned by individuals, land often in the same family for generations. In some cases, whole towns were moved.

Besides outright taking (through mandatory sale), some state laws also allow use of the power to obtain rights-of-way. The March/April 1992 issue of *Harrowsmith Country Life* reported the story of an artist who bought land in Wyoming's Owl Creek Range, looking forward to peace and quiet. That ended when a judge upheld an obscure state law to let a Denver oil company take over, widen, and use a road through the middle of her property to move well-drilling equipment to a site on U.S. Bureau of Land Management land.

The article exposed the fact that condemnation laws in most western states give private companies eminent domain powers normally reserved only for governments. The purpose is to encourage natural resource development by private firms.

Backing up to or being surrounded by a national forest or other government-owned land seems like a good thing. Often it is not. If the federal government or its lessees need access for a logging operation, forest improvement, oil drilling, or any other authorized activity, and the shortest route is across your land, guess what? They *will* go across your land. If you object, an eminent domain proceeding almost certainly will be decided in favor of the government. That may mean that you will endure the noise and dust of logging trucks rumbling past your house from sunup to sundown, or worse. And, after the forest is denuded, or the oil rigs are in operation, your view will not be nearly as pleasant as before.

Eminent domain proceedings are rarely to the property owner's satisfaction. The potential threat of eminent domain can destroy your peace of mind. Absent overriding advantages, avoid buying property with discernible eminent domain potential.

The other reason not to buy land adjoining government land is that you will likely never have the option of buying it, should you wish to enlarge your acreage.

Isolation

This is more of a warning about the downside of isolation than a condition to avoid. I am not quite an isolationist but I do like more privacy than most people seem to require. The caveat to being way out in the boonies is this: while isolation and peace and quiet go hand in hand, a personal subjective result may be loneliness. If you usually stay busy and you attend to your social needs on a regular basis you may never become lonely. But if you are accustomed to the hubbub of city activity you may find country seclusion almost overwhelming, especially after you get settled in.

Odds and ends—local conditions

Your contentment will be affected by the lifestyle and values of those who already live where you will go. Consider the nature of a place. Cattle, hog, sheep, and poultry producers have different values than vegetarians. In certain areas, old-timers still kill hawks, eagles, coyotes, and wolves on sight—laws be damned. This may merely sadden most of us but would wound passionate birders and environmentalists. If these people become your neighbors, how will their activities impact your values and lifestyle?

Specific places and conditions to avoid

(In all cases, places downwind or downwater from pollution sources are at greatest risk.)

- Old landfill areas. Landfills always eventually leak or overflow.
- Toxic and hazardous waste sites. No matter how well built—and many were not—they all eventually leak or overflow.
- Toxic waste incinerator vicinities. Smoke and ash from these devices can be deadly.
- Mining areas. Toxic tailings and water-filled mines contaminate groundwater and surface waterways.
- Agribusiness areas. Pesticide drift and groundwater contamination.
- "In addition to the San Joaquin Valley in California, there are major concentrations of pesticide use throughout the Midwest, especially Iowa and Illinois, as well as along the Mississippi River, in a band across the Southeast coastal plain, and in the states of Florida and Washington. Iowa, Illinois, Minnesota, Indiana, and Ohio all account for larger shares of pesticide use than does California" (Goldman—see Recommended reading below).
- Near nuclear reactors.
- Industrial areas. Western Pennsylvania. Wherever there is industry there are hazardous wastes. Three-quarters of all hazardous waste produced in the United States originates in chemical companies.
- Near paper mills. Paper mill effluents contain deadly dioxin compounds and sulfites. Dioxin's effects on laboratory animals are so lethal that some scientists rank it among the most poisonous substances known.
- Along major rivers with industry or agribusiness upstream. Jim Robbins reports that a billion gallons of waste pour into the Columbia river every day from agricultural and municipal sewage.
- "The world's largest hazardous waste site sits between Geiger and Emell [Alabama]" (Setterberg and Shavelson).
- "National Wildlife magazine once called Triana, Alabama the 'unhealthiest town in America'" (Setterberg and Shavelson).
- Yucca Mountain, 80 miles northwest of Las Vegas, may become the nation's nuclear waste disposal place. So far, three billion dollars have been spent studying the site.

Other places to avoid

- Towns with parking meters—the people who run the town either have a parking problem, a tax problem, or a values problem—all conditions to stay away from.
- Places with strong chambers of commerce pushing for growth.
- Places with planning boards or commissions. If there are none and also no building department to torment you with fees, regulations, quadruplicate plans, and inspections you may have hit the jackpot.
- Any place within sound of a highway or commercial business.

And, from writer Richard Todd:
> You should be able to drive away from your farm in either direction and reach a tractor dealer before you come to a fast-food outlet.

(*Harrowsmith Country Life*, January-February 1992, "A Place in the Country.")

Resources and recommended reading

A Livestock Producer's Legal Guide to Nuisance, Land Use Control, and Environmental Law costs $12 from American Farm Bureau Federation, 225 Touhy Avenue, Park Ridge, IL 60068.

For more information on contaminated military installations, contact Environmental Research Foundation at 410-263-1584.

- Garreau, Joel. *Edge City: Life on the New Frontier.* New York: Doubleday, 1991.

- Goldman, Benjamin A. *The Truth About Where You Live: An atlas for action on toxins and mortality.* New York: Times Books/Random House, 1991.

- Setterberg, Fred and Lonny Shavelson. *Toxic Nation: The Fight to Save Our Communities from Chemical Contamination.* New York: John Wiley & Sons, 1993.

And for a more sane solution to prison overcrowding than simply building more prisons, read *Ain't Nobody's Business If You Do: The Absurdity of Consensual Crimes in a Free Society*, by Peter McWilliams, Prelude Press, Los Angeles, 1993. If it's not in your local bookstore, call: 800-LIFE-101.

28
Toxic
pollution

Can anyone believe it is possible
to lay down such a barrage of poisons
on the surface of the earth
without making it unfit for all life?

RACHEL CARSON
SILENT SPRING, 1962

A short course in
species self destruction

The grim news is that pollution exists in every state, probably in nearly every county. The good news is that there are still places where we can live on clean soil, breathe clean air, and drink pure water. If we become aware of how to live properly we can keep it that way. If we are discerning in our product purchases, we can help clean up the rest of the world.

Toxic pollution is a depressing subject but it is a problem that must be addressed in our search for the ideal home. We can avoid fouling our own nest, but first we must avoid making our nest in a foul place. And we all must develop a greater awareness of the problem so we may become part of the solution.

Most pollution is in the form of chemicals. The U.S. chemical industry is a huge, capital-intensive business, a major player in the U.S. economy. It has changed the source of consumer products from wood and iron and cotton and wool to petroleum products. It has made possible pipe that won't rust, shirts that won't wrinkle, and shoes that help athletes jump. Its technology is high science, transforming crude oil into molded dashboards and designer sunglasses. It has caused artificial to become accepted as natural. And we are killing ourselves and our children with its byproducts.

It is impossible to maintain a safe human environment in the presence of large numbers of toxic chemicals now in common production and use. There are laws governing the production, transport, use, and disposal of chemicals, products of chemicals, and chemical wastes. They are not enough. We know this because of the sickness and death these materials and their use are causing. Our most basic requirements for life—air, water, and food—are poisoning us.

It is uncomfortable to face up to, but each of us is responsible for toxic pollution. We all buy products whose production and disposal create pollution. We all buy, use, and dispose of poisonous products. Household cleaning items, painkillers, and cosmetics are leading sources of accidental poisonings in the home. Our carpet, our furniture, and our vehicles emit toxic fumes. Not only do chemicals permeate our food, our clothing, our homes, and our cars, they *are* our food, our clothing, our homes, and our cars. No wonder there is so much cancer.

Tragically, our children suffer most from toxic contamination. In *Toxic Nation* Fred Setterberg and Lonny Shavelson report:

> Beyond the paradoxical attractions of toxic dumps, kids come into greater contact with dangerous chemicals simply because they eat more than adults in proportion to their body weight—including more pesticide residues from fresh vegetables, fruits, and juices. The EPA classifies as possible carcinogens over 65 percent of the 560 million pounds of herbicides and fungicides sprayed annually on U.S. crops. The average child consumes four times the amount of these suspect chemicals than an adult.

Setterberg and Shavelson quote Dr. Herbert Needleman,

> the nation's foremost researcher on childhood lead exposures. 'We're twenty years behind on the study of pesticides. . . . There is no question that pesticides impair children's brain functions as insidiously as lead. I will tell you without fear of contradiction that exposing children to excessive levels of pesticides is impairing their health, eroding their mental abilities, and shortening their lives.'

DDT is bioaccumulative, that is, it is retained within the body of the consuming organism and is concentrated with each ensuing level of the food chain. Rachel Carson's *Silent Spring,* published in 1962, warned of the danger from DDT. Its use was banned in the U.S. in 1972. End of story? Hardly. American chemical companies still produce and export tons of DDT to other countries, knowing full well that food products produced there using the poison will be exported—to American grocery shelves. Profit at any price.

Pesticides and herbicides are designed to kill food crop pests. Arsenic is part of their recipes. Like lead and mercury it accumulates in the body. Like the wife who fed her husband small quantities of arsenic until enough accumulated to kill him, our chemically treated foods are slowly filling us with lethal residue.

The resistance to eliminate the sources of toxic poisoning reminds me of how information presented 30 years ago about the link between cigarettes and lung cancer was dismissed as "inconclusive" by smokers and tobacco companies. The former continue to die of lung cancer. The latter continue to reject overwhelming evidence and to put profit above life, aiming seductive advertising at susceptible young people.

Air pollution

*. . . the thoughts of Plato and Machiavelli . . . don't seem
quite enough armor for a world beset with splitting the atoms,
urban guerrillas, nineteen varieties of psychotherapists,
amplified guitars, napalm, computers, astronauts,
and an atmosphere polluted simultaneously
with auto exhaust and TV commercials.*

JOHN FISCHER

Air pollution is caused by emissions from power plants, solid waste incinerators, factories, and vehicles. The six major types of air pollutants are carbon monoxide, hydrocarbons, nitrogen oxides, particulates, sulfur dioxide, and photochemical oxidants. Air pollution on a regional scale is in large part the result of city and industrial air pollution that has spread out to encompass areas of many thousands of square miles. Meteorological conditions and landforms influence air pollution concentrations at any given place.

Even huge natural areas far downwind from pollution sources are affected. Jim Robbins wrote about the Grand Canyon in *Last Refuge:*

> Air pollution from coal-fired power plants and places like Los Angeles gets caught up in prevailing winds and makes its way to the Grand Canyon, where, because of temperature differences, it often sinks and stubbornly sits. 'The canyon,' says Carl Bowman, an air quality specialist for the Park Service, 'is a catch basin for pollution.' He has a picture on his office wall of the canyon filled to the rim during a haze episode.

Acid rain

Acid rain is created when sulfur dioxide and nitrogen dioxide combine with atmospheric moisture to form rain, snow, or hail containing sulfur and nitric acids. Burning coal produces carbon monoxide and sulfur dioxide. In 1980 in the United States, more than 60 percent of the man-made sulfur dioxide emissions was attributed to coal-fired electrical generation plants. Anti-pollution regulations have caused sulfur dioxide emissions to decrease substantially, but acid rain has diminished only slightly, because the incidence of acid-neutralizing substances has also dropped.

Acid rain raises the acidity (lowers the pH level) of surface water to a level that kills freshwater aquatic life and marine life in coastal waters. It kills trees and other vegetation. It damages croplands, erodes structures, and contaminates drinking water. In the beautiful bayou country of Louisiana, air pollution and acid rain have killed the Spanish moss on many of the giant oak trees.

Jim Robbins relates that:

> . . . ozone and acid precipitation show up in high levels in Sequoia and Kings Canyon. Ozone has contributed to the death of Jeffrey pine trees in Sequoia and has caused visible damage to ponderosa pines.

Talk about a downer subject. And that is not intended as a pun. Acid rain is real, it's pervasive, it's deadly, and it's unnecessary.

The major factors controlling transport and dispersion are the character and movements of meteorological systems. Winds can carry pollutants thousands of miles from their source. Greatest acid rain damage in the U.S. exists in streams, lakes, and forests of the Northeast. Damage also exists in forests of the South and Midwest.

Pollutants move both with strong air movements—storm centers that gather them quickly, and with weak, slow-moving high pressure systems that allow sufficient time for thorough mixing to take place. I have duplicated the major storm track map from chapter 9 here so you easily may compare storm patterns with acid rain incidence. As you look for your property you will want to avoid land downwind from pollution sources.

Radiation pollution

Radiation pollution is any form of ionizing or nonionizing radiation resulting from human activities. The best-known radiation is from the detonation of nuclear devices and the controlled release of energy by nuclear power plants. Other sources of radiation include spent-fuel reprocessing plants, byproducts of mining operations, and experimental research laboratories. The 1979 accident at the Three Mile Island nuclear power plant near Harrisburg, Pennsylvania, and the 1986 explosion at Chernobyl in the former U.S.S.R. clearly illuminated radiation danger.

The environmental effects of exposure to high-level ionizing radiation have been extensively documented through postwar studies on Japanese survivors of the Nagasaki and Hiroshima bombings. Some forms of cancer show up immediately, but latent maladies of radiation poisoning have been recorded from 10 to 30 years after exposure. The effects of exposure to low-level radiation are not yet understood.

Radioactive wastes cannot be disposed of like chemicals. They must be stored in heavily shielded containers in areas remote from living things. The "safest" of current storage sites are impervious deep caves and abandoned salt mines. Some radioactive wastes have half-lives of thousands of years and no storage method has been found that is certainly safe.

MAJOR CLIMATOLOGICAL STORM TRACKS

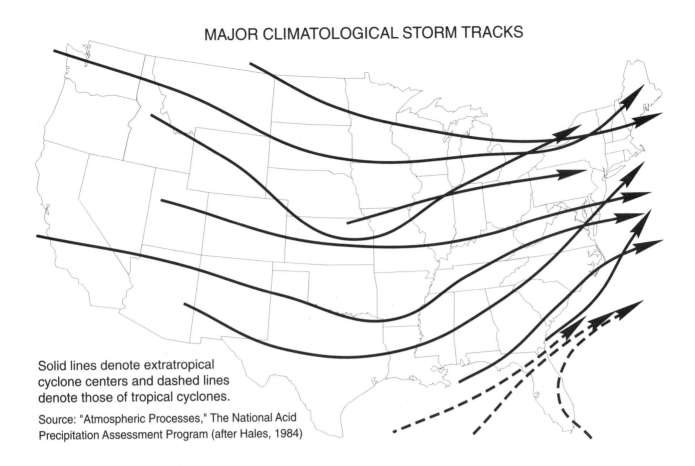

Solid lines denote extratropical cyclone centers and dashed lines denote those of tropical cyclones.

Source: "Atmospheric Processes," The National Acid Precipitation Assessment Program (after Hales, 1984)

GROUND AND WATER ACIDITY CAUSED BY ACID RAIN

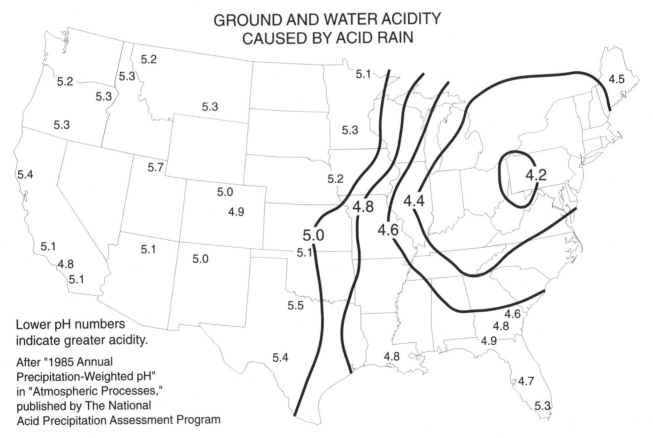

Lower pH numbers indicate greater acidity.

After "1985 Annual Precipitation-Weighted pH" in "Atmospheric Processes," published by The National Acid Precipitation Assessment Program

Water pollution

In the Great Lakes and St. Lawrence Seaway area, water quality is an oxymoron. The Great Lakes are polluted by toxic chemicals called organochlorines from agricultural pesticides and industrial wastes. Fish from the Great Lakes are so full of chemicals and heavy metals that some states have banned them for human consumption. Beluga whales in the St. Lawrence River are dying from eating fish and eels full of toxic substances. PCBs were almost completely banned in 1979, yet in 1993 dead belugas still showed such high concentrations of PCBs that their corpses could be classified as hazardous waste.

The Mississippi River Delta region is one of the most polluted areas in the country. The Mississippi River drains 41 percent of the contiguous 48 states. A legacy of chemical agriculture and industry, the river is a gruesome brew of over 100 toxic chemicals, increasingly worse downstream. There is a 4,000-square-mile area at its mouth called the dead zone—so distinct that it shows up on satellite photographs.

The huge San Joaquin and Sacramento valleys of California are intensively farmed using chemical fertilizers, herbicides, and pesticides. Setterberg and Shavelson state in *Toxic Nation: The Fight to Save Our Communities from Chemical Contamination* that

> . . . potentially cancer-causing chemicals had already seeped into almost one-third of the [California] state's drinking water wells at *levels deemed safe.* (My emphasis)

Thus far, agribusiness lobbying power has evaded responsibility for numerous cases of childhood cancer in these areas.

Thermal (heat) pollution

Thermal pollution is the discharge of waste heat into cooling water and subsequently into nearby waterways. The major sources of thermal pollution are fossil-fuel and nuclear power generating facilities and cooling operations associated with industrial manufacturing, such as steel foundries, other primary-metal manufacturers, and chemical and petrochemical producers. An estimated 90 percent of all water consumption, excluding agricultural uses, is for cooling or energy dissipation.

The discharge of heated water into a waterway often causes major fish kills near the discharge source. The increased temperature accelerates chemical-biological processes and decreases the ability of the water to hold dissolved oxygen. Thermal changes affect the aquatic system by limiting or changing the type of fish and other water life able to live in the waters.

Land pollution and destruction

Land pollution is the degradation of the land surface through misuse of the soil by poor agricultural practices, mineral exploitation, industrial waste dumping, and indiscriminate disposal of urban wastes.

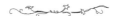

When an agribusinessman hires an expensive crop duster to spray for alfalfa weevils, he may increase this year's alfalfa production. He may also kill his neighbor's bees and his own earthworms and beneficial insects. He may pollute well-water downslope from his fields. If he is not very careful, he will do all these things.

DONALD McCAIG
AN AMERICAN HOMEPLACE

Soil erosion—primarily a result of poor agricultural practices—removes rich topsoil developed over many years through natural processes and strips the land of valuable nutrients. Strip mining for minerals and coal ruins thousands of acres of land each year, subjecting the area to widespread erosion. Clearcutting hillside forests destroys the soil's water-holding ability; sediment loads in adjacent streams may increase as much as 500 to 1,000 times.

Radon

Radon occurs more from natural conditions than from man-made conditions, but you need to be aware of it, know how to avoid it, and know how to deal with it if it enters your home.

Radon is the second most prevalent cause of lung cancer. It is an invisible, odorless gas naturally produced from decaying radium, which comes from uranium, which is found in about 150 minerals. Among these are granite, phosphate, and shale. In *Radon: The Invisible Threat*, Michael LaFavore notes that:

> . . . large deposits of uranium ore, pure enough to mine for atomic fuel, are located in parts of western Colorado, eastern Utah, northeastern Arizona, northwestern New Mexico, Wyoming, Texas, and western Canada.

Uranium mine tailings emit huge quantities of radon. Heavy rains leach radioactive particles out of mine tailings and contaminate groundwater. Before radon was publicly recognized as a health threat, tailings were used to make concrete products and even as landfill under and around new homes. In *The Menace of Atomic Energy*, Ralph Nader and John Abbotts report that as many as 3,300 homes were built on radioactive tailings in Grand Junction, Colorado. And at least one school was built of masonry composed of tailings.

Most U.S. areas have "safe" low levels of radon. While the presence or absence of certain minerals indicates greater possibility, homeowners should satisfy themselves as to safety by having a radon test performed. Uranium concentrations can be very narrow—the absence or presence of radon in one home may not be repeated in a neighboring home. How a house is built can increase its risk. If high levels of radon are found, corrective work can be performed but it may be costly if excavation work is needed to place vent pipes.

In addition to the resources listed at the end of this chapter, state health departments often have radon contact agencies. These agencies and the regional offices of the EPA (see Resources) are good sources of general information about the health risks of radon, radon measurements in your home, and correction of radon problems.

I drew the following map based on a color radioactivity map in *The Geology of Radon* published by the U.S. Department of the Interior (ordering information at end of chapter). The following numbered comments are also those of the Department. Note that #10 and #16 are areas of *low* radon potential.

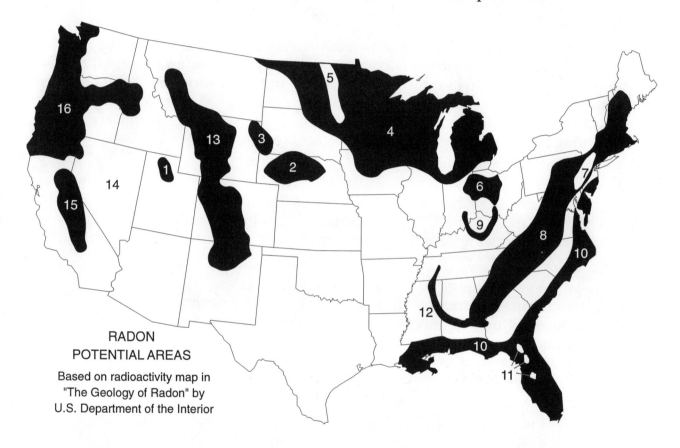

RADON
POTENTIAL AREAS

Based on radioactivity map in
"The Geology of Radon" by
U.S. Department of the Interior

1. Great Salt Lake: Water absorbs gamma rays so it shows as no data area on the map.
2. Nebraska Sand Hills: Wind has separated the lighter quartz sand from the clay and heavier minerals that usually contain uranium.
3. The Black Hills: A core of granites and metamorphic rocks high in radioactivity is surrounded by less radioactive sedimentary rocks and gives a distinctive pattern.
4. Pleistocene glacial deposits: The area has low surface radioactivity, but uranium occurs just below the surface. Thus it has a high radon potential.
5. Deposits of glacial Lake Agassiz: Clay and silt from a prehistoric glacial lake have higher radioactivity than glacial drift surrounding it.
6. Ohio Shale: Uranium-bearing black shale with a narrow outcrop zone was scooped up and spread over a large area in west-central Ohio by glaciers.
7. Reading Prong: Uranium-rich metamorphic rocks and numerous fault zones produce high radon in indoor air and in ground water.
8. Appalachian Mountains: Granites contain elevated uranium, particularly in fault zones. Black shales and soils above limestone also contain moderate to high levels of uranium.

9. Chattanooga and New Albany Shales: Uranium-bearing black shales in Ohio, Kentucky, and Indiana have a distinctive outcrop pattern clearly defined by radioactivity.

10. Outer Atlantic and Gulf Coastal Plain: This area of unconsolidated sands, silts, and clays has one of the lowest radon potentials in the United States.

11. Phosphatic rocks, Florida: These rocks are high in phosphate and associated uranium.

12. Inner Gulf Coastal Plain: This area of the Inner Coastal Plain has sands containing glauconite, a mineral high in uranium.

13. Rocky Mountains: Granites and metamorphic rocks in these ranges contain more uranium than sedimentary rocks to the east, resulting in high radon in indoor air and in ground water.

14. Basin and Range: Granitic and volcanic rocks in the ranges, alternating with basins filled with alluvium shed from the ranges, give this area a generally high radioactivity.

15. Sierra Nevada: Granites containing high uranium, particularly in east-central California, [show as red areas].

16. Northwest Pacific Coastal Mountains and Columbia Plateau: This area of volcanic basalts is low in uranium.

Sewage, oil, and mining pollution

Most cities have sewage problems because sewage volume and ingredients exceed the capabilities of treatment facilities. Untreated and partially treated sewage from municipal systems and rural septic tanks put significant quantities of nutrients, suspended solids, dissolved solids, oil, and heavy metals into waterways.

More than 13,000 oil spills occur in the U.S. yearly. Thousands of environmentally untested chemicals are routinely discharged into waterways. An estimated 400 to 500 new compounds are marketed each year. In addition, strip mining for coal releases acid wastes that poison the surrounding waterways.

Beware of western mining towns inundated and surrounded by toxic mine tailings. In *Last Refuge,* Jim Robbins reports:

> All but a small part of the city of Butte is a Superfund site, and around town there are three million cubic yards of old mine tailings, rocks, dirt, soil and other mining detritus, filled with high levels of such toxic elements as arsenic, lead, cadmium and mercury. . . . The six-thousand-acre site where the Anaconda smelter separated the [gold] metal from the ore for ninety-six years is number forty-eight on the national Superfund list. . . There are 185 million cubic yards of poisoned tailings here . . . Arsenic is also widely scattered across the countryside near Anaconda. . . . one rancher twelve miles downwind lost a thousand cattle, eight hundred sheep and twenty horses to arsenic poisoning in a single year. . . . High levels of arsenic have been found in children in the area. Butte is not the only place where miners have been replaced with toxic-waste remediation workers. Toxic-waste sites can be found near any number of western mining towns, waiting, like huge, festering wounds, to be treated. Bunker Hill in the Silver Valley of northern Idaho. The Yak Tunnel on the headwaters of the Arkansas River near Leadville, Colorado. . . . The copper wastes near Miami and Globe, Arizona, east of Phoenix. Telluride, Colorado. The Bingham Canyon Mine, near Salt Lake City. It's estimated that twelve thousand miles of American rivers and streams have been polluted by mining.

Solid waste

U.S. municipal wastes—the solid wastes from households and businesses sent to local landfills and other waste-disposal facilities—measure about two billion tons per year. Additional solid wastes amass from mining, industrial production, and agriculture. Although municipal wastes are the most obvious, the accumulations of the other types of waste are far greater, in many instances are more difficult to dispose of, and present greater environmental hazards.

The most common and convenient method of disposing of municipal solid wastes is in the sanitary landfill. Sanitary landfills work reasonably well for domestic waste cleared of hazardous materials. But industrial wastes are often commingled with domestic wastes, leading to groundwater contamination from toxic chemicals. Space for landfills is running out and all landfills eventually leak, so a saner system must be embraced.

Toxic industrial wastes, although often in liquid form, are generally treated the same as solid wastes. Hazardous waste disposal sites are often simply lined ponds. No one has solved the problems of leakage and overflow from rain. Perimeter shallow wells are promoted as adequate for testing for leakage and pumping contaminated water from the ground but to where can we pump if the cess pool is full? William T. Cahill was one of the first to phrase the obvious:

> We must realize that we can no longer throw our wastes away because there is no 'away.'

Incineration

Incineration is touted as an efficient method for disposing of solid wastes by those who hope for a simple solution. Incinerators use solid wastes as fuel, burning refuse and using the heat to make steam for electricity generation. Wastes must be burned at very high temperatures, and incinerator exhausts must be equipped with sophisticated scrubbers and other devices for removing dioxins and other toxic pollutants. There are serious flaws with incineration: incinerator ash contains concentrations of heavy metals, becoming a hazardous waste itself, scrubbers sometimes fail, and incinerators discourage the use of recycling and other waste reduction methods.

Update: The U.S. Supreme Court ruled today (5-2-94) that municipal garbage-to-energy plants must treat the resultant ash as hazardous waste. Let's hear it for the Supremes!

Toxic pollution—just how widespread is it?

Setterberg and Shavelson offer compelling vignettes from all over the country. Here is a sampling:

> In Pilcher, Oklahoma, abandoned copper, lead, and zinc mines overflowed during heavy rains, bubbling up from 'a 10 billion gallon vat of subterranean poison' . . . The extruded acid water burned grasslands, scalded horses' hooves,

and ate through a five-gallon metal bucket. 'Fish had open sores,' recalled one Pilcher resident, 'like somebody took a knife and cut a chunk out of them.'

In Toone, Tennessee, several farming families spent four years in what seemed to be chronic depression, until they discovered chloroform in their drinking water.

In Brookhurst, Wyoming, residents abandoned their chemically contaminated homes, turning the neighborhood into a ghost town and leaving their houses marked with anti-toxics graffiti.

In Oxnard, California, Linda Paxton moved away from her two-story duplex after learning that it had been built upon a field of underground liquid toxic waste pools; she painted one side of her abandoned home with a huge skull-and-crossbones, announcing: *Oxnard's Love Canal. Our Home Toxic Dump.*

[Love Canal refers to a neighborhood in Niagara Falls, New York, where homes were built on land poisoned by toxic waste disposal. After a huge fight, the government bought most of the homes.]

In Pompano Beach, Florida, tiny white particles of vinyl chloride descended from the skies like snow . . . This extremely powerful carcinogen was being pumped into the air from a nearby polyvinyl chloride pipe factory. A health study organized by the local residents found high incidences of liver, heart, and kidney disease and cancer.

In Pearland, Texas, the chances of contracting cancer are calculated as being the highest in the nation—with industrial pollution factored as a leading cause.

In Springfield, Vermont, the residents of a mobile home park didn't realize they were sitting on a vast wasteland of arsenic, benzene, cyanide, and lead—what the regional EPA administrator called 'a chemical time bomb'—until 'there were people in white suits and rubber gloves and rubber boots walking around' testing the soil.

In *The Truth About Where You Live*, Benjamin A. Goldman tells of the 400 Ponca City, Oklahoma, families who were successful with a class-action suit against Conoco oil company, which had poisoned the community's groundwater. The company paid $23 million to buy the homes so the residents could start new lives elsewhere.

It may be impossible to locate far enough downwind to avoid all chemical drift. In "Troubled Waters Run Deep" in the 1993 National Geographic Special *Water*, Michael Parfit wrote:

> At Lake Laberge, way up in the Yukon Territory, a study of fish flesh turned up a variety of chemicals, including the insecticide toxaphene, which has been widely used in Russia. It probably blew east, and rain raked it in.

Don't even consider buying property near agribusiness operations. Setterberg and Shavelson reported the heart-wrenching stories of parents losing children to various cancers, from California's San Joaquin Valley to Yellow Creek, Kentucky, to New York. Interminable bureaucratic jungles, chemical company personnel, and agribusiness owners thwart efforts to end the horror of children born with no hands or feet, or impaired mental ability. In many places, even though tests of well water show contamination from various chemicals, current allowed concentrations preclude decisive action.

Current media reports show that even so-called clean industries are creating health hazards. High rates of miscarriages and low-birthweight babies have become evident in California's Silicon Valley. Suspected are water supplies fouled by the solvents used to clean computer chips.

Part of the solution to toxic pollution—recycling

Recycling is practical for much municipal and some industrial waste materials, and a small but growing proportion of wastes is being recycled. When wastes are mixed, recycling becomes far more difficult and costly. New processes of sorting ferrous and nonferrous metals, paper, glass, and plastics have been developed, and many communities with recycling programs now require refuse separation. Crucial issues in recycling are devising better processing methods, inventing new products for the recycled materials, and finding new markets for them.

Composting is increasingly used to treat some agricultural wastes, as well as such municipal wastes as leaves and brush. Composting systems can produce usable soil conditioners, or humus, within a few months.

Although the movement toward recycling and energy production from wastes may help contend with waste-disposal loads, it is not expected to reduce them so long as a high-consumption, throwaway society continues to generate increasing quantities of discarded material. The most sane plans for managing the solid-waste dilemma are to reduce consumption, eliminate waste, make all containers recyclable, and require all producers to take back their used products and recycle them into new ones. The solution to pollution can begin with more responsible consumer buying practices. Each of us must be part of the solution.

Final thoughts

Even with increased EPA regulation, new pesticides and hundreds of other new compounds are marketed each year. Many are not intended ever to enter the environment, although through waste and accidents most eventually do. The EPA attempts to ensure safe management of an estimated 303 million tons of hazardous waste produced annually in the U.S. The EPA has compiled an inventory of 32,000 sites that may contain hazardous wastes.

Prediction: Americans will increasingly turn to organically-grown produce. Chemical-farming areas will be shunned by informed moderns turning to rural life. Eventually, such land will only be used for food exports to other, hungrier nations.

Land without chemical contamination is still available. Most subsistence farmers were too poor to use the expensive products of the chemical companies, so their old homesteads often make good home sites. Land far removed from industrial and agribusiness areas is available in many parts of the country.

Organic certification programs require soil tests to prove the absence of chemical poisoning. If ground has been subjected to chemical products it may

Our ideals, laws, and customs
should be based on the proposition
that each generation in turn becomes the custodian
rather than the absolute owner of our resources
—and each generation has the obligation
to pass this inheritance on
to the future.
ALDEN WHITMAN

take decades before it is clean of chemical residue. Uncontaminated land is becoming increasingly more valuable and more jealously protected.

Check with local planners to see if incinerators, landfills, or hazardous waste sites exist or are being considered for the area. Determine local attitudes toward recycling. Someone at the local recycling center may know the answers or will direct you to someone who does.

Resources

The 1984 Union Carbide chemical escape disaster in Bhopal, India which killed more than 2,500, and the much less serious chemical release in West Virginia shortly thereafter prompted Congress to pass the Emergency Planning and Community Right-to-Know Act. A brochure is available which explains the Act, including how to get information on chemical releases in any community. To order *Chemicals In Your Community: A Guide To The Emergency Planning And Community Right-To-Know Act,* write:
Emergency Planning and Community Right-to-Know Information
OS-120
U.S. EPA
Washington, DC 20460

EPA Right-To-Know Hotline: 800-535-0202. An information specialist will direct you to a state agency that can give you information about toxic conditions in specific locations.

EPA Hazardous Waste, Superfund Hotline: 800-424-9346. Provides information and interpretation of federal hazardous waste regulations. Will provide referrals regarding other hazardous waste matters.

EPA Pesticide Hotline: 800-858-7378. Provides information on health hazards, cleanup and disposal of pesticides. Will refer callers to human and animal poison control centers in their states if necessary.

EPA Radon Hotline: 800-SOS-RADON for free radon information, including a copy of *Reducing Radon Risks.* It includes state radon contact phone numbers.

The Geology of Radon includes a radioactivity map and is available free from:
U.S. Geological Survey
Branch of Distribution
P.O. Box 25286
Denver, CO 80225

The National Priorities List (Superfund sites) is available from the EPA. If a later list is not available, ask for a copy of the Federal Register/Vol. 57, No. 199/ Wednesday, October 14, 1992/Rules and Regulations. (Hand printed at the top of mine is: NPL-FRU11-1-14, perhaps a file code.) It contains a list of the 1,208 then-designated Superfund sites in all states.
United States Environmental Protection Agency
Public Information Center, PM-211B
401 M Street SW
Washington, DC 20460

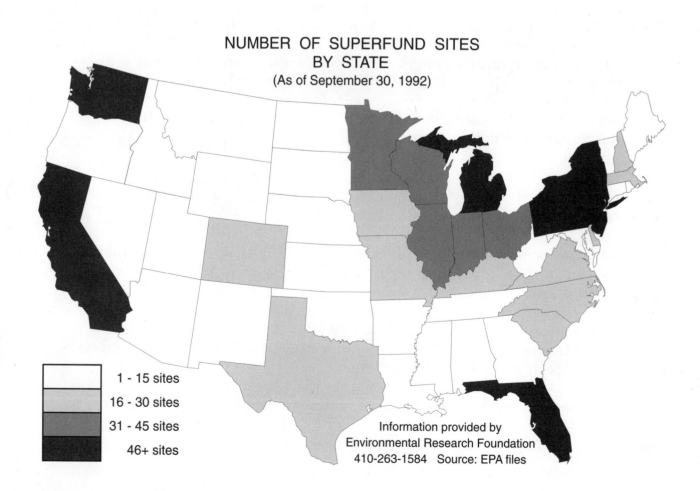

NUMBER OF SUPERFUND SITES
BY STATE
(As of September 30, 1992)

1 - 15 sites
16 - 30 sites
31 - 45 sites
46+ sites

Information provided by
Environmental Research Foundation
410-263-1584   Source: EPA files

Greenpeace
1436 U Street NW
Washington, D.C. 20009
Large number of available environmental publications. Ask for catalog.

Center for Environmental Research Information
26 West St. Clair Street
Cincinnati, OH 45268

Citizen's Clearinghouse for Hazardous Wastes
P.O. Box 6806, 119 Rowell Court
Falls Church, VA 22040
For most people, a crisis center, helpful in dealing with community environmental problems. Source of plain-language publications.

Environmental Research Foundation
P.O. Box 5036
Annapolis, MD 21403-7036
Publishes weekly newsletter *Rachel's Hazardous Waste News* (named after Rachel Carson), provides free rapid-response information service for grass-roots environmental activists, maintains on-line computerized database. Ask for publications list.

- Ford, Norman. *The 50 Healthiest Places to Live and Retire in the United States.* Bedford, MA: Mills & Sanderson, 1991.

- Goldman, Benjamin A. *The Truth About Where You Live: An atlas for action on toxins and mortality.* New York: Times Books/Random House, 1991. Contains many maps showing unhealthful counties.

- LaFavore, Michael. *Radon: The Invisible Threat.* Emmaus, Pennsylvania: Rodale Press, 1987.

- Robbins, Jim. *The Last Refuge.* New York: Morrow, 1993.

- Setterberg, Fred and Lonny Shavelson. *Toxic Nation: The Fight to Save Our Communities from Chemical Contamination.* New York: John Wiley & Sons, 1993.

It is impossible to divorce the question of what we do
from the question of where we are—or, rather, where we think we are.
That no sane creature befouls its own nest is accepted as generally true.
What we conceive to be our nest, and where we think it is,
are therefore questions of the greatest importance.

WENDELL BERRY

29
Finding your ideal area

The method of the enterprising is to plan with audacity,
and execute with vigor; to sketch out a map of possibilities;
and then to treat them as probabilities.

BOVEE

he United States of America is comprised of 50 states, 3,032 counties, 19,083 municipalities, 16,083 townships, and 5,600 towns of fewer than 2,500 residents. Climate zones range from arctic to subtropical. Topography flows from seashore to desert to mountains to great plains to rolling hills and forests. We have land bordering two oceans, a huge gulf, great lakes, medium lakes, small lakes, ponds, rivers, streams, creeks, and springs. It is reasonable to believe that within all this there is for each of us—an ideal place. Let's find yours.

The path to your ideal area

Now that you have pondered all the factors of place and completed your criteria worksheet, it is time to identify your ideal area. If you study pertinent research materials and cover each point, no disaster will befall you if you proceed in a casual, meandering fashion. However, I believe the following guidelines will save you time and prove most pleasurable and successful.

If you have already decided on an area, this is the time to use your iron-willed discipline. Cool down—or chill out, depending on your age group's vocabulary—

and work your way through these steps. You may end up choosing what you have already identified. That's fine, but you will feel good forevermore knowing you have objectively, logically, intelligently arrived at your decision.

1. Using your criteria worksheet, make your criteria list. You may wish to weight each item or to arrange all items in order of importance to you.
2. Use the national maps in this book to identify the regions that meet your criteria for place-related lifestyle, climate, topography, and water quantity. The state maps show low-density areas. Write down all of the appropriate states in those regions—this is your beginning list. Don't be alarmed if this list is fifteen—or only one. After all, there's only one Everglades, and if you want *that* topography, well, that's it—you're headed for Florida.
3. Order materials from the private and public sources listed in this book for those states that appear to most satisfy your needs. Study those materials, plus atlases, and encyclopedias to eliminate states that do not meet your demographic criteria. Ask reference librarians for help—they are worth their weight in data bases.
4. Apply your financial criteria: prices and economic opportunities. Reduce the list to no more than three states.
5. Apply the remaining criteria for lifestyle, air quality, water quality, and health. Narrow your list to a subregion or bioregion. Let's call this your area.
6. Using chapters 27 and 28 on places to avoid and toxic pollution, contact the appropriate sources and get information about the area.
7. Choose towns in areas most free from pollution. Subscribe to their newspapers to check the pulse of the area. Newspapers are excellent sources of cost-of-living figures. In addition to real estate firms, local markets and retail stores often advertise in the local paper.
8. Place an ad in the Personals section of the classifieds requesting contact with others who have moved there from the city. This is a way to get information and maybe make friends—possibly a place to stay when you visit. Expect to hear from every real estate agent in the area. Treat them as a resource—use their area expertise to further inform yourself.
9. Find out about local conditions, taxes and services. In addition to those listed after each chapter, sources of information for local weather, prices, taxes, pollution, crime, density, politics, and economic conditions are real estate agents, chambers of commerce, and bank officers, plus the agriculture extension agent, sheriff, tax assessor, and tax collector
10. Experience the area. Walk the towns. Drive the countryside. Listen to local radio stations. Talk shows quickly reveal local attitudes and concerns. Talk to all you meet. Interview the owners or managers of your bed and breakfast, motel, or campground. Eat in local restaurants. Visit schools. Get lost and ask for help.

If an initial visit indicates that the area is ideal, the very best way to learn all about local conditions is to rent or caretake a property similar to what you want.

Living through all four seasons will allow you to see the area at its best and its worst. To find a vacant property whose owners want caretakers, place an ad in the local newspaper similar to the one successfully used by our friends, shown in chapter 18.

Consider living at an intentional community for a year. This is a way to experience the seasons and conditions and to learn country living skills. A directory is listed at the end of chapter 26.

A way to experience an area for a shorter term is to utilize a home exchange service. For a fee, participants' home information is published and distributed to all subscribers. "Exchangers" trade homes with others for holidays or extended vacations. One such service is listed below.

Home exchange service

Intervac U.S.
30 Corte San Fernando
Tiburon, CA 94920-2014
415-435-3497

30
Real estate
and
real estate agents

For identification, California merchants ask
check writers for their real estate license.
Not everyone in California has a driver's license.

Dennis G. Blair

Real property versus personal property

irst the basics. Real property is all property that is not personal
property and personal property is all property that is not real property.
That is a true statement—but will not help us decide which type of
property such items as rose bushes, fences, and satellite dish antennas
represent.

Real property is primarily land and that which is attached to it. In the case
of the above-mentioned items, they may be real property or personal property
depending on their method of attachment to the land and depending on the
intention of the owner—these conditions are considered by courts in case of
dispute. A satellite dish sitting on a concrete pad, secured by guy wires, may be
considered personal property by its owner and the law. A satellite dish bolted to a
steel post set in the same concrete pad is probably real property.

Typically, the only time these questions become an issue is when a property is sold and the buyer takes possession, only to discover that the prize-winning rose bush and its buried container have been taken away, the split-rail fence has been loaded and hauled away, and the satellite receiver has been unbolted and removed from the site.

There is only one certain item that will prevent misunderstanding about what will and will not remain with the real property—a written contract, spelling out what is included in the sale price. My advice is this: have your agent write and attach to the sales contract a personal property addendum listing all items of personal property that you would like to have stay with the property and especially list all items that are in the gray area between personal and real property. These include but are by no means limited to television antennas, FM antennas, window coverings, bed spreads that match window coverings, fireplace inserts, free-standing dishwashers, refrigerators that are built-in, chandeliers and other special light fixtures, stained-glass windows, ceiling fans, window air-conditioners, and mail boxes on posts in old milk cans. In some places, those cans actually cost money—after this book becomes wildly successful they will likely become downright expensive.

Andrew Jackson's birthplace, Mecklenburg County, North Carolina, c. 1893

Laws of agency

Agents

The basic law of agency is that an agent owes the principal (in real estate that's usually the seller) a *fiduciary responsiveness* founded on trust and confidence. The agent must at all times act in the best interests of the principal. The agent has an obligation to disclose all known facts which the principal may use to make a decision. The agency relationship between seller and agent is established by the listing contract.

Buyer's agents are becoming more common. A buyer can retain a real estate broker to find a suitable property. The buyer agrees to pay a fee to the broker upon performance. The terms of the agreement should be in writing to eliminate misunderstanding and to be enforceable. The broker may not receive compensation from the seller without the buyer's permission and only upon full disclosure to the buyer.

Conflict of interest

In most cases a real estate agent, through the listing agreement, is legally working for the seller. Some believe this means that the buyer is on his own and is likely to be mistreated by the agent. Let's examine this carefully.

First, in most states there are laws that require full disclosure to buyers of all known conditions that affect the value of the property. That's right, no secrets. If the seller knows that the basement floods every spring, he must disclose that fact to the agent and the agent must disclose it to the buyer. If the roof leaks, if the well runs dry every September, if the neighbor is a retired general who drives a Sherman tank up and down the road early every morning, if the dishwasher dances into the middle of the kitchen every Thanksgiving evening, these conditions must be reported to the buyer. If they are not, both the seller and the agent may be liable for damages. Judges take a dim view of willful nondisclosure and even have the power to set a sale aside, in addition to damages and criminal penalties. And the agent could lose his or her real estate license.

While the agent gets paid by the seller (with money from the buyer), guess who really makes the deal work or not? The buyer. And in most cases the agent gets not one dollar until the transaction is successfully completed. So an agent is highly motivated to help *everybody* get what they want, so that the sale closes and the commission gets paid. Also, after the transaction is closed, the buyer/owner is now a prospective seller for the agent. Keenly aware of this from the beginning, it is understandable that the agent wishes to impress the buyer with professionalism.

A full-time agent who has operated in an area for a year or two and who enjoys a good reputation in the community is succeeding in a demanding business by helping people get what they want. As to the information source of reputations, sellers often leave the area; buyers *are* the "reputation community."

Agent motivation

Real estate licensees live with the pressure of uncertain income, as do all who are paid only by commission. Let's be candid—like anyone who works for a living, an agent wants to be paid. So the agent wants to make the deal work. The agent wants the buyer to make an offer that the seller will accept. If the buyer makes a low offer, then the agent wants the seller to either accept it or to make a counter-offer that the buyer will accept. A good agent will continue to write counteroffers rather than rejections as long as the seller wants to sell and the buyer wants to buy. The agent will continue to do everything legally possible to help the seller and buyer find agreement and complete the sale. That's how agents get paid.

Real estate agents

Real estate agent is a generic term used to describe anyone who, for a commission, lists, sells, exchanges, rents, or leases real property. This generally means brokers and salespersons licensed by the state wherein they do business. Brokers can conduct business on their own; salespersons must work under the supervision of a broker, who is responsible for their actions. A salesperson may be an employee or an independent contractor in the view of the IRS.

Each state sets its own licensing requirements for education and continuing education for salespersons, and education, experience, and continuing education for brokers. Required salesperson education ranges from none in Alaska, Maine, Montana, New Hampshire, Rhode Island, and Vermont, to 180 classroom hours in Texas. Broker experience (as a salesperson) requirements range from none in Wisconsin to five years in Delaware.

Persons exempt from licensing laws include property owners dealing with their own property, lawyers conducting a transaction as an incidental part of their duties as an attorney, trustees and receivers in bankruptcy, legal guardians, administrators and executors handling an estate, government agency employees dealing in agency business, and persons operating under powers of attorney.

Realtors®

Not all real estate agents are Realtors®. Realtors® are licensed agents who belong to the National Association of Realtors® (NAR) and subscribe to a strict code of ethics. This is not to say that Realtors® are inherently more ethical than non-Realtors®, but NAR provides an extra layer of protection for the public, namely the local real estate board's ethics and arbitration committee and the hearings it conducts. Hearings are available at low or no cost to any seller or buyer who believes a Realtor® has done them wrong. During my years as ethics and arbitration committee chairman and as board president I monitored many

John Adams House, Quincy, Massachusetts, c. 1893

such hearings. My experience is that Realtors® tend to hold their peers to a higher standard than does the public. Realtors® are highly motivated to upgrade their image. Complainants therefore receive fast and fair justice—always faster, and oftentimes fairer, than with the courts.

Ethics hearings address questions of conduct; arbitration hearings adjudicate money matters. Ethics hearings are most commonly brought by one Realtor® against another. Arbitrations typically settle client complaints against a Realtor® regarding financial matters, although Realtor® versus Realtor® is not uncommon. A court of law will uphold the decision of a properly conducted arbitration hearing. If you ever feel you have been wronged by a Realtor® do not hesitate to register a complaint with the local real estate board. A complaint must be in writing.

Country real estate agents are less likely to be Realtors® than city agents because of distance considerations. I do not downgrade country agents for not being Realtors® if there is no real estate board within a reasonable driving distance. I bought my property using a non-Realtor®.

As in any profession, education, experience, ability, and integrity are the qualities of excellence. For the first months I was in real estate, I expected someone to notice my naiveté and ask me how long I had been an agent. No one ever did. They should have. Country real estate agents typically do not handle as many transactions per year as their city cousins, so experience does not equate on a year-for-year basis.

Part-time agents

From extensive personal experience I am biased against part-time agents. Of the many part-time agents I have known, only one was top-notch. When part-time agents are at their regular jobs they are not available to take care of their clients' business. Some part-time agents partner with another agent who covers for them when they are not available. As with doctors and dentists who have others cover for them while they are on vacation, this does not provide optimum personal service for the client, and the back-up person cannot know all details of each case or transaction. My recommendation is to work with an experienced full-time agent.

Of course even some full-time agents are not worth their salt. Others are invaluable. What you want is a professional person who is very knowledgeable about properties, financing, laws, conditions, and values in your target area. Take your time and use your very best judgment choosing an agent. Do not feel obligated to agents

just because they have spent time talking to you. Like any professional, an agent needs to earn your respect and support. Once you decide on an agent, treat him or her with the same respect that you desire and that you would give any other professional.

Why I recommend using an agent

Agents are valuable not only for their specialized knowledge and experience but because they are third parties, emotionally removed from the egos of the principals. Agents who specialize in a given field will always be more knowledgeable and effective than a seller or buyer who tries to represent himself/ herself. Buyers and sellers are emotionally involved and may damage or destroy a transaction due to temperament. Ballplayers, movie stars, writers, attorneys, and many others use agents to represent them on important matters. A buyer who represents himself may not have a fool for a client but he will likely have unprofessional representation.

Real estate agents are experts in real estate transactions *in their area*. They know local values, financing, escrow procedures, laws, customs, and who best provides the many and various needed inspections and services. Agents are strongly motivated to have a successful transaction and are experts in making that happen.

You may feel I recommend using an agent because I am an ex-Realtor®. Although I had nearly eight years full-time experience as a real estate agent, including six years as broker of my own office at the time, I used an agent to handle the purchase of the property that is now my permanent home—the most important real estate transaction of my life. I did so for all of the above reasons.

And, in case you are wondering, I neither asked for nor received any special consideration or commission referral fee. I did, however, write the purchase contract.

How to choose an agent

Judging integrity is like guessing the weight of an elephant—it's easy to be fooled by presence. So ask many people in your target area who is good and who is not. Certain names will recur—in both categories.

Ask for recommendations from escrow officers and bank loan officers. You are likely to be in an area where you know no one. Certain criteria are useful. Is the agent a Realtor®? Does he/she subscribe to a multiple listing service? Not all rural areas have one, but if there is one and an agent does not use the service, that agent cannot show you all of the listings available in the area. How long has he/she been in real estate? Is he/she full-time? Ask for an estimated purchase cost sheet; if the agent hems and haws, excuse yourself and go on down the street to the next office. Ask about local financing, title, and escrow customs. Ask how the agent feels about being the sellers' agent and serving you at the same time. Ask for a list of the buyers' names and phone numbers for the last five closed transactions. Call some of them and ask for their feelings about how the agent handled their transaction. Glowing recommendations from past clients are indicative of competence but are not a guarantee; those transactions may have been much simpler.

Observe how agents handle themselves. Careful interviewing is a sign of a professional agent, as the process saves everybody's time. Good agents will take the time to clearly understand what you want and what you wish to pay. If you will need a loan to finance your purchase, they will determine your qualifications, either themselves or through a loan agent who will take your information. Agents will make a list of appropriate properties to show you and will call for appointments with the owners—at the same time making sure that the property is still available.

Don't go out looking at properties with an agent you are not comfortable with—for any reason. Looking at country property is time- and fuel-consuming. Although you are not legally obligated to stay with a particular agent, once that agent has spent considerable time, energy, and fuel showing you properties, you are both going to feel pretty bad if the relationship abruptly ends. Make sure you are satisfied with an agent's qualifications before looking at listings. If the vibes are bad, state honestly that you'd like to interview other agents.

Open listings—a country condition

In my experience, country agents operate similarly to city agents but differently in one practice that is notable. For sound reasons many city brokers and multiple listing services will not accept open listings.

An *open listing* is a nonexclusive listing given by a seller to one or several real estate brokers; a commission is paid only to the broker procuring a buyer, *and* the seller reserves the right to sell the property with no obligation to any broker. Unscrupulous sellers sometimes try to cheat brokers out of a commission by dealing directly with potential buyers brought to the property by the broker. The act is called "going around the broker." Brokers cannot justify spending time and advertising dollars on a listing that may be sold any day by another broker or the seller, with no compensation to the first broker. In spite of these dangers, in many rural areas agents regularly take open listings, especially in those areas without a multiple listing service.

Open listings and the lack of a multiple listing service (MLS) create a negative condition for buyers. Under such conditions buyers must visit several brokers to be sure that they are aware of all available properties, which can be very time consuming. There is no way around it; if you find that in your target area agents do not have or belong to an MLS then you will have to use multiple agents to be sure of seeing all available properties.

An *exclusive listing* can come in two flavors: *exclusive agency* and *exclusive right to sell*. An exclusive agency listing means that the seller agrees to pay a commission to the listing broker even if another broker provides the buyer. In that case the listing and selling brokers usually split the commission according to their prior agreement. Exclusive agency listings allow sellers to sell their property and not owe a commission. An exclusive right to sell listing is where the seller agrees to pay the listing broker a commission no matter who sells the property, including the seller. The advantage to the broker is obvious. The advantage to the seller is that the broker will spend money on advertising, will submit the listing to the MLS, and will generally expend all possible effort to sell the property because of the certainty of getting paid if successful.

FSBOs

If you happen to find a property for sale by owner (FSBO, pronounced fizbo) and you wish to buy it, I recommend that you use an agent to draw the contract according to the terms you dictate, to advise you on financing, and to recommend termite, structural and other inspectors if you want them, appraisers, surveyors, lenders, escrow agents, and title companies. Negotiate a fee with the agent, to be paid from escrow upon successful closing of the transaction. Have the agent type up a simple agreement stating what services will be provided and the fee you will pay. Once you both sign, it is an enforceable contract.

If you choose to act as your own agent

Educate yourself. Learn the language of real estate; start with the glossary in this book. Study real property descriptions (U.S. Survey method, metes and bounds, and lot and block, all of which may be used for country property), rights of way and easements, title insurance and title opinions, escrow procedures and customs, types of financing and instruments used with each, mechanics liens, appraisers and methods of appraising, surveys, and inspections—health inspections of wells and septic systems, soil tests, structural inspections, termite inspections, energy-efficiency inspections, etc.

Know that all matters pertaining to real estate contracts, agreements, and understandings are rarely enforceable unless they are in writing, so study contract law and learn to write contracts. Basic contract forms are available but rarely include room for the appropriate conditions and addendums often needed in country property transactions.

Expect your real estate education to take time. If you are willing to spend the time educating yourself, if you learn the customs and procedures appropriate to your target area, and if you intend to pay cash for your property then you will only be restricted by your available time, ego, patience, and competence.

Be sure to have the property appraised by a licensed appraiser. This will probably cost you between $250 and $500 but is the most reliable estimate of value you can get without using an agent familiar with area values.

Expect real estate agents to be uncooperative—they are not keen on helping novices who are cutting into their business. You will probably have to find properties that have not been listed, which means that most properties will not be available to you. You will likely be limited to FSBOs and properties you find yourself the same way that real estate agents do, by making a lot of phone calls.

Expect something to go wrong. If you would like to know *most* of what can go wrong, spend a few days talking to an experienced escrow officer. She (most often female) will turn your hair gray with real estate horror stories.

On using a lawyer to help with a real estate transaction

I am biased against lawyers being involved in most residential and rural land real estate transactions because of my experiences where they caused deals to be lost through their insistence on some contract condition that caused one of the principals to back out of the deal, or because they caused delays.

Some lawyers specialize in real estate and are competent to help buyers or sellers in their area. Unless they are very active in real estate, lawyers are rarely knowledgeable about property values, and price is usually the most important factor in any real estate transaction. I have expressed my feelings above on the subject of part-time real estate agents; lawyers who occasionally handle real estate transactions belong in the same category.

Lawyers are good for reviewing contracts that an unrepresented buyer or seller has written. In their effort to protect their client they tend to unnecessarily complicate contracts. In real estate transactions, time is of the essence. Lawyers sometimes cause transactions to be delayed and made more difficult by taking too long to do their work. And they add to the cost of the transaction.

Lawyers are not supposed to act as real estate agents except as an incidental part of their work for a client, for instance as part of their duties as trustees or executors/executrixes. In my considered opinion, a lawyer who wants to be a real estate agent should first obtain a real estate license. Then they should handle a large number of real estate transactions each year so they stay informed as to local values and conditions.

George Washington was a surveyor.
He took the exact measure of the British
and surveyed himself out about the most valuable
piece of land in America at that time, Mount Vernon.
George could not only tell the truth but land values.
WILL ROGERS

The father of our country and his country home

George Washington
Daguerrotype of Gilbert Stuart painting, 1853

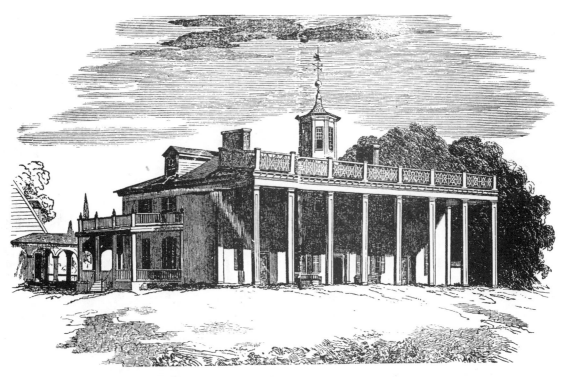

Mount Vernon (built 1774-1787: John Ariss, architect), Fairfax County, Virginia, c. 1848

31
Looking at
country property

It is finally time to find your ideal country place. Do try to exercise patience—you've come too far to make a mistake now by hurrying. Take your time—look at a lot of properties before you make a decision. Yes, it is possible that the first one you look at will be the right one, but keep looking anyway, or you will always wonder. In this case, resist falling in love before the marriage.

We have a neighbor who, after seeing our place, expressed the common buyer's lament: "We didn't look enough." He and his wife have a sound house on 40 acres, garden space, plenty of forest for firewood, and at the lower back of their property the downstream part of our creek. They are very nice people and we hope they stay, but his statement needs little interpretation.

When to do it

The great French Marshall Lyautey once asked his gardener to plant a tree.
The gardener objected that the tree was slow growing and would
not reach maturity for 100 years. The Marshall replied,
"In that case, there is no time to lose; plant it this afternoon!"
JOHN F. KENNEDY

We Americans have a cultural quirk to take actions according to the calendar. In the doldrums period following Christmas and New Year's we fret about who, what and where we are, and we often resolve to initiate change. Our social conditioning programs us to initiate change, to be more bold, to do things that we have been putting off—and to do them at the beginning of a week, a month, or a year. Imagine the intensity of energy that will occur on the first day of the year 2000! Mercy! A new millennium!

Throughout my real estate career in northern California I found that the first four months of each year registered the heaviest sales activity. In northern-tier states, real estate sales activity tends to follow the habits of plants: with spring warmth comes activity—with the snow comes hibernation. Northern sellers know that buyers are few when the days grow short and the white stuff falls. The reverse is true of states such as Arizona and Florida. Boiling hot summers and wilting humidity rarely motivate serious activity.

Financially, the worst weather time of the year is the best time to buy. Prices and interest rates tend to rise with strong sales activity. There is often a correlation between interest rates and election years. As national elections approach, politicians try to win voters with low interest rates and an infusion of federal (read your/my) money.

Time of year

The ideal number of times to inspect property is four, in each of the seasons. That will be impractical unless you are living in the area and unless the owner of your dream property has Job-like patience. Realistically, determine what conditions are like during the worst times of the year: when it rains the most— when mud and flood enter each conversation, when it is the hottest and the coldest, when snow and ice cancel all travel. If you like a property during those conditions you will love it during better times.

My advice is to look at property after the school year begins. I struck the deal on my place in late September. Droughts most often occur in late summer and early autumn, so look at property in the fall when water supplies are most strained. Grass will be brown. Sellers will be more realistic about prices and terms as they look forward to winter in a place they no longer wish to be. Tourists will have gone home and the community will be most like what it is during the majority of the year. Local people will have more time to talk to you.

Depending on the area, the inventory of available properties may be smallest in the fall and winter. One strategy is to find a place you like in the fall, then wait until spring when listings are most numerous, look at all the new listings and, unless you see one you like better, buy the one you found last fall. A plus is that you will have seen the property during two different seasons. The downside to this plan is having to resist the hungry real estate agent's logic that buying during the winter will likely get you the best price. Expect many phone calls. And of course there is the chance that another offer may be submitted while you wait.

Time of the week

Weekday and weekend sounds and activities are often drastically different. The property that looks ideal on a quiet Saturday or Sunday afternoon will be awful on Monday through Friday when garbage trucks thunder by, stirring up clouds of dust on their way to the landfill at the end of the road. That is exactly the case with friends of ours. Conversely, the road that is quiet during the week may explode with weekend traffic heading for the local swimming hole, fishing stream, and picnic spot. So there is no ideal time of the week. Once you find a property you like, make your second inspection when conditions are most likely to be different than when you first saw it.

Time of the day

The action of the sun may make a cheery kitchen in the morning and create hot boxes of rooms exposed to the burning rays of afternoon. Again make your final inspection at a different time of day than your first visit.

Looking at properties

Looking at country property requires attention to many more details than when looking at city property. Without city streets, codes, ordinances, utilities, and services to insulate you from natural and human conditions you will want to consider essentially everything.

Make appointments with real estate agents a few days before you will see them. Help agents help you best by being open about your needs and your financial position. Explain completely the type of property you are looking for. Tell them your priorities. "We want a nice place in the woods that's not too expensive" doesn't get it. To hold back pertinent information is to waste your time and the agent's time. Do not wait until after you've been shown several places to tell your agent that he or she is on the wrong track.

After an agent has shown you everything available, move on to the next agent in the next town. If there is not a local multiple listing service you will have to see several agents in each town to make sure you have seen everything. Repeat the process. Tell each agent the features of properties you have seen and what you did and did not like. Keep a scoresheet on each property.

If your agents tell you that there is nothing available that meets your requirements, move on to the next agent. If you get the same response from several agents, you may wish to rethink your demands.

How many places to look at

In *Harrowsmith Country Life* (January-February 1992) Richard Todd offered "The Eleven Farm Theory."

> Look at ten farms. Buy none, but rank them in order of appeal. Then buy the next farm that you like better than the one you liked best.

Todd tried it. He made it nearly through the first ten before he fell in love with a place that, well, for the rest of the sad tale I refer you to that issue. Suffice to say the theory *might* work for you. Don't feel guilty if you, too, fall in love before ten. It's as good a time to fall in love as any other. Sorry. *No, I'm not.*

If you find yourself confronted with too many places to look at, you have given your agent too much latitude. Narrow your instructions down: "We want no fewer than X acres and no more than X. The house must face south or southeast. There must be at least X space open around the house. There must be at least X acres of hardwood forest for firewood. There must be live water." Like that. By giving specific information on items that are most important to you, you will shorten the list of possible places.

I found my ideal place on the third day of my search. It was tempting to make an immediate offer but I continued to look for many more days at dozens of additional properties, found nothing to match it, came back, looked at it again and made an offer. If I had not looked at those extra dozens of places I might wonder if I missed something better. As it is, I know I bought the place best for me out of everything available.

Problems commonly overlooked

It is easy to overlook an item or condition of importance. Commonly overlooked conditions include access problems, easements, water taste, sanitation, potential development, and noise from commercial activities or nearby highways.

When inspecting homes, buyers are often shy about opening closets, cupboards, and drawers. Don't be. This is your potential home. Look at and into anything that will help you know that place. If you are not sure what you are seeing, ask. Do not be embarrassed about not understanding a pressure pump system, a gravity-flow wood furnace, a chicken self-feeder, a compost bin, or any of the countless other items found with country homes.

Building sites

Building site evaluation is similar whether the property has been improved with a house or the land is bare. Any building site must have stable soil and good drainage, especially in high-rainfall areas. A slightly sloping site is ideal. Flat land is most suspect. Look for low spots that do not drain well after a heavy rain.

Waterways, side hollows, and other obvious drainage areas should be inspected for signs of flooding. Past flooding will have left leaves, weeds, pieces of bark, and other detritus in the low branches of trees and shrubs in the stream or drainage area. This evidence often will be found many feet above the ground.

Flat land in high-rainfall areas often has drainage problems, especially where the soil is heavy. Such conditions often make it difficult to install a good septic tank and leach field system for waste disposal. If in doubt a percolation test should be made a contract condition and performed after contract acceptance.

Ridgetop and valley pros and cons

Ridgetops usually have nice views, freedom from flooding, good access, and good air flow. Disadvantages include well depths, dryness, susceptibility to fires (fires burn upward), rocky or thin soil, and high winds.

Valley advantages include springs and streams, abundant groundwater, and good soil. Disadvantages include steep access roads, flooding, and a later sunrise and earlier sunset. Cold air drainage from above is a negative in wintertime but pleasant during the summer.

Access

Ask your real estate agent to verify the fact of legal ingress and egress rights. If the property does not front on a public road there should be a *deeded* easement for road purposes. If in doubt make that a condition in the contract.

Dependable year-round access requires a good road. South-facing slopes will be drier and will melt snow most quickly. During cold weather, north-facing slopes hold snow and ice, alternately thawing and freezing, making roads dangerous or

Example of property with excellent water, great views, and poor access

even impassable. Unless built up with gravel, lowland and flatland roads are prone to rut, hold water, and grow mud after rain, which becomes ice in the winter.

Solar exposure

The house site, garden site, and other cropland will ideally have effective solar exposure. South slopes receive maximum solar exposure both summer and winter. Southwesterly exposure is warmer than southeasterly because late afternoon sun is hotter than early morning sun. For gardens I prefer southeasterly slopes because they receive first light, warm earlier in the spring, and are protected from cold winds coming out of the northwest.

During the growing season, the warmest land is that which is most perpendicular to the sun's rays. South-facing slopes are typically drier, sunnier, warmer—roses, grasses, tomatoes, oaks and pines do well there with adequate rainfall. North-facing slopes are cooler and more moist—good for ferns, azaleas, rhododendron, blueberries, and fruit trees—to lessen the chance of premature bloom and late-freeze damage. North-facing slopes might be preferred house sites in very hot dry climates.

Utilities

The main thing here is to ensure that electric and telephone service are installed or, if not, determine what it will cost to bring them in versus the cost of an independent solar and generator-backup system. If you will be working with a computer you will want to discover conditions such as telephone line static, electrical voltage fluctuations, and frequency and duration of outages. If the agent or owners do not seem to be forthcoming about utility problems you may wish to talk to the neighbors. Check with the phone company on the availability and cost of a private line.

Do not assume that neighbors will allow an easement across their property. If power lines must be brought in, make getting a legal easement a contract condition.

Views

While evaluating views, keep in mind that trees grow. If they are yours, you can trim them or cut them down and replace them with shorter varieties. If they are a neighbor's you will likely have to live with them. Many trees reach 100 or more feet at maturity.

Wind

Learn wind directions and speeds. A homestead exposed to strong, hot summer winds and cold winter winds can be a disaster. The exposed side and the lee side of a hill can be like two different worlds. Trees work well as a windbreak if they are large enough and thick enough.

This homesteader has property with great access, excellent views, and unlimited building sites

If you are considering using wind to generate electricity, know that wind plants require an average monthly wind speed of 8 to 14 miles per hour. Sites should be clear of upwind obstructions.

Use the property scoresheet

Some recommend using a property checklist. Yep, there's a house. Check house. Yep, there's a tree. Check tree. Garden? Check. Road? Check.

I prefer to use a property scoresheet. Let us not just make sure everything is there; let us decide what it is worth to us. So make copies of the property scoresheet on the following page and use one to rate each place you look at. It is the only way to effectively compare properties. After you have looked at ten to fifteen places, there is no other way you will remember the details of even several of them.

If you have a camera, take a picture or two of each place. Be sure to make a note on the scoresheet of some unique features shown in each picture so they can easily be matched with the correct property.

Now let's learn how to make a final evaluation before making an offer to purchase.

Dedicated real estate agent inspecting rural property

PROPERTY SCORESHEET

Address _____

Contact person and phone_____

Acreage_____ Price _____ Terms _____

Occupancy conditions _____

Score 0 to 10 points for each item. Zero is non-existing, 1 is poor, 10 is excellent. With multiple items, (spring, stream, well) circle what is found and assign score.

Water source: spring, stream, well_____ Supply system _____

Water quantity _____ Water quality _____

Solar exposure _____ Windbreak _____

Soil quality: garden_____ fields _____ woodlot _____

Woodlot_____ Orchard_____ Yard _____ Pasture _____

Fencing: garden _____ pasture_____ fields _____

Topography _____ Scenery _____

Drainage: road, house, garden, yard, woodlot, fields _____

Access road: surface material, width, well graded _____

Electricity _____ Telephone _____

Waste system: septic, outhouse, composting toilet_____

House size_____ Rooms _____ Quality _____ Roof _____

Foundation _____ Siding _____ Doors/windows _____

Heating system_____ Plumbing system _____

Special features _____

Other buildings: garage, barn, shop, chicken coop _____

Notes _____

_____

_____

32
Making a final evaluation before purchase

If decisions were a choice between alternatives,
decisions would come easy.
Decision is the selection
and formulation of alternatives.
KENNETH BURKE
TOWARDS A BETTER LIFE, 1932

Don't fall in love until after the marriage

es, I know. You have painstakingly developed your criteria, have researched the entire northern hemisphere, have looked at every place available in your chosen area, and have found your absolutely perfect piece of property without which you will not be able to live. Congratulations. But, as the young folks say, chill out. This is the time to keep your cool, maintain complete composure, evidence dignity and mature calculating discernment. You've come too far to blow it now.

Try harder.

Once you have seen the place that appears to be "it" you must return at another time to inspect it thoroughly. To not do so is to risk overlooking a condition you cannot live with. An equal risk is paying too much, which will brand you as a dumb city person and is the sort of thing for which newcomers are derided in all communities.

You already will have filled out the property scoresheet when you first looked at the property. Review each item with a low score and decide if you can live with the condition, or determine what the cost will be to correct it. Such costs should be deducted from the price you would be willing to pay for the property if it were in top condition. You will need those dollars to correct the deficiencies.

Water

If you did not determine at the initial visit that water is both plentiful and of good quality, now is the time to do so. Water is a clearly understood necessity, so, if there is a correctable problem you may be able to persuade the seller to fix it.

A good test for quantity is to open an outside faucet and let it run while continuing the property evaluation. It should be running just as strongly an hour

This is what happens when essential country skills are not taken seriously. These boys failed to learn Essential country skill #44: driving a horse. They have ignored Instruction #1: At all times insist on being in charge. If the horse disagrees with you, pull over to the side of the road and talk to the horse in a calm manner until it is mutually understood that you are in charge. Talk as long as necessary.

after turning it on. If there is a problem with a well running dry the seller will likely bring it up at this point and ask that the water be turned off to avoid a household shortage.

Look at the pressure system equipment and ask how old it is and what problems have been experienced. In cold-weather areas the pressure tank and piping must be protected from freezing. Run each faucet to determine if the flow is sufficient and steady. With most home water systems the strength of water flow and temperature fluctuates slightly as the pump motor cycles on and off. The better systems have a large pressure tank and three-quarter inch or larger piping. With such a system, if the pressure switches are correctly adjusted, pressure fluctuation will be minimal. This is essential—especially adequately-sized piping— to avoid the dangerous spectacle of a naked human being (you) doing the hula dance to avoid butt-burn in the shower.

With a small pressure tank, pressure fluctuation may not occur with even only one faucet wide open as the pump may run continually. Turn the shower on and observe it. Flush the toilet and see if the pressure drops. While running faucets, observe how well the drains work.

Water system problems are unlikely to be of great enough magnitude for you to reject the property but you should be aware of them, as you may use them to affect the price and terms of purchase.

Quality may first be checked by tasting the water. Expect well water to taste different than the chlorinated city water to which you are accustomed, but it should not have an off taste. Toilets, shower heads, and faucet nozzles may show color or crust buildup which indicates a high mineral content and which may cause plumbing problems.

Soil

If farming or market gardening is your intention make your acceptance of soil tests a condition of the purchase contract. You can observe the general condition of the soil by what is growing well in the garden and in fields and woods. You may wish to review the material on soil quality in chapter 10.

Houses

Structural and energy-efficiency inspections are typically made after contract acceptance. If you feel inspections are important make them a contract condition, with your disapproval adequate reason for the contract to be cancelled. At this point you should satisfy yourself, by asking and by looking, of the general condition of the house. Items to check include quality and condition of foundation or basement, siding, roofing, insulation, doors and windows, heating system— including a lined masonry flue, electrical and plumbing systems, and general overall condition. Deficiencies may be acceptable if they are reflected in the asking price.

New homes may have more problems than old ones that have been well-maintained. In *Crumbling Dreams*, Ruth S. Martin details personal and national problems with incompetent and sleazy builders.

Property lines

The only sure way to know what you are buying is to walk the property lines. Country property corners are usually identified by surveyors with monuments—pipes driven into the ground, or large stones, or stone piles, often painted red. Property lines running through wooded land are indicated by red surveyor's tape tied to branches—they will be close but are often off the line somewhat. Occasionally a tree will be blazed by cutting off the bark and marking the smooth wood with red paint.

Fences and roads should not be relied upon as property-line proof. For many reasons they may have been built within or beyond true property lines. One of the fences on our property is about thirty feet north of the line marked by surveyors.

Country surveyors are like people in other professions—they are limited by their training, experience, and integrity. In some places they are not required to be certified or licensed. Additionally, large parcels of relatively inexpensive acreage leads to an attitude of "it's not important to get the lines marked perfectly—a few feet one way or the other is of no consequence." And rough, hilly land is difficult to walk easily, let alone survey or carefully mark. A place originally surveyed "on the ground" may be deeded as "40 acres more or less." Surveyed using modern instruments, the same property may be many acres less. If in doubt, you may wish to make your offer based on dollars per acre, so you only pay for what you receive.

We have friends who built a house on what they believed was the edge of their land. Years later they discovered their house was on their neighbor's land. Such a situation is at least embarrassing, and could be very expensive to correct.

All of which is to alert you to the possibility of mismarked property lines. If the value of your target property is substantially affected by a feature—a building, a spring, a cave, or a certain tree close to the property line—you may wish to hire a licensed surveyor to make another survey.

Take your time

Take plenty of time inspecting the property. Do not allow yourself to be hurried by the agent or the seller. Satisfy yourself that this is indeed your ideal country home. Make notes of all deficiencies that money can correct. Tell your agent to ask the seller to correct them, in writing, in your offer. Expect the seller to counteroffer. You may do the same. Once you have an accepted contract and are certain of your financing you can start falling in love.

You've come a long way. I sincerely hope you have enjoyed the journey. Happy country living!

Believe nothing,
no matter where you read it,
or who said it
—even if I have said it—
unless it agrees
with your own reason
and your own common sense.

THE BUDDHA

Essential country equipment
#4: chickens

Chickens come in designer colors and models. The ones with shorter rear plumage are hens. Hens are hard workers. They are sweet, gentle things that produce the main ingredient in omelettes and Angel's Food cake, and the second most important ingredient in egg nog.

Male models are the original design alarm clock which require no electricity, batteries, or winding. Fuel with corn and stones. Alarm goes off about 4 A.M. and continues until midmorning, strangulation, or axing, whichever you choose. Snooze buttons are not an option. Other than providing this uncontrollable alarm service, males—also called cocks, roosters, and several unprintable names— are best known for being oversexed macho terrorists.

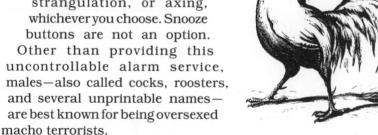

Appendix A
Resources

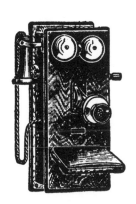

*The soul of our quest
for the simple life . . .
reflects a need to reestablish
control of our lives.*

National information sources

United States Information Centers

Alabama, Birmingham, Mobile 800-366-2998
Arizona, Phoenix 800-359-3997
Arkansas, Little Rock 800-366-2998
California, L.A., San Diego,
      San Francisco, Santa Ana . . . 800-726-4995
      Sacramento 916-973-1695
Colorado, Colorado Springs,
      Denver, Pueblo 800-359-3997
Connecticut, Hartford, New Haven 800-347-1997
Florida, Fort Lauderdale,
      Jacksonville, Miami, Orlando,
      St. Petersburg, Tampa,
      West Palm Beach 800-347-1997
Georgia, Atlanta 800-347-1997
Illinois, Chicago 800-366-2998
Indiana, Gary 800-366-2998
      Indianapolis 800-347-1997
Iowa, All locations 800-735-8004
Kansas, All locations 800-735-8004
Kentucky, Louisville 800-347-1997
Louisiana, New Orleans 800-366-2998
Maryland, Baltimore 800-347-1997
Massachusetts, Boston 800-347-1997
Michigan, Detroit 800-347-1997
Minnesota, Minneapolis 800-366-2998
Missouri, St. Louis. 800-366-2998
      All other locations 800-735-8004
Nebraska, Omaha. 800-366-2998
      All other locations 800-735-8004
New Jersey, Newark, Trenton 800-347-1997
New Mexico, Albuquerque 800-359-3997

New York, Albany, Buffalo,
        New York, Rochester 800-347-1997
North Carolina, Charlotte 800-347-1997
Ohio, Akron, Cincinnati, Cleveland,
        Columbus, Dayton, Toledo . . .800-347-1997
Oklahoma, Oklahoma City, Tulsa . . 800-366-2998
Oregon, Portland 800-726-4995
Pennsylvania, Philadelphia,
        Pittsburgh 800-347-1997
Rhode Island, Providence 800-347-1997
Tennessee, Chattanooga   800-347-1997
        Memphis, Nashville 800-366-2998
Texas, Austin, Dallas, Fort Worth,
        Houston, San Antonio 800-366-2998
Utah, Salt Lake City 800-359-3997
Virginia, Norfolk, Richmond,
        Roanoke 800-347-1997
Washington, Seattle, Tacoma 800-726-4995
Wisconsin, Milwaukee 800-366-2998

United States Department of the Interior

U.S. Geological Survey
Branch of Distribution
Box 25286
Denver, CO 80225
Excellent source of catalog of maps and free booklets on water, ground water, wastewater, rain, earthquakes, radon, and more. Ask for their list: General Interest Publications of the U.S. Geological Survey.

National Cartographic Information Center

U.S. Geological Survey
507 National Center
Reston, VA 22092
Or call: 800-USA-MAPS
Ask for the *Catalog of topographic and other Published Maps* for the states you wish to study in detail.

U.S. Environmental Protection Agency

EPA Region 1
JFK Federal Building
Boston, MA 02203

EPA Region 2
26 Federal Plaza
New York, NY 10278

EPA Region 3
841 Chestnut Street
Philadelphia, PA 19107

EPA Region 4
345 Courtland Street N.E.
Atlanta, GA 30365

EPA Region 5
230 South Dearborn Street
Chicago, IL 60604

EPA Region 6
1445 Ross Avenue
Dallas, TX 75202-2733

EPA Region 7
726 Minnesota Avenue
Kansas City, KS 66101

EPA Region 8
One Denver Place, Suite 1300
999 18th Street
Denver, CO 80202-2413

EPA Region 9
215 Fremont Street
San Francisco, CA 94105

EPA Region 10
1200 Sixth Avenue
Seattle, WA 98101

Water resources information

Questions about water resources in general and about the water resources
of specific areas can be directed to:
Hydrologic Information Unit
U.S. Geological Survey
419 National Center
Reston, VA 22092
703-648-6817

Government land

"Does the Federal Government ever sell public land? The answer is yes." So begins the free brochure *Are There Any Public Lands For Sale?* available upon request from:
U.S. Department of the Interior
Bureau of Land Management
Room 5600, Building MIB
Washington, DC 20240-0001

United States Government Printing Office

8660 Cherry Lane, Laurel, MD 20707
301-953-7974

Real estate

United National Real Estate
P.O. Box 11400, 4700 Belleview
Kansas City, MO 64112
800-999-1020

United National Real Estate catalogs provide the most available country properties of any single source of which I am aware. Their motto is: "No one knows the country like we do," and I am inclined to believe it. I found my property with the help of a United affiliate in 1976.

United National catalogs showcase rural properties listed by their affiliates in 41 states. The national catalog *United Country* is available for $4.95 by mail. Allow three to four weeks for delivery or send $7.95 for first-class delivery, which they say will get it to you in seven to ten days. They accept credit card orders by phone. Or, you can receive the catalog free of charge at any of their affiliated offices. After you have decided on an area, call them at the toll-free number and they will send a free regional catalog. You will then receive brochures of available properties from affiliates in that area. They also publish *American Treasures*, a catalog of historical properties, many of which are listed on the National Register. *American Treasures* costs $3.95, whether you pick it up or have it delivered by pony express.

Rural Property Bulletin
Box 37
Sparks, Nebraska 69220
402-376-2985

Published monthly for nearly 14 years now. Contains ads for properties all over the U.S. plus Canada. Also lists businesses. Subscriptions are $16 per year. Free classified ad to new subscribers.

Home exchange (temporary)

International Home Exchange Service
P.O. Box 190070
San Francisco, CA 94119
415-435-3497

Newsletters

The Caretaker Gazette, Box 342, Carpentersville, IL 60110.

Rocky Mountain Institute, 1739 Snowmass Creek Road, Snowmass, CO 81654-9199. 303-927-3851.

RMI is a nonprofit research and educational foundation, the child of Amory Lovins, a brilliant and caring physicist, and his lawyer-wife, Hunter. Lovins developed the theory of "negawatts" a concept by which utility companies make greater gains through energy conservation than through building new generating facilities. RMI's goal is to foster efficient and sustainable use of resources as a path to global security. Subscribe to its newsletter and give it as much support as you can.

Greener Pastures Institute Gazette ($25/yr.)
P.O. Box 2190
Henderson, NV 89009
818-355-1670

Magazines

BackHome, P.O. Box 70, Hendersonville, NC 28793. 800-992-2546. Quarterly. $16/yr.

The magazine of basic independent family living. Owned and published by the former staff of a well-known, back-to-basics magazine that left the country and is now run by New York City editors. *BackHome* is the real stuff.

Concentrates on energy, gardening, recycling, home schooling, home business, home construction, and much more. Here is a list of article titles from past issues:

Weed-Free Gardening, Shop for a Used Truck, Nontoxic House Construction, Living on Solar Power, Building Log Homes, Seed Starting Simplified, Make Water Pump Itself, Baking With Kids, Forming a Food-Buying Group, Homeschooling Methods, Aquafarming as a Business, Hand-Built Masonry Heaters, New Organic Pesticides, Cut Your Power Bills in Half, Household Rainwater System.

Countryside & Small Stock Journal, W11564 Hwy 64, Withee, WI 54498. 800-551-5691. Bi-monthly. $18/yr.

Small Stock Magazine was founded 1917; *Countryside* was founded 1969. Much of the editorial content of this highly useful magazine is written by readers who are living on the land. This is the *Countryside* philosophy:

> It's not a single idea, but many ideas and attitudes, including a reverence for nature and a preference for country life; a desire for maximum personal self-reliance and creative leisure; a concern for family nurture and community cohesion; a certain hostility toward luxury; a belief that the primary reward of work should be well-being rather than money; a certain nostalgia for the supposed simplicities of the past and an anxiety about the technological and bureaucratic complexities of the present and the future; and a taste for the plain and functional.

COUNTRYSIDE reflects and supports the simple life, and calls its practitioners *homesteaders*.

Harrowsmith Country Life, Ferry Road, P.O. Box 1000, Charlotte, VT 05445-9984. 303-447-9330. Bi-monthly. U.S. $18/yr.; Canadian $24/yr.

Harrowsmith was first published in Canada in 1976 and has won numerous national awards. It provides useful authoritative information on home/shelter, gardening, food/cookery, investigative journalism, and outdoors/environment. Its readers have above-average education and income and live in small communities, on an average of 4.1 acres.

Organic Gardening, P.O. Box 7304, Red Oak, IA 51591-2304. Nine issues per year. Discount subscription cards in Harrowsmith currently state $18.94/yr., a 30% saving.

Published by the Rodale people, who also put out a prodigious collection of country-skill books—at last count, we have about 20 of their titles, including the definitive *Organic Gardening Encyclopedia*.

Raise the Stakes, the periodical of Planet Drum Foundation, P.O. Box 31251, San Francisco, Shasta Bioregion, CA 94131.

Planet Drum is "A Voice for Bioregional Sustainability, Education and Culture." It asks the question: "What approach can people take to go beyond environmental protests and actually begin living sustainably wherever they are located?" Membership is $20.00 and includes two issues of *Raise the Stakes*, a surprise publication, and a 25% discount on all Planet Drum Publications.

American Demographics, 127 West State Street, Ithaca, NY 14850. 800-828-1133. Monthly—$69/year. Primarily directed toward the business community, *AD* provides a lot of pertinent and timely information on what's happening with people in the U.S. Much of the demographic information in this book was found there.

Alternative Technology

The New Alchemy Institute, 237 Hatchville Road, East Falmouth, MA 02536.

Started in about 1970 by John Todd and Bill McLarney, New Alchemy performs wonders on its 12 acres. It serves students, teachers, households, and small-scale farmers with research and education projects on food, energy, water, and waste treatment systems. Its mail-order catalog is available upon request. They are reorganizing so expect a delay.

Kansas Wind Power, Route 1CS4, Holton, KS 66436. 913-364-4407.

KWP's catalog ($4) offers independent power systems and energy-saving devices, including solar electric modules, batteries, DC equipment and supplies, ram pumps, refrigerators, and composting toilets.

Real Goods Trading Corporation, 966 Mazzoni St., Ukiah, CA 95482-3471. 707-468-9292; order line: 800-762-7325.

Real Goods publishes the *Real Goods Catalog* (remember the Solar Turtle in chapter 24?) and the *Alternative Energy Sourcebook* which is a combination catalog and primer on home electric generation systems, energy-efficient lighting, water pumps and purification systems, non-toxic household products, and recycling products and aids. The *Sourcebook* costs $16. I have the 7th Edition, which is over 500 pages. You can become a member of The Real Goods Hard Corps for $40 and get the *Sourcebook* plus a 5% discount on all purchases.

State information sources

State Government Information Centers

Alabama 205-242-8000
Arizona 602-542-4900
Arkansas . . . . .501-682-3000; in AR only: 800-482-5850
California . . . . . . 916-322-9900 north; 213-620-3030 south
Colorado 303-866-5000
Connecticut . . . . 203-566-2750; in CT only: 800-842-2220
Delaware 302-739-4000
Florida 904-488-1234
Georgia 404-656-2000
Idaho 208-334-2411
Illinois 217-782-2000

Indiana . . . . .317-232-1000; in IN only: 800-382-1563
Iowa 515-281-5011
Kansas 913-296-0111
Kentucky 502-564-3130
Louisiana 504-342-6600
Maine . . . . .207-289-1110; 207-582-8880 for info. svcs.
Maryland 301-974-3431
Massachusetts . . 617-727-7030; in MA only: 800-392-6090
Michigan 517-373-1837
Minnesota 612-296-6013
Mississippi 601-359-1000
Missouri 314-751-2000
Montana 406-444-2511
Nebraska 402-471-2311
Nevada . . . . 702-687-5000; in NV only: 800-992-0900
New Hampshire . .603-271-1110; in NH only: 800-852-3456
New Jersey 609-292-2121
New Mexico 505-827-4011
New York 518-474-2121
North Carolina . . 919-733-1110
North Dakota . . . 701-224-2000
Ohio 614-466-2000
Oklahoma . . . . . .405-521-1601; in OK only: 800-522-8555
Oregon 503-378-3131
Pennsylvania 717-787-2121
Rhode Island . . . .401-277-2000; in RI only: 800-752-8088
South Carolina . . 803-734-1000; in SC only: 800-922-1367
South Dakota . . . 605-733-3011
Tennessee 615-741-3011
Texas 512-463-4630
Utah 801-538-3000
Vermont 802-828-1110
Virginia . . . . .804-786-0000; in VA only: 800-422-2319
Washington . . . . .206-753-5000; in WA only: 800-321-2808
West Virginia . . . 304-348-3456
Wisconsin 608-266-2211
Wyoming 307-777-7220

State chambers of commerce

A good source of maps, tourist guides, demographics, climate information, industry, taxes, etc. Tell them what you want. The volume of material you receive will be indicative of the priority placed on attracting tourists and new residents. Be ready to be sold. Contact through the appropriate state government information center listed above.

Local information sources

Local chambers of commerce

U.S. Chamber of Commerce
1615 H Street NW
Washington, DC 20062
301-468-5128

Source for addresses of local chambers. Most chambers will send you packets of information including maps and real estate company listings. Some rural chambers are so small they can't afford to mail information packages—perhaps an indication of a superior place to live. In that case you will have to rely on the state chamber.

You can also find chamber of commerce listings in the annual *World Wide Chamber of Commerce Directory*, available in most libraries.

County agricultural extension agents

Ag agents are good sources of information on soils and local conditions. Telephone numbers and addresses for these state and county government agencies are in the telephone book or available from the national or state information centers.

Newspapers

Source for subscription information about each of the U.S.'s 1,651 daily newspapers is *Editor & Publisher's International Yearbook*. For information on the nearly-7,000 weekly papers, check out the *IMS Directory of Publications* or *Gale's Directory of Publications*.

Libraries

The *National Atlas of the United States of America* contains 765 maps and charts. It is out of print but can be found in many public libraries.

The *Rand McNally Commercial Atlas & Marketing Guide 1994* includes maps and information on a large amount of useful material, including substantial data for each county. It shows all major military installations.

There is a set of books, one for each state, titled *America The Beautiful*, listed in the bibliography under Joan Downing, the project editor. Although classified as juvenile literature, I found them in the adult book section of my library, and the ones I have used seem to be well researched, written, and designed. Subjects include geography, history, government, economy, industry, and culture. These books were the source for the density patterns of the state maps in appendix B.

Essential country equipment #8: the dog

The dog is available in many colors, sizes, and configurations, with and without tails, pointy ears, hanging-down-droopy ears, etc. Preferred fuel is what's on your plate.

The dog is needed for bird and rabbit chasing, for jumping on visitors, and for licking your face when you are taking a nap. Some models are large enough to ride or pull farm machinery—these require fuel available in very large sacks at feed stores.

Appendix B
State Maps

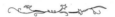

We go forth all to seek America.
And in the seeking we create her.
In the quality of our search
shall be the nature
of the America that we created.

WALDO FRANK

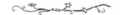

The Michiganers are called Woolfverines,
the Illinois Suckers, the Indianians Hooshers,
and the Missourians Pukes, and the N. Yonkers Eels,
and the People of Detroit Hollow Heads.
Although there is many Peculiarities in their manners
they all appear to be very friendly to Strangers.

SEA CAPTAIN MORRIS SLEIGHT
Letter to his wife, July 9, 1834

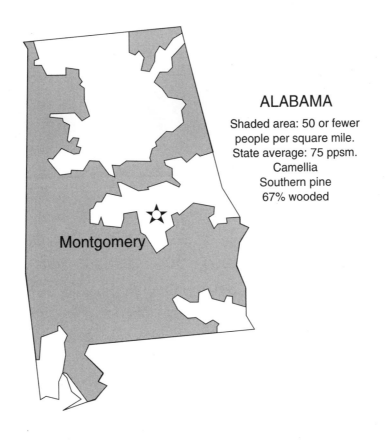

ALABAMA

Shaded area: 50 or fewer
people per square mile.
State average: 75 ppsm.
Camellia
Southern pine
67% wooded

Montgomery

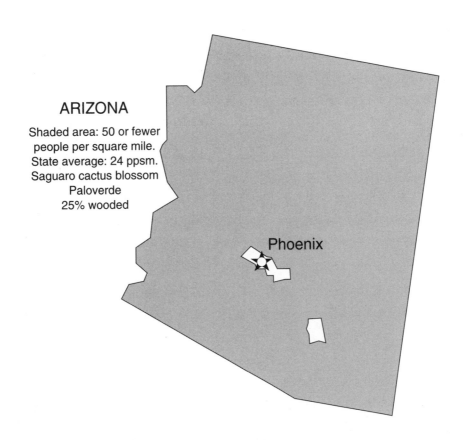

ARIZONA

Shaded area: 50 or fewer
people per square mile.
State average: 24 ppsm.
Saguaro cactus blossom
Paloverde
25% wooded

Phoenix

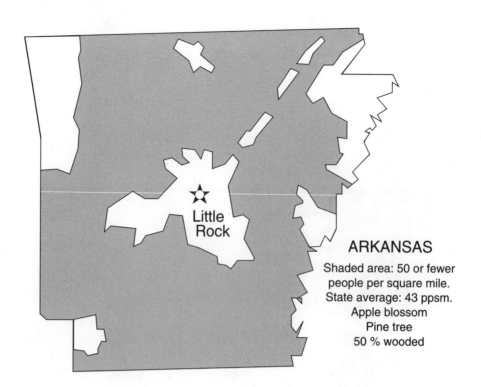

ARKANSAS

Shaded area: 50 or fewer
people per square mile.
State average: 43 ppsm.
Apple blossom
Pine tree
50 % wooded

CALIFORNIA

Shaded area: 50 or fewer
people per square mile.
State average: 149 ppsm.
Golden poppy
California redwood
45% wooded

COLORADO

Shaded area: 10 or fewer
people per square mile.
State average: 28 ppsm.
Rocky Mountain columbine
Colorado blue spruce
33% wooded

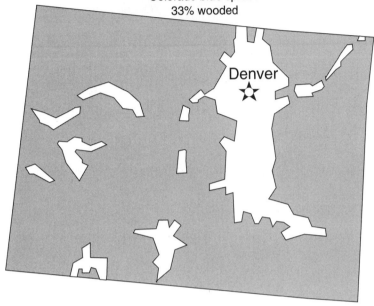

CONNECTICUT

No area of 50 or fewer
people per square mile.
State average: 619 ppsm.
Mountain laurel
White oak
60% wooded

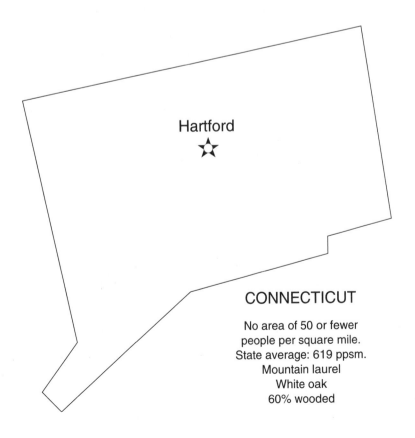

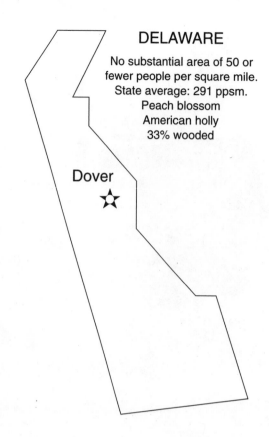

DELAWARE

No substantial area of 50 or
fewer people per square mile.
State average: 291 ppsm.
Peach blossom
American holly
33% wooded

Dover

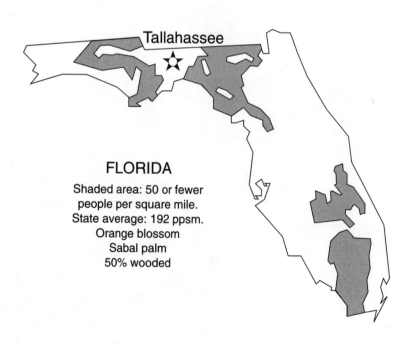

Tallahassee

FLORIDA

Shaded area: 50 or fewer
people per square mile.
State average: 192 ppsm.
Orange blossom
Sabal palm
50% wooded

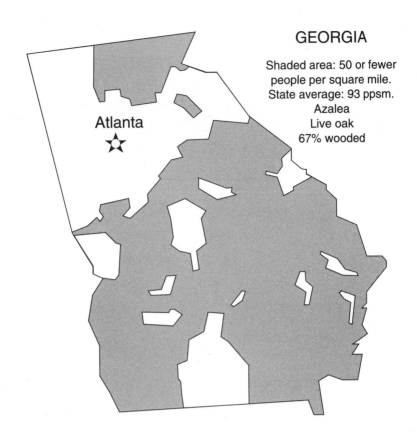

GEORGIA

Shaded area: 50 or fewer
people per square mile.
State average: 93 ppsm.
Azalea
Live oak
67% wooded

Atlanta

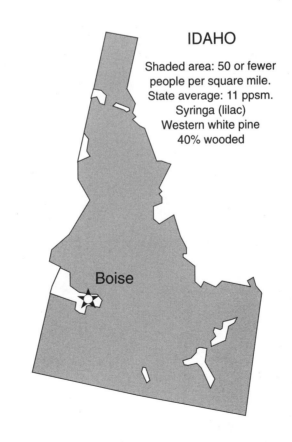

IDAHO

Shaded area: 50 or fewer
people per square mile.
State average: 11 ppsm.
Syringa (lilac)
Western white pine
40% wooded

Boise

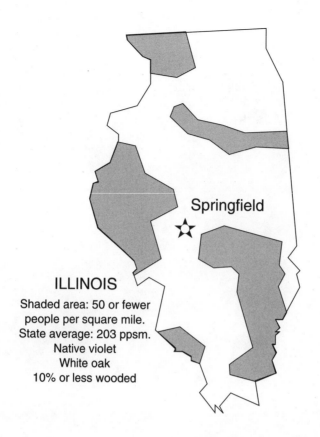

ILLINOIS

Shaded area: 50 or fewer
people per square mile.
State average: 203 ppsm.
Native violet
White oak
10% or less wooded

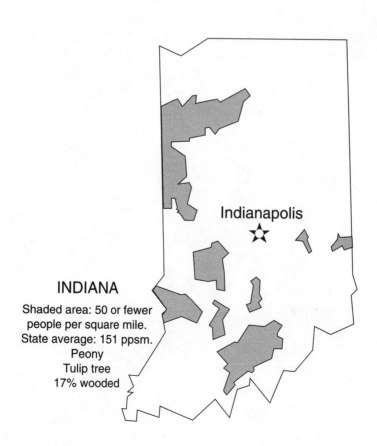

INDIANA

Shaded area: 50 or fewer
people per square mile.
State average: 151 ppsm.
Peony
Tulip tree
17% wooded

IOWA

Shaded area: 50 or fewer
people per square mile.
State average: 52 ppsm.
Wild rose
Oak
3% wooded

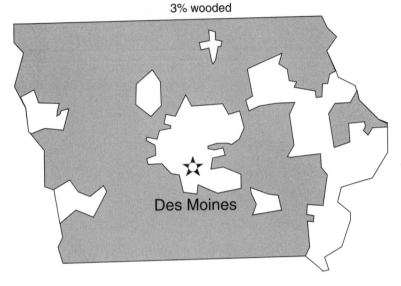

KANSAS

Shaded area: 50 or fewer
people per square mile.
State average: 29 ppsm.
Sunflower
Cottonwood
Minimally wooded

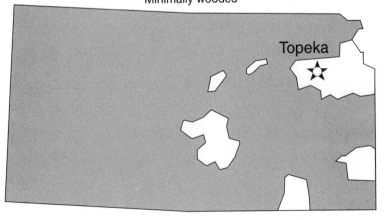

KENTUCKY

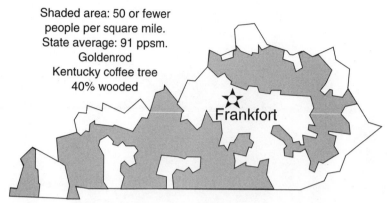

Shaded area: 50 or fewer
people per square mile.
State average: 91 ppsm.
Goldenrod
Kentucky coffee tree
40% wooded

LOUISIANA

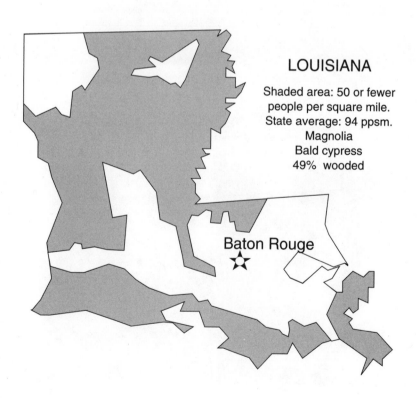

Shaded area: 50 or fewer
people per square mile.
State average: 94 ppsm.
Magnolia
Bald cypress
49% wooded

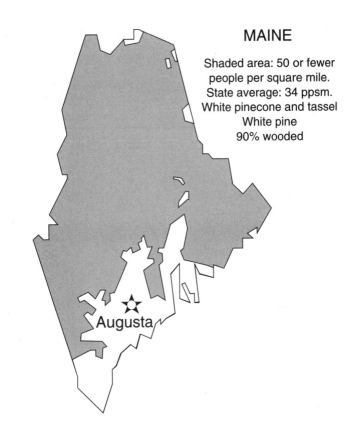

MAINE

Shaded area: 50 or fewer
people per square mile.
State average: 34 ppsm.
White pinecone and tassel
White pine
90% wooded

Augusta

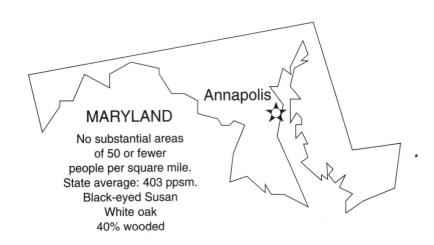

MARYLAND

No substantial areas
of 50 or fewer
people per square mile.
State average: 403 ppsm.
Black-eyed Susan
White oak
40% wooded

Annapolis

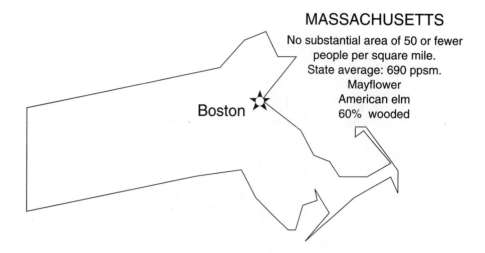

MASSACHUSETTS

No substantial area of 50 or fewer
people per square mile.
State average: 690 ppsm.
Mayflower
American elm
60% wooded

Boston

MICHIGAN

Shaded area: 50 or fewer
people per square mile.
State average: 158 ppsm.
Apple blossom
White pine
51% wooded

Lansing

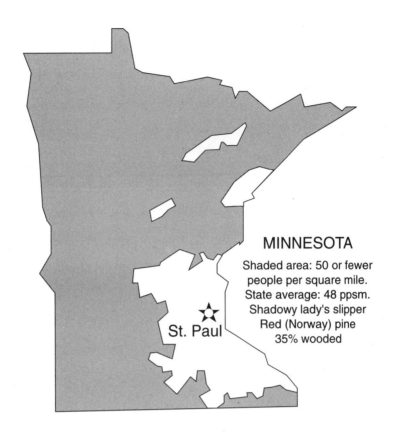

MINNESOTA

Shaded area: 50 or fewer
people per square mile.
State average: 48 ppsm.
Shadowy lady's slipper
Red (Norway) pine
35% wooded

St. Paul

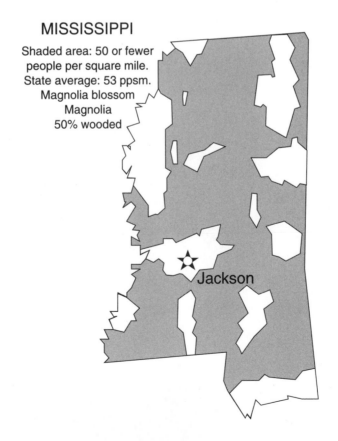

MISSISSIPPI

Shaded area: 50 or fewer
people per square mile.
State average: 53 ppsm.
Magnolia blossom
Magnolia
50% wooded

Jackson

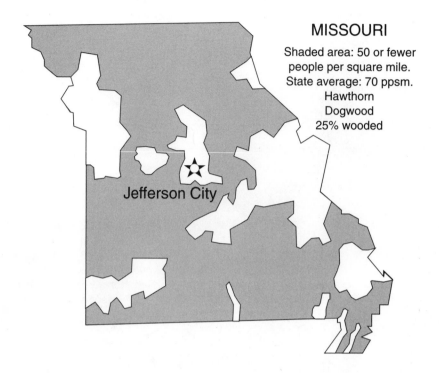

MISSOURI

Shaded area: 50 or fewer
people per square mile.
State average: 70 ppsm.
Hawthorn
Dogwood
25% wooded

Jefferson City

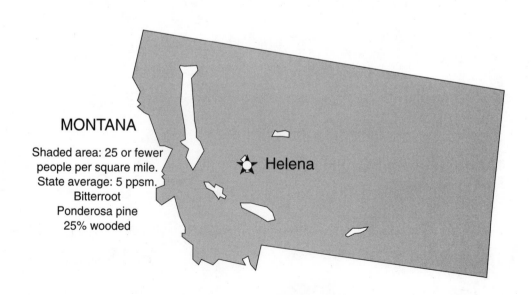

MONTANA

Shaded area: 25 or fewer
people per square mile.
State average: 5 ppsm.
Bitterroot
Ponderosa pine
25% wooded

Helena

NEBRASKA

Entire state is sparsely
populated other than towns.
State average: 20 ppsm.
Goldenrod
Cottonwood
Minimally wooded

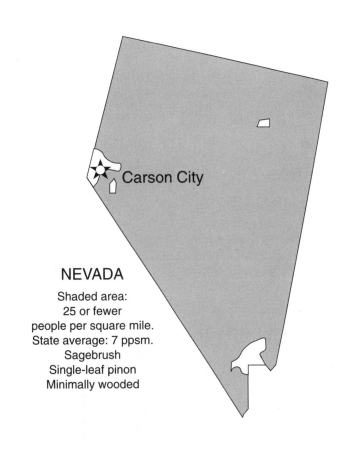

Lincoln

Carson City

NEVADA

Shaded area:
25 or fewer
people per square mile.
State average: 7 ppsm.
Sagebrush
Single-leaf pinon
Minimally wooded

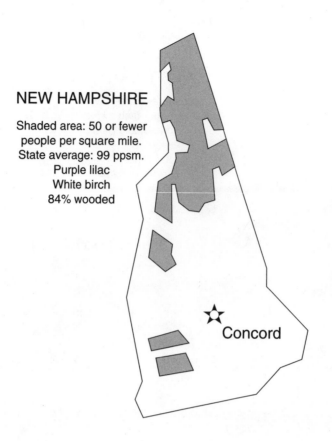

NEW HAMPSHIRE

Shaded area: 50 or fewer
people per square mile.
State average: 99 ppsm.
Purple lilac
White birch
84% wooded

Concord

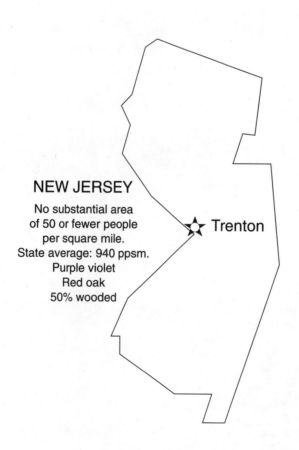

NEW JERSEY

No substantial area
of 50 or fewer people
per square mile.
State average: 940 ppsm.
Purple violet
Red oak
50% wooded

Trenton

NEW MEXICO

Entire state is sparsely
populated other than towns.
State average: 11 ppsm.
Yucca flower
Pinon (nut pine)
Minimally wooded

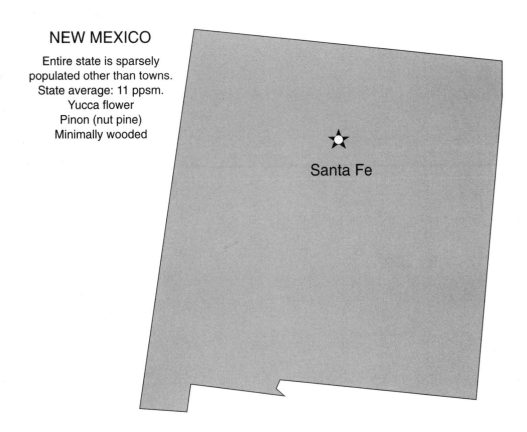

Santa Fe

NEW YORK

Shaded area: 50 or fewer
people per square mile.
State average: 358 ppsm.
Rose
Sugar maple
51% wooded

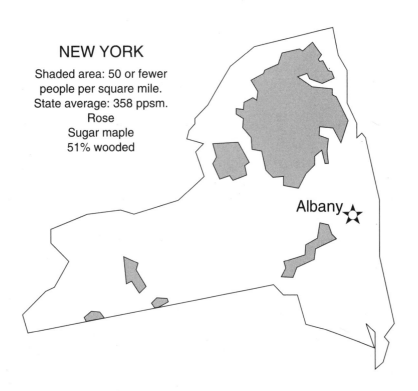

Albany

NORTH CAROLINA

Shaded area: 50 or fewer
people per square mile.
State average: 112 ppsm.
Flowering dogwood
Pine
60% wooded

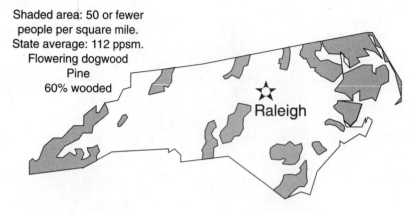

NORTH DAKOTA

Shaded area: 25 or fewer
people per square mile.
State average: 9.2 ppsm.
Wild prairie rose
American elm
1% wooded

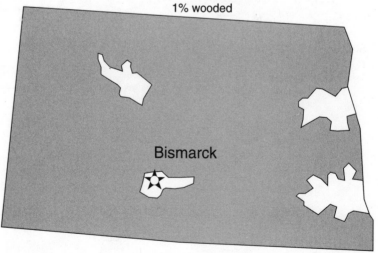

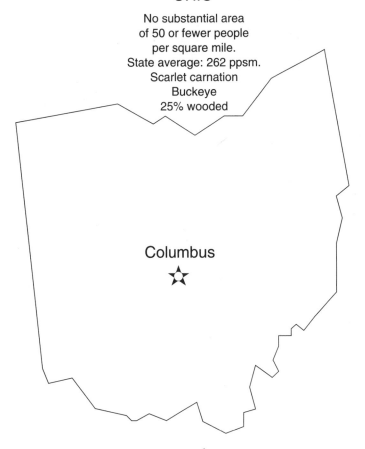

OHIO

No substantial area
of 50 or fewer people
per square mile.
State average: 262 ppsm.
Scarlet carnation
Buckeye
25% wooded

Columbus

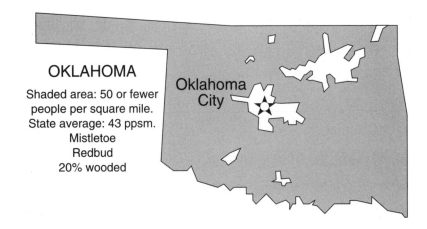

OKLAHOMA

Shaded area: 50 or fewer
people per square mile.
State average: 43 ppsm.
Mistletoe
Redbud
20% wooded

Oklahoma
City

OREGON

Shaded area: 50 or fewer
people per square mile.
State average: 28 ppsm.
Oregon grape
Douglas fir
50% wooded

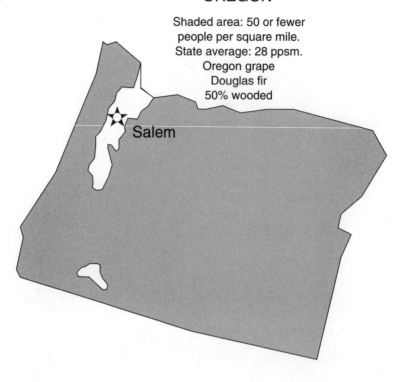

Salem

PENNSYLVANIA

Shaded area: 50 or fewer
people per square mile.
State average: 262 ppsm.
Mountain laurel
Eastern hemlock
60% wooded

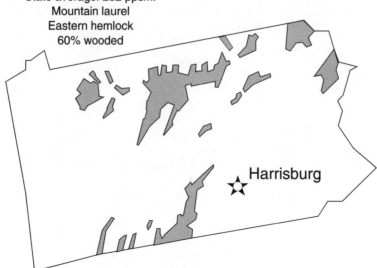

Harrisburg

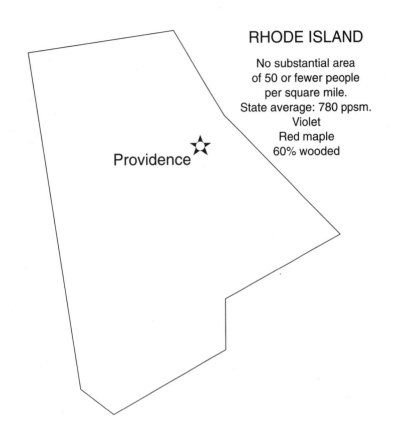

RHODE ISLAND

No substantial area
of 50 or fewer people
per square mile.
State average: 780 ppsm.
Violet
Red maple
60% wooded

Providence

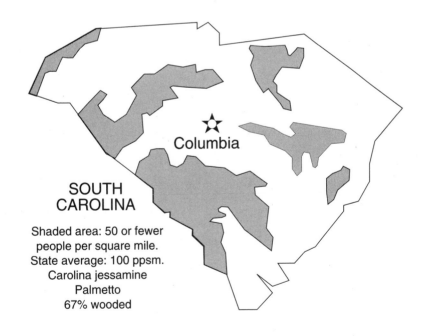

Columbia

SOUTH
CAROLINA

Shaded area: 50 or fewer
people per square mile.
State average: 100 ppsm.
Carolina jessamine
Palmetto
67% wooded

SOUTH DAKOTA

Shaded area: 25 or fewer
people per square mile.
State average: 9 ppsm.
American pasqueflower
Black Hills spruce
4% wooded

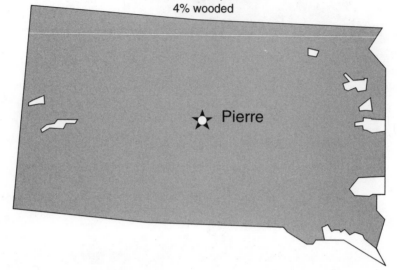

TENNESSEE

Shaded area: 50 or fewer
people per square mile.
State average: 109 ppsm.
Passionflower
Tulip poplar
49% wooded

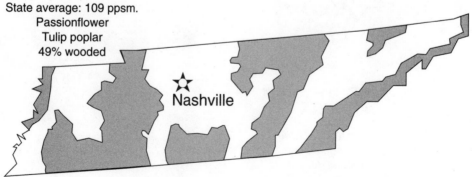

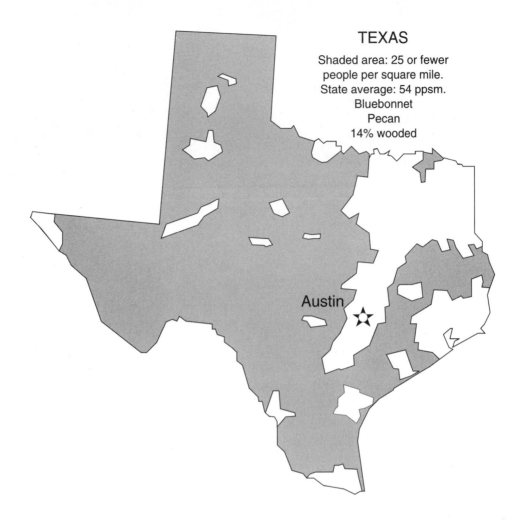

TEXAS

Shaded area: 25 or fewer
people per square mile.
State average: 54 ppsm.
Bluebonnet
Pecan
14% wooded

Austin

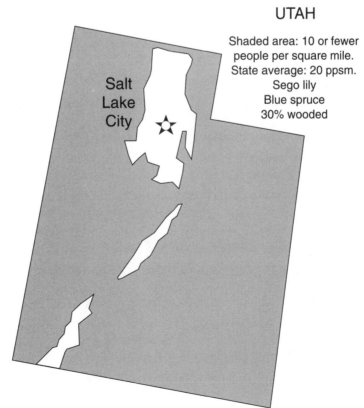

UTAH

Shaded area: 10 or fewer
people per square mile.
State average: 20 ppsm.
Sego lily
Blue spruce
30% wooded

Salt
Lake
City

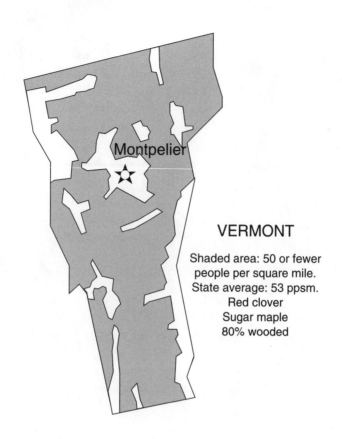

VERMONT

Shaded area: 50 or fewer
people per square mile.
State average: 53 ppsm.
Red clover
Sugar maple
80% wooded

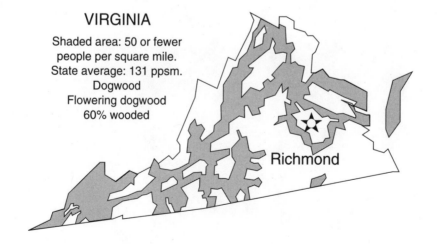

VIRGINIA

Shaded area: 50 or fewer
people per square mile.
State average: 131 ppsm.
Dogwood
Flowering dogwood
60% wooded

WASHINGTON

Shaded area: 25 or fewer
people per square mile.
State average: 61 ppsm.
Coast rhododendron
Western hemlock
49% wooded

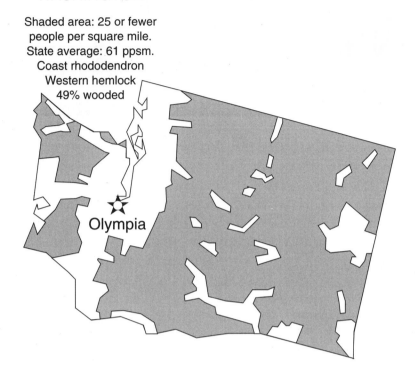

Olympia

Charleston

WEST VIRGINIA

Shaded area: 50 or fewer
people per square mile.
State average: 80 ppsm.
Rhododendron
Sugar maple
80% wooded

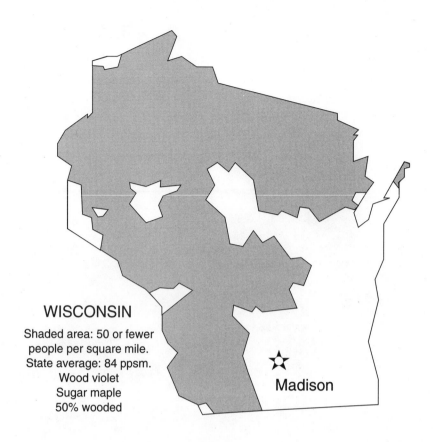

WISCONSIN

Shaded area: 50 or fewer
people per square mile.
State average: 84 ppsm.
Wood violet
Sugar maple
50% wooded

Madison

WYOMING

Shaded area: 50 or fewer
people per square mile.
State average: 5 ppsm.
Indian paintbrush
Plains cottonwood
16% wooded

Cheyenne

Glossary

abstract of title: A chronological summary of all recorded documents that affect title to a property, usually going back to a government patent or Spanish land grant. Often simply called an abstract. Old abstracts were often bound in leather, like a little book.

acceleration clause: A condition in a *security instrument* that accelerates the time of final payment, for instance, non-payment of taxes, non-maintenance of improvements, or failure to make payments. Usually allows the lender to demand immediate payment.

adjustable rate mortgage. See *ARM*.

adverse possession: A legal condition allowing a stranger to a real estate title to gain title by performing certain acts for a prescribed period of time, most notably being in possession of the property contrary to the interests of the owner.

agent: In real estate law, one who acts for another and owes a *fiduciary* duty to perform. A real estate broker is usually the agent of a seller (a seller is the agent's *principal*) through a listing agreement. She may also be the agent of a buyer through an agreement. She may not be an agent of both buyer and seller at the same time without full disclosure and agreement by the principals. A real estate salesman acting for the broker is an agent of the broker and a sub-agent of the seller. Another real estate broker working through a multiple listing authority is a sub-agent of the seller.

agency: The legal relationship whereby one (the agent) may act on behalf of another (the *principal*).

APR: Annual percentage rate, as defined by the Truth-in-Lending Act; the total finance charge expressed as an interest rate.

appraiser: One who investigates and evaluates real property. Appraiser licensing laws vary from state to state.

appraisal: An estimate of value, usually by a licensed appraiser.

arbitration: A non-judicial process by which a monetary dispute is heard and decided. Although there may be only one arbitrator, typically the plaintiff and defendant each select one arbitrator and then those two agree on a third, who acts as the chairman or chief arbitrator at the proceedings. Realtor® boards offer arbitration, often at no cost to members of the public who have legitimate disputes with Realtors®. Usually three board members, who have no relationship with the defendant, comprise the arbitration panel. Contrary to what one might think, Realtors® tend to deal harshly with their peers who injure the public. Most courts uphold and enforce the decision of an arbitration panel.

ARM: Adjustable rate mortgage. The interest rate rises and falls with changes in certain published indexes, such as CDs or treasury notes. ARMs can be good under certain circumstances but disastrous under others. Ask for a blank copy of the note and deed of trust you will be required to sign so you can read it at your leisure. Make sure you understand how fast and how much the interest rate can rise.

assessed value: County tax assessors place a value on property that is usually well below market value. The tax rate multiplied against the assessed value (usually per hundred) determines the tax liability.

assessment: An assessment is a lien for a special purpose, for instance to pay off water or sewer bonds, and usually means special taxes are due to some agency on a regular basis.

bioregion: A term so new it is not in my dictionaries. A bioregion is a definable natural area containing distinct climate, topography, minerals, plants, and animals. Bioregions have natural boundaries, as contrasted with the artificial boundaries of states and counties. A bioregion is often defined by a watershed.

broker: A licensed real estate agent who may or may not be a Realtor®. A broker-associate has a broker's license but works as a salesman for another broker.

broker-salesperson: A real estate agent qualified as a broker but working as the salesperson of another broker.

buyer's agent: A real estate broker who works solely for a buyer, by contract, as opposed to the norm, in which the broker works for the seller.

CC&Rs: Covenants, conditions, and restrictions. These are encumbrances on the property usually placed by a subdivider to protect the economic integrity of the subdivision. A typical covenant is that the owner will not conduct a business on the property. A condition may require that any building plans be approved by a committee before construction will be allowed. Get a copy of the CC&Rs and read them carefully to be sure you will not be prevented from doing as you wish with the property. If you are an insomniac, reading CC&Rs will be less expensive and less injurious to your body than sleeping pills.

caveat emptor: Let the buyer beware. But of course you already knew that. Well, just in case you've led a sheltered life.

closing: The act of completing a transaction, where the buyer gets title to the property and the seller gets the purchase price. If you hear closing escrow, it means the same thing. Some areas still use the word settlement.

closing instructions and statements: The escrow agent prepares instructions according to the orders of the buyer, seller, and lender, including monetary demands by persons such as termite inspectors, appraisers, and insurance agents. The instructions list all monies and documents to be given and to be received. Instructions usually contain estimates, such as for interest and insurance prorations. After closing, the escrow agent prepares buyer's, seller's, and lender's statements reflecting final disbursements.

contract of sale: An uncertain, confusing term. Some use the term to mean an offer to purchase, which, if accepted, becomes a legally enforceable contract.

Also known as contract for sale, land contract, contract for deed, and installment land contract. Is sometimes used instead of a mortgage or note and deed of trust to act as a security instrument, typically for sellers who carry the financing on the sale of their property. Potentially dangerous for buyers, as the contract often allows the seller to easily regain the property if the buyer fails to perform any condition on time, with the buyer losing all deposits, down payments, and payments on the contract. See *installment land sales contract.*

country: In this book, country means a place outside the obvious influence of a city. Country places don't have parking meters or traffic congestion. They do have store clerks and bank tellers who smile, address you by your name, ask how you're doing—and listen to your answer. Country is—well, you'll know it when you feel it.

covenants, conditions, and restrictions: *See CC&Rs.*

deed: A deed is a written instrument by which a seller transfers legal interest to a buyer. Examples of common deed types follow.

warranty deed: The grantor warrants to the grantee that the title is clear of encumbrances and he will defend the grantee's title against all other claims. Various states include other warranties.

grant deed: Typically, a warranty deed that limits warranties to two: 1) the grantor has good title and the power to convey, and 2) there are no encumbrances on the property that would harm the grantee.

sheriff's deed: In some counties, when properties are sold for back taxes or to settle a disputed estate, the sheriff conducts the sale (usually an auction) and a sheriff's deed is given to the purchaser. If the sheriff is bona fide, the deed most likely is also.

trustee's deed: In states using deeds of trust to evidence a security interest in property, a trustee's deed is given in a foreclosure.

quitclaim deed: The grantor gives the grantee all the interest that he has in the property. This may be little or none as there are no implied warranties. Quitclaim deeds are useful in clearing clouds on title, such as the potential claim of an ex-spouse. Perhaps it will be helpful to your understanding of this deed if I tell you that it would be perfectly legal for me to give you a quitclaim deed to the Tower of Pisa. Stand back!

deed of trust: A deed of trust creates a security interest for a lender and spells out the conditions of default, for instance, if the buyer does not make payments, fails to maintain the property in good condition, or fails to provide fire insurance; and the method the trustee may use to effect the foreclosure.

deposit receipt: Much more than a receipt for money, "DRs" are binding purchase contracts if certain conditions are met.

earnest money deposit: Cash, promissory note, check, or other item of value given by a buyer with a purchase contract. Not legally required, but shows serious intent to a seller. Amount is negotiable between buyer and seller. Most contracts call for forfeiture of deposits to the seller upon buyer default or, if seller defaults, deposit returns to buyer.

easement: A right to use someone else's land as a right-of-way, or for some other legal purpose.

ecosystem: A system of interaction of organisms with their environment. Modernly used to depict a distinct geographic area, as, the Greater Yellowstone ecosystem.

eminent domain: The power of government to take property for the public good. An eminent domain proceeding is the legal process for determining if the taking is proper, and what shall constitute fair compensation. The power may also be used to use your property to gain access to a nearby property.

encumbrance: A claim, lien, charge, or liability attached to and binding on real property. Includes mortgages, assessments, leases, and easements.

escrow: A neutral depository of funds and documents.

escrow agent: Also called escrow officer. A person who accepts and holds escrow funds and documents, and takes instructions for closing the sale: recording the appropriate documents, delivering them to the proper parties, and disbursing funds in agreement with the signed instructions of the parties, typically the buyer, seller, and lender. Depending on the area, escrow agents may be real estate brokers, lawyers, employees of title insurance companies, or independent escrow agents. Escrow officers are much like Santa Claus, but they require that you pay in advance for your present.

escrow instructions: See *closing instructions*.

estimated purchase cost sheet: Prepared by real estate agents for buyers so there are no financial surprises at closing. Shows all anticipated costs of purchase, including down payment, escrow fee, title insurance policy fee, recording fees, loan fee, appraisal fee, termite inspection fee, property insurance premium, and prorations of taxes, insurance, and interest if appropriate.

ethics hearing: A hearing conducted by a board of Realtors® to decide if a member has violated the Code of Ethics of the National Association of Realtors®. The hearing may be initiated by a Realtor® or a member of the public. Monetary disputes are resolved through an *arbitration*.

exclusive listing or exclusive right to sell: A listing agreement in which the seller agrees to pay a commission to the broker in the agreement no matter who provides the buyer, even if the seller finds the buyer.

FHA: Federal Housing Administration, which insures loans.

fiduciary: Sometimes used synonymously with agent. An agent has a fiduciary obligation to his principal—a very high degree of confidence and trust.

foreclosure: The procedure by which a property is taken from an owner who has failed to meet certain conditions of a mortgage.

forty: Originally a square parcel of land containing approximately 40 acres, one-quarter mile per side, and being one-sixteenth of a section. Now used loosely to describe any parcel containing 40 acres.

grantor: The party that grants a real property interest, i.e., the owner-seller.

grantee: The party that receives the interest, usually the buyer, and usually in the form of a deed. You would be a happy grantee if your Aunt Mabel left her country estate to you as a small part of your inheritance.

GRI: Graduate of Realtor's® Institute. A designation awarded upon completion of a prescribed course of study.

homestead: May refer to property obtained by the Homestead Act of 1962. The last of such programs ended in 1977. Homestead exemptions may be recorded in some states, protecting one's primary residence from foreclosure for certain reasons, but not from default on a security device. Also used loosely to decribe a country home place with garden, orchard, chickens—that sort of thing.

installment land sales contract: Also known as land contract, conditional sales contract, contract for deed, and agreement of sale. A contract that calls for the deed to be given to the buyer only after all payments have been completed. You don't want this because, if you miss one payment the seller can keep the property plus all monies you have paid. Also, if the contract is not recorded, the seller may use the property as collateral for loans. Sellers who carry the financing like this contract because, in case of default, they need not go through a foreclosure proceeding to regain title to the property. See *contract of sale.*

lawyer's title opinion: See *title opinion.*

lien: A legal encumbrance on land, ensuring payment of a debt, obligation, or duty.

lis pendens: A legal notice that a lawsuit is pending, the outcome of which could affect real estate title.

listing agreement: A contract between a property owner and a real estate broker, providing a commission to the broker if he procures an acceptable buyer—but see *open listing* and *exclusive agency listing.*

marketable title: Title that is free from encumbrances and third-party rights or interests incompatible with the use, enjoyment, and ownership of the title holder. Not perfect title but considered reasonably free of potential legal challenges.

metropolitan area: In 1970, Standard Metropolitan Statistical Areas were designated by the Census Bureau wherever there was an urban center of 50,000 or more people. Neighboring commuter counties of metropolitan character were also included in these areas, to the county borders. All other counties were nonmetropolitan. In 1980 the designation was changed. It is now simply a thickly populated county or counties of at least 50,000 population. Peripheral counties are included if they meet certain criteria. "Both rural and urban areas are found in metropolitan and nonmetropolitan sectors of the country" (Fuguitt, Brown, Beale, *Rural and Small Town America, 1989).* These changing and confusing designations have made the statistics of metropolitan\nonmetropolitan\rural migration patterns less meaningful. Who cares—we know where we're going, even if the statisticians don't.

monument: A permanent physical object marking the corner point of a land survey, as an iron pipe driven into the ground, or a pile of rocks, sometimes marked with red paint.

mortgage: Commonly used as a term to describe a loan made with property as security, a mortgage is a document which makes property security for the repayment of a debt.

MAI: Member of Appraisal Institute. The MAI designation is awarded only upon successful completion of various classes and after substantial experience.

maintenance agreement: Generally for upkeep of a private road used by two or more parties. Also used in subdivisions that contain common areas used by the various owners.

metropolitan statistical area: See *metropolitan area.*

mechanics lien or materialmen's lien: A lien against real property available to those who have provided services or materials used to improve real property. These are the responsibility of the seller; make sure they are paid before you take title.

microclimate: A pocket of localized climate different than nearby or surrounding areas. The lee side of hills, valleys, and large bodies of water create microclimates.

note: Also called a promissory note. A document evidencing a debt, typically stating the amount, the interest rate, and the terms of repayment. Usually secured by a deed of trust or a mortgage, otherwise it is simply a promise to pay. Some states use a bond for the same purpose.

offer to purchase: The first step in a real estate sale. The buyer makes a written offer to the seller, which if accepted, becomes a contract. The term also is used to reference a document used for this purpose. See *purchase agreement.*

open listing: A nonexclusive listing given by a seller to many real estate brokers; a commission is paid only to the broker procuring a buyer. The seller reserves the right to sell the property without incurring a commission liability.

personal property: All property that is not real property.

point: Each point charged by a lender is equivalent to one percent of the loan amount.

prepayment penalty: A lender's charge to a borrower when the loan is paid off before the maturity date. This can be a very painful surprise—shop for your loan carefully and ask if there will be such a penalty.

principal: In a real estate sale, the primary principal is generally the seller, who employs the real estate broker as his agent. An increasingly common arrangement is the *buyer's agent*, where a buyer is the principal of the agent who represents him.

purchase agreement: Also known as purchase contract, deposit receipt, offer and acceptance, purchase offer, and purchase and sales agreement. Four key parts: 1) receipt of the buyer's deposit; 2) terms of the buyer's offer; 3) provision for the seller's acceptance; 4) provision for payment of the broker's commission. Usually preprinted forms; specific wording and clauses vary from state to state.

radon: A colorless, odorless, tasteless, naturally occurring radioactive gas formed by radium decay.

real estate broker: One licensed to sell, rent, or buy property and collect a commission. Especially in the country, may not be a Realtor®.

real estate salesperson: A person licensed to perform real estate activities, but must work under the authority of a broker.

real property: Land and that which is affixed to it, including buildings, vegetation, and minerals. A tree purchased at a nursery is personal property; once planted, it becomes real property.

Realtor®: A licensed real estate broker who is a member of the National Association of Realtors®, which membership includes a pledge to adhere to a strict Code of Ethics.

Realtor® Associate: A licensed real estate salesperson who is a member of the National Association of Realtors® and works for a Realtor®.

recording: The process of placing important documents such as deeds and deeds of trust into the public record. Serves as constructive notice to the public.

right-of-way: The right to use the land of another for a certain purpose, typically as a roadway or for utility lines. This is very handy if it's the only way to access your property but a real nuisance if someone else has one over your land.

riparian rights: Water rights of a property owner whose property touches the water. The extent of riparian rights varies from state to state.

rural: The Bureau of the Census defines rural as the population outside incorporated or unincorporated places with more than 2,500 people and/or outside urbanized areas, the latter being defined as a central city or cities which together with surrounding closely settled territory (density of more than 1,000 persons per square mile) has a minimum population of 50,000.

sales associate: A real estate salesperson who works for a broker.

second mortgage or lien: Also simply called a second. A lien that is in a junior position. Sellers often "take back a second" if the buyer does not have all of the down payment required by the first lender.

section: A square parcel of land surveyed according to the United States rectangular survey system, containing approximately 640 acres and being approximately one mile on each side.

security instrument or device: Notes, deeds of trust, mortgages, and other agreements that pledge property as security for a loan.

settlement: In some places this term is used synonymously with *closing.*

SRA: Senior Residential Appraiser.

subdivision: Division of land into smaller parcels. In many counties, a subdivider must comply with various state and county regulations as to roads, utilities, minimum lot size, and others. If the subdivision map has not been accepted and recorded, no building permits will be issued. Subdivision lands sold through interstate commerce must comply with federal regulations.

subordination: A clause that allows a lien to be moved into a junior position, as when a seller finances the sale but allows the buyer to obtain a bank loan for house construction. The bank will insist on being in first position; this will only be possible if the initial first loan contains the subordination clause.

taxes: The rent that the king (or governor) charges you for using his property.

title: The right to or ownership of property. The evidence of ownership, as a deed.

title insurance: For a one-time fee, a title insurance company issues to a property buyer a policy indemnifying loss against any factor listed in the policy occurring before the purchase. I dislike insurance on general principles, but I have a high regard for title insurance. Title insurance contributes to peaceful sleep.

title opinion: Also called lawyer's title opinion. A lawyer's written statement of the quality and condition of real property title. Lawyers usually issue a statement that they have studied the abstract of title and, in their opinion, the seller has clear and marketable title. Among other potential problems, examining an abstract does not reveal forgeries—and the lawyer is not responsible for same. If a lawyer makes a mistake he or she may be liable but unable to pay your loss.

And if lawyers are not honest they may squeeze out of liability. You will have much more protection if you buy title insurance.

trustee: The person or company that will take your property away from you if you fail to meet your payments or other requirements of the lender.

truth in lending: An indecipherable rule decreed by Big Brother to make sure we aren't fooled into paying more for our loans that we thought we were. Gave birth to APR—annual percentage rate, by which charges other than interest are calculated to determine the true cost of a loan to a borrower.

VA: Veteran's Administration. Helps veterans obtain loans by *guaranteeing* payment of the loan to the lender. Differs from the FHA, which is available to all citizens, and which *insures* loans.

VIR: Variable interest rate. The note contains provisions for increasing the interest rate that you will pay. Make sure you understand the terms of any loan before agreeing to it.

watershed: The total land area from which rainfall drains into a stream. Extends from ridgetop to ridgetop. Watersheds are often *bioregions.*

wrap-around mortgage: A mortgage that includes an existing smaller mortgage. We used "wraps" during the early period of rising interest rates, to keep assumable low-interest-rate loans alive. Many lenders refuse to allow their loans to be wrapped and, if they discover the transaction (often through insurance policies), will demand immediate payoff. This can create a most awkward situation, especially if the borrower cannot quickly obtain another loan.

You'ns and us'ns oughta get together sometime: Mid-south country version of "Let's do lunch." More likely to be sincere than city version.

Essential country equipment #5: the duck

The duck is primarily useful as a swimming coach. Watch how the duck moves while on the water. Perform similar actions while floating and you will be swimming like a duck. Olympic hopefuls take note.

Bibliography

Bailey, Liberty Hyde. *The Outlook to Nature.* New York: The MacMillan Company, 1924.

Bennett, Hal Zina & Susan J. Sparrow. *Follow Your Bliss.* New York: Avon Books, 1990.

Berry, Wendell. *The Unsettling of America: Culture & Agriculture.* San Francisco: Sierra Club Books, 1977.

———. *Sex, Economy, Freedom & Community.* New York: Pantheon Books, 1993.

Bowman, Thomas F., Ed.D.; George A. Giuliani, Ph.D.; M. Ronald Minge, Ph.D. *Finding Your Best Place to Live in America.* New York: Red Lion Books, 1981.

Boyer, Richard & David Savageau. *Retirement Places Rated.* Chicago: Rand McNally, 1987.

———. *Places Rated Almanac.* New York: Prentice Hall, 1989.

Brabec, Barbara. *Homemade Money: The Definitive Guide to Success in a Homebased Business.* White Hall, VA: Betterway Publications, 1989.

Bromfield, Louis. *Pleasant Valley.* New York: Harper & Brothers Publishers, 1945.

Campbell, Carlos C. *New Towns: another way to live.* Reston, VA: Reston Publishing Company, 1976.

Conway, H. McKinley & Linda L. Liston. *The Weather Handbook.* Atlanta: Conway Research, Inc., 1974.

Crampton, Norman. *The 100 Best Small Towns in America.* New York: Prentice-Hall, 1993.

Davidson, Osha Gray. *Broken Heartland: The Rise of America's Rural Ghetto.* New York: The Free Press, 1990.

Dickerman, Pat. *Farm, Ranch & Country Vacations.* New York: Farm & Ranch Vacations Inc., 1983.

Dickinson, Peter A. *Retirement Edens Outside the Sunbelt.* Glenview, Illinois: Scott, Foresman, 1987.

Downing, Joan, project editor. *America The Beautiful* (separate book for each state in the set). Chicago: Childrens Press, 1987-1992.

Dychtwald, Ken. *Age Wave.* Los Angeles: Jeremy P. Tarcher, Inc., 1989.

Ford, Norman. *The 50 Healthiest Places to Live and Retire in the United States.* Bedford, MA: Mills & Sanderson, 1991.

Garreau, Joel. *Edge City: Life on the New Frontier.* New York: Doubleday, 1991.

Germer, Jerry. *Country Careers: Successful Ways to Live and Work in the Country.* New York: John Wiley & Sons, 1993.

Gilligan, Gerald S. *A Price Guide for Buying and Selling Rural Acreage.* Stamford, Connecticut: Gerald S. Gilligan & Associates, 1974.

Goldman, Benjamin A. *The Truth About Where You Live: An atlas for action on toxins and mortality.* New York: Times Books/Random House, 1991.

Graves, William, ed. National Geographic Special Edition: *Water: The Power, Promise, and Turmoil of North America's Fresh Water.* Washington, DC: The National Geographic Society, 1993.

Gusewelle, C.W. *Far From Any Coast: Pieces of America's Heartland.* Columbia, MO: University of Missouri Press, 1989.

Hall, Bob and Mary Lee Kerr. *1991-1992 Green Index: A State-By-State Guide to the Nation's Environmental Health.* Washington D.C.: Island Press, 1991.

Haywood, Julie and Ken Spooner. *Goodbye City Hello Country.* Grand Junction, CO: Highland Books, 1985.

Healy, Robert G. and James L. Short. *The Market for Rural Land: Trends, Issues, Policies.* Washington, DC: The Conservation Foundation, 1981.

Heenan, David A. *The New Corporate Frontier: The Big Move To Small Town, USA.* New York: McGraw-Hill, Inc., 1991.

Herbers, John. *The New Heartland: America's Flight Beyond the Suburbs and How It Is Changing Our Future.* New York: Time Books, 1986.

Hiss, Tony. *The Experience of Place.* New York: Alfred A. Knopf, 1990.

Joseph, Stanley and Lynn Karlin. *Maine Farm.* New York: Smallwood and Stewart, 1991.

Kimble, George H.T. *Our American Weather.* New York: McGraw-Hill, 1955.

LaFavore, Michael. *Radon: The Invisible Threat.* Emmaus, PA: Rodale Press, 1987.

Levering, Frank, and Wanda Urbanska. *Simple Living: One Couple's Search for a Better Life.* New York: Viking Penguin, 1992.

Little, Charles E. *Louis Bromfield at Malabar: Writings on Farming and Country Life.* Baltimore: The Johns Hopkins University Press, 1988.

Long, Charles. *Life After The Country: A Harrowsmith Guide To Rural Living.* Camden East, Ontario: Camden House Publishing, 1989.

Martin, Ruth S. *Crumbling Dreams: What You Must Know Before Building or Buying a New House (or Condo).* Cleveland: Lakeside Press, 1993.

McCaig, Donald. *An American Homeplace.* New York: Crown Publishers, 1992.

McGill, Robert. *Moving to the Country.* Reeds Spring, MO: White Oak Press, 1987.

McPhee, John. *Basin and Range.* New York: Farrar • Straus • Giroux, 1981.

McWilliams, Peter & John-Roger. *Do It!: Let's Get Off Our Buts.* Los Angeles: Prelude Press, 1991.

Mitchell, John Hanson. *Living At The End Of Time.* Boston: Houghton Mifflin Company, 1990.

Morrison, Peter A., ed. *A Taste of the Country: A Collection of Calvin Beale's Writings.* University Park, PA: The Pennsylvania State University Press, 1990.

Nader, Ralph, and John Abbotts. *The Menace of Atomic Energy.* New York: W.W. Norton & Company, 1977.

Naisbitt, John. *Megatrends.* New York: Warner Books, 1982.

Naisbitt, John and Patricia Aburdene, *Megatrends 2000, Ten New Directions for the 1990's.* New York: William Morrow and Co., 1990.

Nearing, Scott and Helen. *Living the Good Life: How to Live Sanely and Simply in a Troubled World.* New York: Schocken Books, 1970.

———. *Continuing the Good Life: Half a Century of Homesteading.* New York: Schocken Books, 1979.

Popcorn, Faith. *The Popcorn Report.* New York: Doubleday, 1991.

Ringholz, Raye C. *Little Town Blues: Voices From the Changing West.* Layton, UT, Gibbs Smith, 1992.

Robbins, Jim. *The Last Refuge: The environmental showdown in Yellowstone and the American West.* New York: Morrow, 1993.

Rosenberg, Lee & Saralee. *50 Fabulous Places To Raise Your Family.* Hawthorne, NJ: Career Press, 1993.

———. *50 Fabulous Places To Retire In America.* Hawthorne, NJ: Career Press, 1991.

Ross, Tom & Marilyn. *Country Bound!* Buena Vista, CO: Communication Creativity, 1992.

Rossiter, Phyllis. *A Living History of the Ozarks.* Gretna, LA: Pelican Publishing Company, 1992.

Ruegg, Frank, and Paul Bianchina. *You Can't Plant Tomatoes in Central Park.* Far Hills, NJ: New Horizon Press, 1990.

Sale, Kirkpatrick. *Dwellers in the Land: The Bioregional Vision.* San Francisco: Sierra Club Books, 1985.

Savageau, David. *Retirement Places rated: All you need to plan your retirement or select your second home.* New York: Prentice-Hall, 1990.

Schaeffer, John, ed. *Alternative Energy Sourcebook: 7th Edition.* Ukiah, CA: Real Goods Trading Corporation, 1993.

Scher, Les and Carol Scher. *Finding & Buying Your Place in the Country.* Chicago: Dearborn Financial Publishing, 1992.

Setterberg, Fred and Lonny Shavelson. *Toxic Nation: The Fight to Save Our Communities from Chemical Contamination.* New York: John Wiley & Sons, 1993.

Shattuck, Alfred. *The Greener Pastures Relocation Guide: Finding the Best State in the United States for You.* Englewood Cliffs, NJ: Prentice-Hall, 1984.

Snyder, Gary. *No Nature: New and Selected Poems.* New York: Pantheon Books, 1992.

Steila, Donald. *The Geography of Soils.* Englewood Cliffs, NJ: Prentice-Hall, 1976.

Teaford, Jon C. *Cities of the Heartland: The Rise and Fall of the Industrial Midwest.* Indianapolis, IN: Indiana University Press, 1993.

Thomas, G. Scott. *A Rating Guide to Opportunities in America's Metro Areas.* Buffalo: Prometheus Books, 1993.

———. *The Rating Guide to Life in America's Small Cities.* Buffalo: Prometheus Books, 1990.

Toffler, Alvin. *Future Shock.* New York: Random House, 1970.

Vinz, Mark and Thom Tammaro, eds. *Common Ground: A Gathering of Poems on Rural Life.* Moorhead, MN: Dacotah Territory Press, 1988.

Whatley, Booker T. *Booker T. Whatley's Handbook on How to Make $100,000 Farming 25 Acres.* Emmaus, PA: Regenerative Agriculture Association, 1987.

Index

H

habits 59, 62
Hammerstein, Oscar 89
hardwoods 100
Harlin, John Conklin "Uncle Johnny" 183
Harrowsmith Country Life 282, 284, 342
Hart, Lorenz 75
having it all 61
Hayward, Julie 272
hazardous waste, amount produced in U.S. 298
hazardous waste dump 280
Hazel, John Tilghman Jr. 269
health 163-174
  and place 163
  author's bias 171
  community connection 178
  environmental factors 164
  equals fewer doctors 164
  helpful hints, list of 172-173
  home-grown food benefits 169-170
  mental 167
  mortality reductions 165
  places to avoid 276-280
  soil connection 169-170
health care
  chemical agriculture connection 170
  services 165
  tele-medicine 166
healthfulness
  geography of 166-167
healthiest people
  states where found 169
heart disease
  states with high rates of 168
heat
  too much 72
heating costs 109
Heenan, David A. 117, 118
Herbers, John 166, 240, 257
herbicides 288
Hershey Chocolate Company, Hershey, Pennsylvania 268
Hiaasen, Carl 267
Highland County, Virginia 154
Hiss, Tony 14, 137
Hmongs 188
Holmes, Oliver Wendell 204
home businesses 121-124
  successful 123
home exchange services
  Intervac U.S., address 305
  International Home Exchange Service 341

home workers 121-124
homeowners associations 258
homestead
  definition 59-60
Homestead Act of 1862 59
homesteaders 28-29
  state destinations 232
homesteading 28-29
homophobia 200
hospitals, rural 165-166
hostility toward newcomers, natives' 196, 201, 232
house sites 101
houses, existing and old
  considerations 213
Hubbard, Frank McKinney "Kin" 66, 272
Hudlow, Michael 146
humidity 76-77
hurricanes 69, 83
hydrangeas act like litmus paper 96
hydrologic cycle 144-145
hydrocarbons as pollution 289

I

IBM 119
ice 74
Idaho
  groundwater use 142
  healthy people 169
  property price example 218
  Silver Valley pollution 295
  toxic waste sites in 295
ideal home place
  water, water sources 145
ideal life
  author's concept 13
  having it all 61
  includes working at home 116
illegal immigrants 188
Illinois
  Bloomington 119
  foreign immigration, native outmigration 188
Immigration Act of 1990 188
immigration and ethnicity 187-189
improved property considerations 212-213
incineration of wastes 296
  Supreme Court ruling 296
income, average farm 131
independence of rural people 197
Indians-versus-settlers war 272
industrial wastes 296
inspecting homes 322
inspections of property 331

About the author

The author with winter beard. The camera that took this picture has been donated to a recycling center. The photographer has requested anonymity.

Reared in rural Wisconsin, Gene GeRue was mistakenly loosed upon the world. After wandering aimlessly for years he became a real estate broker and college instructor in northern California. Looking forward to becoming an urban burnout, he researched the 48 contiguous states by phone, mail, books, travel, and a lot of really hard thinking. He found his ideal country home in 1976 and moved there in 1983. Since then, in addition to enjoying country living, he has been publications director for a national home energy-efficiency company and a freelance editor and graphic designer. He has written two regional books, *Ozark Country Pizza* and *Show Me Fishing in Ozark County* and has edited too many newsletters. *How To Find Your Ideal Country Home* is his first major book and may be his last unless you recommend it to your friends. In addition to writing, editing, illustrating, designing, and publishing books, he enjoys gardening, hiking, building, and watching trees grow.

To order this book by phone, call 800-RURAL-22 (800-787-2522)

If you prefer to order by mail, please send a check or money order for $25.00 to Heartwood Publications, HC 78, Box 1105, Zanoni, MO 65784. For the extra nickel we will pay the postage and tax. (You get a good deal and we are able to do our bookkeeping using fewer fingers.)

Returns policy: If at any time you are dissatisfied with one of our books that you have purchased from us we will sob but we will give you a full refund. Simply return the undamaged book to us. Upon receipt, we will send your refund.

Help us help others

One of our future books will tell the stories of individuals, couples, and families of diverse backgrounds who have moved from city to country. Reading of their challenges and solutions will help others make the transition a most pleasant experience. If you would like your story to be part of that book, write to us now of your present situation and intentions. Then, after you have settled into your country home, tell us your story. Of course we can make no promise of inclusion. We also want to know how this book helped and how you feel the next edition would be improved. Write to Gene and Chris GeRue, HC 78, Box 1105, Zanoni, MO 65784. We'll be in touch.